The Power and Vulnerability of Love

The Power and Vulnerability of Love

A Theological Anthropology

Elizabeth O'Donnell Gandolfo

Fortress Press
Minneapolis

THE POWER AND VULNERABILITY OF LOVE

A Theological Anthropology

Cover design: Laurie Ingram

Cover image: *Rest on the Flight into Egypt*, ca. 1597; © HIP/Art Resource, NY

Library of Congress Cataloging-in-Publication Data is available

Print ISBN: 978-1-4514-8467-0

eBook ISBN: 978-1-4514-9420-4

The paper used in this publication meets the minimum requirements of American National Standard for Information Sciences — Permanence of Paper for Printed Library Materials, ANSI Z329.48-1984.

Manufactured in the U.S.A.

This book was produced using PressBooks.com, and PDF rendering was done by PrinceXML.

To the loves of my life:
David, Tess, Davey, Gabriel, and Joseph

In memory of Rufina Amaya

Nothing is more practical
than finding God,
than falling in Love
in a quite absolute, final way.
What you are in love with,
what seizes your imagination,
will affect everything.
It will decide
what will get you out of bed in the morning,
what you do with your evenings,
how you spend your weekends,
what you read,
whom you know,
what breaks your heart,
and what amazes you with joy and gratitude.
Fall in Love,
stay in love,
and it will decide everything.

~Fr. Pedro Arrupe, SJ

Contents

Acknowledgments

I preface this book with a deep and heartfelt acknowledgment of those who have contributed to its conception, gestation, and birth, not only because the practice is customary, but because of the fundamental place my theological anthropology carves out for acknowledging the relationality and interdependency of the human condition. Because interdependency is so complex and pervasive in human life, it is hard to know where to begin to thank all of the individuals and communities that have contributed to my growth and formation as a person and a scholar, and who have thus played a role, big or small, in the production of this book. There are so many of you without whom this project would not have happened. And so I begin at the beginning, by thanking the woman who made everything possible: my mother, Gertrude O'Donnell. She brought me into this world, taught me how to love, and instilled in me a sense of vocation. Her persistent reliance on the love of God gives testimony to the redemptive possibilities of resilience in the face of tragedy and loss. I pray that she continues to find peace and strength in love.

Throughout the course of my professional journey, friends, mentors, and professors have continually awakened and reawakened my commitment to both critiquing injustice and oppression, and plumbing the depths of the human condition with the riches of the

Christian tradition. At my undergraduate institution, where I was introduced to the relationship between faith and justice, it was Paul Aspan who first alerted me to my gifts in the study of theology, and his confidence in me still keeps me going when the going gets tough; Millie Feske introduced me to the riches of liberation theologies, which have been a continual inspiration and challenge to my work as an aspiring Christian and theologian; and Vincent Genovese, SJ, awakened me to the vocation of human beings, as *imago dei*, to love like God. I have come back to this insight over and over again, and it is a fundamental undercurrent of my scholarship in this book, which asks how such love is possible in the midst of vulnerability, suffering, and violence.

Prior to graduate studies in theology, I spent two years living and working with the ecclesial base communities of El Salvador. I was able to do this thanks to the hospitality of both the communities themselves and the NGO with which I worked, Fundación Hermano Mercedes Ruíz (FUNDAHMER). FUNDAHMER and the base communities bear living witness to the love of God made flesh in the midst of human suffering. In particular, the women of the base communities have captured and formed my theological imagination. Their suffering, hope, and praxis of survival and liberation fuel my own desire to understand the deep connections between the Christian faith, personal healing, and practical engagement for peace and justice in a wounded and wounding world. I offer a specific word of gratitude and solidarity to the mother of the family with whom I lived during my time with the Oscar Romero Base Community of Jardines de Colón. Like her own mother before her, Rosa has experienced far more suffering than any mother or anyone should ever have to bear. Her ability to continue to love astounds and inspires me.

Returning to the study of theology at the University of Notre Dame was another pivotal and formative experience for me. I was encouraged by the faculty there—especially Mary Doak, Matt Ashley, and Cathy Hilkert—to place my experience in El Salvador in dialogue with the rich theological legacy of Catholic social thought, along with liberation, political, and feminist theologies. Cathy Hilkert continues to be a mentor for me as I seek to discern both my identity as a theologian and the future direction of my work. The opportunity to study with Gustavo Gutiérrez at Notre Dame was humbling and invigorating and I thank him for his availability to graduate students who hope to infuse North American theology with his love of the poor and passion for justice.

My transition to doctoral studies at Emory gave me the opportunity to place the insights of the progressive theologies I studied at Notre Dame in mutually critical dialogue with voices from the history of the Christian tradition. First and foremost, I thank Wendy Farley for impacting me with the writings of medieval contemplative women and for encouraging me to think about power and love through engagement with classic Christian texts. She has persistently challenged me, both spiritually and intellectually, to think and write about human suffering with a critical mind and compassionate heart. This book would be something else entirely if it weren't for her influence. Pam Hall has continually reminded me that human vulnerability and the suffering it can entail has the potential to completely destroy the sufferer. Luckily, her infectious sense of humor keeps this insight from sending me straight into the depths of despair! Pam has also been very encouraging and helpful with regard to incorporating narrative as a key imaginative resource for this theological project. Joy McDougall has solidified my commitment to feminist theology, continually asking me to locate myself vis-à-vis other feminist thinkers in their dialogues on vulnerability, suffering, and the nature of God and divine redemption. She also challenges me to claim my heritage as a Catholic theologian, and to discern the location of my own work in that lineage. I am thankful for her insistence on my potential for making an important contribution to the field. Finally, I am grateful to Tom Long—his enthusiasm for my work is heartening and gives me hope for the possibilities of fruitful dialogue between systematic and practical theologies. *Mil gracias* to all of you.

My gratitude also extends to Michael Gibson and the editorial team at Fortress Press, for recognizing something of value in my work and for allowing me to share my passion with the world on the printed page. There is something truly magical about publishing one's first book, and I offer many thanks for the opportunity to do so.

Outside of academia, there are many others who have made their own, more indirect, contributions to this book. I am grateful to the community of mothers that I am a part of in Greenville, South Carolina. In particular, the mothers who live on my street have been such a calming and enjoyable presence in my life, distracting me from the stresses of both motherhood and scholarly work. They keep me sane. Together, we sit in the driveway and talk about anything and everything while our kids run wild. We look out for each other's children, share meals, vent our frustrations, and rejoice in our great fortune as mothers of such beautiful creatures. I am especially thankful to Nicole Carmenates for her friendship, almost daily solidarity, and support throughout this journey.

If it were not for the presence of Yudy Bedoya in my family's life, I would not have felt nearly as comfortable with taking time away from my children to pursue my writing. She has been an "othermother" to my children, whose labor of love gave me great relief as I entered my study to write. My mother- and father-in-law, Betty and David Gandolfo, have welcomed me into their family with open arms and have offered me unwavering love and support on this journey.

To David Gandolfo, my best friend and beloved spouse, you have my heart. You have communicated unbridled confidence in my potential as a scholar since I met you. Our many years together have brought me such joy that it is hard to remain in the space of suffering that my theological work seeks to address. Our conversations always challenge me to think more deeply and critically about my writing and I am ever-inspired by your tireless dedication to scholarship and teaching that speaks to the needs of the world's poorest and most vulnerable populations. You are *la otra mitad de mi naranja*; we are made of the same stuff, and I look forward to many more years of work and struggle by your side.

Thanks to the love that David and I share, I conclude these acknowledgments with a word of deep gratitude to and for our four young children—Theresa, David, Gabriel, and Joseph. Their presence in my life has been revolutionary. It has changed everything. Mothering these little human beings is a spiritual and practical challenge, but it is also the fulfillment of my heart's deepest desires and the inspiration for the theological work that I do in this volume. Together with their father, they confirm for me the words of Pedro Arrupe, SJ: "Fall in love, stay in love, and it will decide everything."

Introduction

For about two weeks following the birth of my first child, I experienced what is commonly referred to as the "baby blues." This phenomenon, common to many new mothers, is induced by a combination of hormonal changes, physical exhaustion, and the enormity of the life and identity transformations that a woman undergoes after the arrival of her first baby. Mothers report experiencing anything from a vague feeling of melancholy to full-blown post-partum depression. My own bout with the baby blues went something like this: In general, I was riding high on the joys of new motherhood and the miraculous presence of my mind-blowingly beautiful daughter. But every evening at precisely seven o'clock, I would have to excuse myself from the dinner table or conversation with visiting family members to go lie in bed and weep.

Some mothers are blue without being able to identify a reason for their sadness. I, however, was overwhelmed with deep sorrow for very specific reasons. I grieved first of all because I was so in love with this tiny creature, who I knew would not forever remain so tiny and perfect, and who would one day grow up and leave me. But my body was wracked with sobs most of all because I could not bear the thought of anything bad ever happening to my precious child. Since life in this world necessarily entails all kinds of suffering,

I wept not only because of the possibility that harm could come to her, but because of the certainty that some kind of harm will come to her. At the very least, she will one day, like all the rest of us mortals, depart from this life. It pains me to even set those words to the page. Thankfully the baby blues only lasted about two weeks for me, and they did not return with the same intensity after the birth of my subsequent children. But I still feel a penetrating ache of sorrow, especially while nursing my youngest son or holding my older children close to read them a story or soothe a hurt. As I cradle my children in my arms, or press my lips to their foreheads, I am often painfully and viscerally aware of their vulnerability, the vulnerability of our relationship, and by extension, the vulnerability of my own happiness.

Looking back on this experience, some important insights about the human condition, suffering, and divine love have emerged from my bout with the baby blues. First, I now not only know in my mind but intimately feel in my body the fleeting nature and inherent vulnerability of the human condition and the contingency of human happiness. But I also have come to understand the power of love, beauty, and connection that is only available in vulnerability. Indeed, as I argue in this book, the redemptive power of divine love itself comes to human beings not in a blaze of glory, but in solidarity with our vulnerable condition. Furthermore, from the maternal perspective I now inhabit, I am more viscerally aware than ever that the radical suffering caused by the violation of vulnerable beings in situations of poverty, abuse, and violence is absolutely intolerable. The life of every human being—each one "some mother's child"[1]—is

---

1. Cf. Eva Feder Kittay, *Love's Labor: Essays on Women, Equality, and Dependency* (New York: Routledge, 1999), 23ff. Kittay reflects on the universal condition of being a mother's child as a basis for claims to entitlement, equality, and empathy. Her argument rests not on the affection of mothers for their children (though this is certainly an element of her ethical reflection), but on the fact of dependency and vulnerability in human life.

as precious and beautiful as the lives of my own children. And the lives of two-thirds of our world's population are far more vulnerable, far less protected by privilege than they. Finally, I have come to realize that as beautiful and fulfilling as human love—in this case, maternal love—can be, it can also contribute to debilitating anxiety, complicity in systems of privilege and violence, and moral blindness to the vulnerability and suffering of other human beings.

It is largely these insights that provided the original impetus for me to root this constructive work of theological anthropology in the fertile soil of women's diverse experiences of motherhood. The anthropological insights that emerge from these maternal experiences are not unavailable elsewhere, but they do emerge in a particular configuration and with particular intensity when considered from the standpoint of maternal experience and practice. Women's diverse experiences of maternity and natality reveal that vulnerability is a fundamental dimension of the human condition. Vulnerability is central to who we are as human beings—it is the milieu in which we experience both suffering and redemption. Vulnerability not only exposes human beings to harm, it is also the condition for the possibility of healing, health, and wholeness. The maternal narratives on which my arguments rest demonstrate that the redemptive human encounter with divine love—experienced here as resilience in the face of harm and resistance to violence and oppression—takes place within the vulnerable human conditions of embodied, relational existence.

Vulnerability, Resilience, and Resistance: Theological Anthropology in a New Key

I define vulnerability as the universal, though diversely experienced and often exacerbated, risk of harm in human life.[2] The theological

2. A new field of interdisciplinary inquiry, Vulnerability Studies, has recently emerged from the global situation of heightened vulnerability. Emory University hosts an interdisciplinary

anthropology that I construct in these pages uncovers the givenness of vulnerability as an inevitable dimension of the human condition. Maternal narratives and analyses provide this lens of "natural" vulnerability, which contrasts sharply with dominant strands of the Christian tradition in which vulnerability and the suffering to which it exposes us are the punitive response of divine justice to human sin. The biblical account of the Fall in the third chapter of Genesis attributes human vulnerability to a curse meted out by God on the human race as punishment for Adam and Eve's transgression. Women's pains in childbearing, human dependence on the land for sustenance, the difficulty of attaining that sustenance, and perhaps even mortality itself—in the biblical narrative, these are all vulnerabilities that are not natural to the human condition, but can be traced back to the Original Sin of our first parents.

Augustine of Hippo's influential appropriation of this narrative places the blame for human suffering and death squarely on the shoulders of human beings themselves.[3] Although his intention is to preserve the original goodness of creation and the human body,

and international "Vulnerability and the Human Condition Initiative," which encourages collaboration among scholars working in this burgeoning field. The Initiative's website is located at http://web.gs.emory.edu/vulnerability/. Theological works on vulnerability *per se* are scarce, although it could be argued that most of Christian theology is an attempt to grapple with vulnerability (human and divine) in one way or another. In contemporary theological literature that addresses vulnerability explicitly, William Placher's *Narratives of a Vulnerable God: Christ, Theology and Scripture* (Louisville: Westminster John Knox, 1994) explores the vulnerable depths of divine love and Christian discipleship, while Kristine Culp's *Vulnerability and Glory: A Theological Account* (Louisville: Westminster John Knox, 2010) identifies vulnerability as the basic openness of the human condition to both harm and transformation. Perhaps the most famous recent treatment of vulnerability is Sarah Coakley's article, "Kenosis and Subversion: On the Repression of 'Vulnerability' in Christian Feminist Writing," which originally appeared in *Swallowing a Fishbone: Feminist Theologians Debate Christianity*, ed. Daphne Hampson (London: SPCK, 1996), 82–111. Academic research and discourse on vulnerability has been popularized by social work professor Brené Brown's widely disseminated audio and print books, as well as her lectures, which are available online. See her website, http://www.brenebrown.com. Her twenty-minute TED talk, "The Power of Vulnerability," has been viewed over fourteen million times on the www.ted.com website.

3. See, e.g., Book XIII of Augustine's *City of God*, trans. Henry Bettenson (London and New York: Penguin, 1972).

the result is a vitiation of real human embodiment in a finite and relational world. In Augustine's view, the vulnerable body is not natural to human beings, but rather represents the unnatural state of affairs that results from sin and that must be overcome to experience salvation. Indeed, for him, "it is not necessary for the achievement of bliss to avoid every kind of body, but only bodies which are corruptible, burdensome, oppressive, and in a dying state; not such bodies as the goodness of God created for the first human beings, but bodies in the condition which the punishment for sin forced upon them."[4] In a laudable attempt to affirm the goodness of the body against philosophical blame of the body for the sins of the soul, Augustine unfortunately denigrates the body as equally as Platonists when he identifies bodily corruption not as the cause of the first sin, but as its punishment.[5] For this influential figure in the history of the Christian tradition, the vulnerability of human beings to bodily harm, relational conflict, temporal perishing, moral ambiguity, and ultimately death is not natural to the human condition. Rather, vulnerability is God's just punishment for sin. Divine redemption, then, involves liberation from enslavement to sin and removal of vulnerability in the world to come.

The maternal narratives and analyses that inform my own theological anthropology offer an alternative framework. Drawing on their practical wisdom, I argue a) that vulnerability is indeed our original condition, b) that vulnerability does play a significant causal role in what the Christian tradition has named sin, and c) that the human experience of redemption—at least in this lifetime—takes place within the vulnerability of the human condition. In this framework, sin is not central to my analysis of the human problem; vulnerability is. This alternative understanding of that which ails

4. Ibid., Book XIII.17, 528–29.
5. Ibid., Book XIV.3, 551.

humanity requires an alternative model of human flourishing and redemption. Therefore, I claim that the redemptive response of divine power to that which ails humanity is not primarily rectification of human sinfulness and removal of vulnerability after death (much less condemnation to eternal suffering). Rather, divine love responds to human vulnerability here and now, within our vulnerable condition, with existential and practical resources for resilience to harm and resistance to violence. These redemptive resources can empower human beings to face our frightening condition with courage, peace, and compassion, rather than egocentrism, anxiety, and violence. Sin is not categorically banished from this alternative framework, but it does take a backseat to the deeper reality of vulnerability as the defining characteristic of the human condition.

The theological framework I propose in this book also offers an alternative—or rather, a complement—to contemporary feminist, political, and liberation theologies in which sin is recast as a social problem that cries out for divine justice enacted through emancipatory human action. These theologies, which have been my primary inspiration for becoming a theologian myself, typically approach human suffering with the tools of social, cultural, economic, and political analysis in order to uncover and dismantle the structural causes of injustice and oppression. For example, feminist thinkers seek to eliminate forms of vulnerability that render women subject to patriarchal domination and abuse. In liberation theologies, suffering and vulnerability are protested as unjust consequences of social (and individual) sin. Political theologians doing God-talk "after Auschwitz" have made great strides toward absolving God of responsibility for suffering by pinning the blame on humanity. Such contributions are invaluable for the progress of Christian theology and practice toward greater authenticity and faithfulness to the gospel. What these approaches can tend to overlook (or can seem to overlook), however, are the root causes of suffering located deep within the vulnerability of the human condition itself. Beverly Lanzetta has apt words to describe this oversight, with specific reference to feminist thought: "While feminism has awakened women to the structural components that generate violence, it has been less successful in analyzing the deeper spiritual causes and consequences that underlie dominating behaviors and subjugating forms of consciousness."[6] To get at the root causes and damaging consequences of the radical suffering inflicted through the violation of vulnerable beings, we must first ask: What is it about our fundamental structure and condition as human beings that makes us capable and even desirous of inflicting terrible suffering on others (and ourselves)? If human beings—not God—are the cause of evils such as extreme poverty, violence, and oppression, it is imperative that we probe the depths of the human heart to uncover why we, who are made in the image of Divine Eros, fail so miserably to love. I locate the key to investigating these questions in vulnerability—a dimension of human existence that causes us great anxiety, which in turn sets in motion tragic attempts by individuals and interest groups to eliminate, or at least mitigate, their own vulnerability at the cost of vulnerable others.

Feminist, liberation, and political theologies also can tend to overlook theoretical and practical resources for countering the spiritual dimensions of this vicious cycle—that is, existential resources for resilience and resistance in the face of vulnerability, suffering, and violence. In addition to a spirituality of prophetic denunciation of oppression and annunciation of a more just and peaceful world, or rather in order to *nourish and sustain* prophetic praxis, human beings need spiritual assets for living courageously, peacefully, and

---

6. Beverly Lanzetta, *Radical Wisdom: A Feminist Mystical Theology* (Minneapolis: Fortress Press, 2005), 1.

compassionately both with the pain of the past and with present forms of vulnerability and suffering that cannot be changed. It is important to make a distinction between vulnerability as a fundamental and unavoidable feature of the human condition and the violation of human vulnerability in situations of injustice, poverty, oppression, and violence (though, admittedly, this distinction is not always unambiguous). Our basic human condition is one that exposes us to great suffering, but it is not the condition itself that we ought to reject; rather, it is the exploitation, abuse, mismanagement, and neglect of our condition that ought to be resisted. Therefore, I worry that we run the risk of throwing the baby out with the bathwater if we reject vulnerability in all of its forms. While social protest of injustice and oppression is indispensible in a world wracked by violent conflict, debilitating poverty, and social oppression, it often lacks the spiritual practices necessary for coping courageously, peacefully, and compassionately with vulnerability and the anxiety it brings. Keeping the focus on vulnerability is itself a helpful spiritual practice, especially in a religious tradition that advocates love of enemies. Unlike prophetic condemnation of oppression (again, very important!), vulnerability points to the universality of human frailty and thus might serve to instill a sense of compassion for even the perpetrators of crimes against vulnerable others. Within this alternative theological framework, neither socio-political self-righteousness nor condemnation to eternal punishment are options. Rather, the vulnerability of each individual is recognized and understood as a factor in his or her moral demise. Such understanding does not offer perpetrators the permission to violate vulnerable others; rather, it seeks to break the cycle of violation through the practice of compassion.

A Few Words on Theological Method

The primary task of theological anthropology is to plumb the depths of human experience in order to better understand the human condition, its ailments, and its openness to a redemptive encounter with the divine. Major figures in twentieth-century theological anthropology such as Paul Tillich and Karl Rahner employed the tools of philosophy and psychology to "turn to the subject" and to uncover the basic structures of the human condition that dispose humanity to sin and guilt, as well as to revelation and grace. More recently, political, liberation, and feminist theologians have built upon this "turn to the subject" but have also challenged the abstract, bourgeois conception of the subject found in liberal theology. These "theologies from the margins" have concretely refocused Christianity's attention on the threatened, yet persistent, subjectivity of the world's poor and marginalized populations. While these and other "contextual" theologies are often less well accepted within the academic discipline of systematic theology, they nonetheless share a methodological goal with more traditional theological anthropology: to understand the dimensions of human experience that a) open human beings to redemptive encounter with the divine and b) threaten the human flourishing offered by this divine-human encounter. In order to pursue these goals, both groups have turned to human experience as the starting point for understanding the human condition, what ails it, and how humanity is transformed by God's loving response.

I take methodological inspiration from both traditional and explicitly contextual approaches to theological anthropology. On the contextual side, I explore the human condition and its disposition to both vulnerability and redemption in light of women's experiences of motherhood, especially maternal suffering. In doing so, I am following the recommendation of Johann Baptist Metz, who advocates for constructive theology that would remember, narrate, and stand in solidarity with suffering humanity. Such theology, he argues, takes place in conversation with actual narratives present in biography, imagination, visions, prayers, and collected experiences.[7] I follow Metz's suggestion, weaving together a theological anthropology from the diverse strands of maternal narratives and practices of vulnerability, suffering, and redemption. The concreteness of these narratives offers a corrective complement to the abstract universalism of much twentieth-century theological anthropology.

On the other hand, I deliberately attend to the core elements that have endured as areas of concern for theological anthropology—namely the topics of creation, fall, and redemption. Attention to these basic theological categories helps to deepen the work of political, liberation, and feminist theologies by pushing beyond social analysis to the root causes of suffering and destruction located deep within the vulnerability of the human condition itself. To get at the root causes of suffering and violence, we must ask the questions of social context but we must also ask a more profound theological question: What is it about human nature fundamentally that makes us capable of inflicting suffering on others and on ourselves? This, therefore, is the question around which this book is organized.

Seeking wisdom about this "universal" anthropological question, however, can never be done abstractly and thus requires a redoubled commitment to engaging the contemporary human situation at the site of particular wounds[8]—not just for the sake of heightened

---

7. See chapter 12, "Narrative," in Johann Baptist Metz, *Faith in History and Society: Towards a Practical Fundamental Theology*, trans. J. Matthew Ashley (New York: Crossroad, 2007), especially 198ff.

understanding, but for the sake of contributing to the healing, transformation, and full flourishing of human beings and all of creation. Casting my lot with feminist, political, and liberation theologies, then, I seek to describe and interpret reality with critical and practical intent. As such, this book as a whole and each section within it contain descriptive, interpretive, and practical elements. Investigating women's experiences of maternity and natality, especially maternal experiences of suffering, provides fertile ground for both interpreting reality as a whole and suggesting practices of compassion and transformation.

Sources

The starting point and primary resource for this theology of the human condition is the diverse and multifaceted experiences and practices of mothers—especially their experiences and practices of vulnerability, resilience, and resistance.[9] Motherhood is an experience

---

8. Cf. Mary McClintock Fulkerson, *Places of Redemption: Theology for a Worldly Church* (Oxford: Oxford University Press, 2007), 13.

9. Since the 1980s, popular and academic writing on motherhood has exploded, leading to the birth of the interdisciplinary field of motherhood studies. Many academic edited volumes have been published recently on motherhood, and an entire book publisher (Demeter Press) has recently been founded for the purpose of focusing solely on motherhood. While secular academic writings on motherhood offer an incredible amount of diversity and scholarly sophistication in their approaches to analyzing the institution and experience of motherhood, they include very little analysis of religious meanings of motherhood that go beyond critiquing the religiously sanctioned institution of patriarchal motherhood. Aside from conservative missives on women's God-given vocation to motherhood, Christian theology has been rather slow to catch on to this upsurge in scholarship on maternity. Nevertheless, momentum is gaining. Notable exceptions to the relative silence on mothering in mainline and progressive Christian theologies include the following: Margaret Hebblethwaite's *Motherhood and God* (London: Cassell, 1984) explores motherhood and its place in a woman's relationship with God from the perspective of personal narrative. Bonnie Miller-McLemore's groundbreaking work, *Also a Mother: Work and Family as a Theological Dilemma* (Nashville: Abingdon, 1994) develops a feminist maternal theology that rethinks human generativity from the perspective of maternal caregiving labor. In the area of God-talk, both Sallie McFague's *Models of God: Theology for an Ecological, Nuclear Age* (Philadelphia: Fortress Press, 1987) and Elizabeth A. Johnson's *She Who Is: The Mystery of God in Feminist Discourse* (New York: Crossroad, 1992) provide extended reflections on imaging God as mother. In *Sisters in the Wilderness: The Challenge of Womanist God-Talk* (Maryknoll, NY: Orbis, 1995), Delores Williams draws on the experience

both of the self as woman and mother, and of another person as a dependent extension of the self and a growing, changing, distancing other. Therefore, I find it impossible to separate out women's experiences of maternity from their experiences of natality, and I find fruitful insights and empowering resources in both categories of thought and practice. The maternal perspective that I describe and from which I argue unavoidably reflects my own socially situated standpoint as a white, middle-class, heterosexual, academic woman and stay-at-home mother of four small children. As my opening reflections indicate, my experience as a mother has impacted me with a visceral awareness of my children's vulnerability and, by extension, my own. Though disaster could strike at any moment, our family's inherited position of privilege offers my children a substantial amount of protection from the violation of their vulnerability. The maternal standpoint that I claim in my writing, however, is not limited to my own socially privileged perspective. In my accounts of motherhood, I rely heavily on the narratives and analyses of other mothers, especially mothers who have experienced radical suffering due to the violation of their own and/or their children's vulnerability. I employ a patchwork of diverse theoretical and imaginative resources for

of black maternal surrogacy and black mothers' God-dependency to provide a foundation for womanist theology. Ethicist Cristina Traina lays out the contours of maternal eroticism, analyzes the phenomenon of child abuse, and offers a full-bodied Christian ethic for selectively cultivating passion as erotic attunement between parents and children in *Erotic Attunement: Parenthood and the Ethics of Sensuality between Unequals* (Chicago: University of Chicago Press, 2011). In the area of theological anthropology, four recent works stand out: Marcia Mount Shoop employs pregnancy and motherhood as metaphors for the relationality and ambiguity of the human condition in *Let the Bones Dance: Embodiment and the Body of Christ* (Louisville: Westminster John Knox, 2010). Michele Saracino offers motherhood as an example of incarnating hybridity in human life on a personal level in *Being About Borders: A Christian Anthropology of Difference* (Collegeville, MN: Liturgical, 2011). Cristina Grenholm's *Motherhood and Love: Beyond the Gendered Stereotypes of Theology* (Grand Rapids: Eerdmans, 2011) critiques and reimagines Christian approaches to gender, maternity, and maternal love. Finally, and most recently, Jeannine Hill Fletcher's *Motherhood as Metaphor: Engendering Interreligious Dialogue* (New York: Fordham University Press, 2013) draws on women's experiences, especially their experiences of motherhood, as a resource for thinking about interfaith encounters and the dynamic relationality of human existence.

speaking about motherhood, including personal testimony and narrative, memoir, literature, poetry, Scripture, historical theology, feminist philosophy and theology, care ethics, and interdisciplinary work in the burgeoning fields of both vulnerability studies and motherhood studies.

Methodological Dangers

Drawing on maternal experience and practice comes with the dangers inherent to saying anything universal about the nature of humanity and divinity, and also with some particular dangers of its own. These dangers make this anthropological project itself vulnerable to certain pitfalls, but they do not doom it to failure. Rather, the rewards are well worth the risks.

First, it is important to note that the insights that arise from mothering are not necessarily unique to mothers or even other nurturers of children. For example, an ethic of care is not distinctively women's territory, nor do mothers have an exclusive claim to its heritage.[10] Indeed, research has shown that African and African American moral traditions give rise to similar patterns of moral reasoning.[11] My aim is not to romanticize mothers, alienate women who are not mothers, exclude fathers, or place mothers at the summit

---

10. In fact, most care ethicists are averse to using the mother–child relationship as the paradigm of care.
11. Take, for example, the research of Carol Stack, who found no gender difference when she tested Carol Gilligan's "Different Voice" theory in an African American community. Cf. Stack, "Different Voices, Different Visions: Gender, Culture, and Moral Reasoning," in *Uncertain Terms: Negotiating Gender in American Culture*, ed. Faye Ginsburg and Anna Lowenhaupt Tsing (Boston: Beacon, 1990), 19–27. See also Joan Tronto, *Moral Boundaries: A Political Argument for an Ethic of Care* (New York: Routledge, 1993), 83. African American feminist and womanist scholars, such as Patricia Hill Collins, Katie G. Cannon, and Emilie M. Townes have also written about the prominence of an ethic of care in African American communities. Cf. Collins, *Black Feminist Thought: Knowledge, Consciousness, and the Politics of Empowerment*, 2nd edition (New York: Routledge, 2000); Cannon, *Black Womanist Ethics* (Atlanta: Scholars, 1988); Townes, *Breaking the Fine Rain of Death: African American Health Issues and a Womanist Ethic of Care* (Eugene, OR: Wipf & Stock, 2006).

of an anthropological or moral hierarchy. Rather, I humbly set forth what I think are some helpful insights that arrange themselves in a particular configuration when we draw out the implications of maternal experience for reflecting on the human condition and divine redemption thereof. It is my hope that the particularity of my maternal sources might serve to build community and solidarity among all women and men of goodwill.

Second, talking about motherhood always runs the risk of reinscribing traditional gender roles that identify women with vulnerability and assign sole, or at least primary, responsibility for care of vulnerable bodies to women. As Bonnie Miller-McLemore points out in her own work on mothering,

> [r]etrieving anything related to the institutions of motherhood, family, and children has its inherent dangers. Women have paid, and continue to pay dearly for nurturing children, costs that men have not known. The constraints of nurturing children are real. Reproductive difference, a potential source of power, is at the same time the source of women's greatest vulnerability.[12]

I argue that maternal experience and practice reveal both the inherent vulnerability of the human condition as a whole and God's compassionate response to our condition. In no way do I wish to reinforce unjust forms of women's dependency and vulnerability that have traditionally been justified as essential aspects of women's "nature." Nor do I intend to buy into the romanticized vision of vulnerability that characterizes the patriarchal institution of motherhood.

Third, talking about motherhood runs the risk of eliding differences in maternal experiences across the lines of sexual orientation, class, race, and culture. While I take this danger very

---

12. Miller-McLemore, *Also a Mother*, 83.

seriously, I share Martha Fineman's concern that overstating the anti-essentialist case can be paralyzing—"silencing or restricting voices as women determine that they cannot speak for anyone other than those women with whom they share major nongender characteristics such as class, sexual preference, or race."[13] Though I do not claim to "speak for" anyone else, I agree with Fineman that strict anti-essentialism can be divisive and problematic for politics (as well as theology and ethics, not to mention ministry). I also believe that solidarity across differences is possible. I do not want to deny the difference that difference makes, but I also want to recognize something basic that mothers generally (though not universally) do share—namely, a commitment to responding to their children's vulnerability by providing resources for their survival and well-being. With Sara Ruddick, I take the risk and identify "maternal" work because "I take a child's demand that her life be protected as a demand *children* make upon the world—a demand intrinsic to the promise of birth that mothers in many cultures around the world can and, so far as I can tell, do organize to meet."[14] This demand, and the maternal labor that responds to it in innumerable ways, can actually be a starting point for dialogue across differences and solidarity in the struggle to overcome that which threatens mothers, children, and human beings everywhere.[15]

13. Martha Fineman, *The Neutered Mother: The Sexual Family and Other Twentieth Century Tragedies* (New York: Routledge, 1995), 44.
14. Sara Ruddick, *Maternal Thinking: Towards a Politics of Peace* (New York: Ballantine, 1989), 55.
15. Cf. Miller-McLemore, *Also a Mother*, 100, where she cites Ursula Pfäfflin's suggestion that we take the "paradigm of motherhood as a starting point for dialogue across differences in sex, age, class, sexual orientation, ethnicity, and worldview. This has the capacity . . . 'not only for overcoming the split between the worlds of women and men but also splits among different cultures nations, races, classes, and religions.'"

Epistemological Issues

In addition to the methodological dangers explored above, using maternal sources for theological reflection on humanity and divinity carries with it the dangers endemic to all contextual theology (and, of course, all theology is contextual). More often than not, human beings project onto God and "universal human nature" the socially situated values, ideals, and even ideologies that they hold most dear and/or that serve to benefit their own self-interest.[16] Does constructing a theological anthropology from an explicitly maternal perspective not fall into the same trap? Christian theology often appeals to the authority of Scripture or Tradition in order to transcend historical contexts and thus avoid ideological distortions that ultimately result in idolatry. The problem with this approach is that it fails to acknowledge that our particular choice of authority is already ideologically charged and the source of the authority itself is imbued with the social, cultural, and political agendas of its authors and time periods. As human beings we can never abstract ourselves from our contexts and the desires that they produce in us. Unless we are to accept total relativism, however, Christian theology must try to say *something* about humanity, who God is, and what the divine will is for creation.

The question is, how can we get closer to the truth? The answer to that question does not (indeed, cannot) involve abstracting ourselves from our respective contexts and desires in order to seek a pure truth, wholly objective and unadulterated by human influence. Nor can it mean a strict appeal to the authorities of Scripture and Tradition. All human apprehension of truth is situated and perspectival, including our interpretation of what we consider to be authoritative sources of

16. This is Ludwig Feuerbach's famous critique of religion in *The Essence of Christianity* [1841] (Cambridge: Cambridge University Press, 2012).

divine revelation. But, as Catherine Keller points out, the dissolute is not the only alternative to the absolute.[17] That truth claims are always contextual does not mean that seeking the truth about God and reality is impossible, that truth simply does not exist, or that Scripture and Tradition are irrelevant. Rather, it means that we need to deliberately seek out perspectives from which to view the world and our textual and ecclesial traditions that can bring us closer to the truth about reality and the will of God for reality. It means seeking out standpoints that have greater epistemological authority and that thus yield better knowledge. It means discerning, from these perspectives, the values and desires that are most authentic and that we *should* identify as meaningful reference points for talking about humanity and divinity.

Political and liberation theologians have adopted a theological method based on the conviction that the truth about God and God's will for humanity is best discerned from the authoritative standpoint of suffering, especially the suffering of those on the underside of history.[18] Edward Schillebeeckx, for example, argues that theological and ethical attempts to determine God's will for human beings must start with "negative contrast experiences," in which resistance to what

---

17. See Catherine Keller, *On the Mystery: Discerning Divinity in Process* (Minneapolis: Fortress Press, 2008).

18. In a secular parallel, feminist standpoint epistemologists, such as Nancy Hartstock and Sandra Harding (among others), argue that subjugated knowledge offers a more comprehensive view of reality than the dominant perspective because the latter actively obscures the former. In their analysis, all knowledge is socially situated, but the social location of the marginalized provides the better starting point for knowledge projects because the activities of the dominant group render invisible the activities, problems, and questions of marginalized. Taking on the perspective of a subjugated population—in this case, mothers—uncovers this previously invisible standpoint and thus provides for stronger truth claims than thinking done from the more severely limited perspective of the dominant group. Cf. Nancy Hartstock, "The Feminist Standpoint: Developing the Ground for a Specifically Feminist Historical Materialism," in *Discovering Reality*, ed. Sandra Harding and Merrill B. Hintikka (Dordrecht: Kluwer Academic, 1983): 283–310; Sandra Harding, "Rethinking Standpoint Epistemology: What Is 'Strong Objectivity'?" in *Feminist Epistemologies* (New York: Routledge, 1993): 49–82; and Harding, ed., *The Feminist Standpoint Theory Reader: Intellectual and Political Controversies* (New York: Routledge, 2004).

negatively threatens the worth and dignity of human beings points to the positive call—the worth and dignity—that the divinely desired *humanum* truly entails.[19] The "no" to radical suffering, injustice, and meaninglessness in history uncover a "yes" to the values that we should consider divine, as well as the human conditions that God desires and must be met for our full flourishing. Unless we tend to the situation of suffering humanity in our world, any positive conception we have regarding who God is, what God's will is, or what it means to be human will be dangerously skewed. Though the epistemological standpoint of the negative contrast experience still projects onto humanity and divinity the objectives, values, and hopes of human beings, it gets us closer to projecting those objectives, values, and hopes that more adequately mirror the divine will for human flourishing. This is because suffering calls into question all of our other desires and agendas (though it does not necessarily invalidate all of them). It cuts through the superficiality of conventional values and ideologies, thus offering a deeper and less illusory perspective on reality.

Liberation theologians have taken a similar approach, with a more explicitly biblical and specifically Christological justification.[20] All theological reflection is situated in a historical context, a "somewhere" that affects the why, how, from whom, and for whom of that reflection. According to Jon Sobrino, the "somewhere" that

19. Cf. Edward Schillebeeckx, *God the Future of Man* (New York: Sheed & Ward, 1968); *The Understanding of Faith: Interpretation and Criticism* (New York: Seabury, 1974); *Church: The Human Story of God* (New York: Crossroad, 1996). Although Schillebeeckx was influenced by Critical Theory in his formulation of the concept of "negative contrast experiences," he was ultimately dissatisfied with the tendency of this school of thought to "intensify the 'no' until it becomes an absolute, [which] in turn favors the growth of a new form of alienation." He insists that the "no" actually "presupposes a hermeneutical process which is based on meaning and not on nonsense." See *The Understanding of Faith*, 127–28.

20. I am not sure if he put this exact phrasing in writing anywhere, but I recall Gustavo Gutiérrez commenting that liberation theologians seek God among the poor because, in the Bible, "that's where God told us He would be!"

matters is not an *ubi*, or a concrete, geographical location (the university, the Vatican, and so on), however significant such settings might be to the style and product of any given theological project. Rather, the "somewhere" in which theology must be embedded is a *quid*, or a "substantial reality" by which theology is illuminated and challenged, and from which it formulates its questions.[21] This is the *locus theologicus*, which not only produces a particular reading of the traditional sources of theology, but also actualizes and make present certain contents of those sources, thus becoming a source itself. Any theology that takes seriously the presence of God in human history, thus avoiding a contemporary form of "theological deism," not only operates out of a specific historical location, but also asks itself how God is actually present in the particular signs of the times that characterize that location.[22]

Sobrino logically maintains that different theological locations produce different interpretations of theology's sources, including biblical texts, the tradition, and the contemporary presence of God in the believing community and in broader society. Each location captures something different about what the texts and the tradition say about the meaning and truth of the Christian faith. However, these varied locations are not all equally adequate because some are closer to what is real than others; that is, some are closer to God's revelatory and active presence in history. For Sobrino, who draws on his martyred Jesuit brother Ignacio Ellacuría here, it is the poor and oppressed majorities who represent the primary socio-theological location in which Christ is present in the signs of the times throughout history: "Among the many signs that are always present, some that stand out and others barely perceptible, there is in each

---

21. Jon Sobrino, *Jesucristo Liberador* (San Salvador: UCA Editores, 1991), 59. All translations from original Spanish sources are mine.
22. Ibid., 54.

time one that is the principal sign in whose light the others must be discerned and interpreted. This sign is always the historically crucified people."[23] The world of the crucified people is the *locus* of Latin American liberation theology because they "constitute the maximum and scandalous, prophetic and apocalyptic presence of the Christian God."[24] This is true *a priori* because of both "the correlation between Jesus and the poor, and his presence in them," and *a posteriori* because theology "obtains a wider and sharper view of everything from the perspective of the situation of the poor."[25] Like the Servant of Yahweh and the crucified Christ, the crucified peoples of the world offer an epistemological advantage, a light by which we might see things more broadly and more accurately.[26] In the words of Kevin Burke, who also takes inspiration from Ellacuría, "the truth of reality becomes most manifest where reality has been crucified."[27]

While I have become increasingly uncomfortable with the language of the "crucified people" due to its tendency to relegate the poor and marginalized to the status of victims lacking agency, my project is located squarely within the methodological genealogy of thinkers like Schillebeeckx and Sobrino, who seek the truth on the underside of history, in the presence of those who suffer. It is my contention that the maternal standpoint, especially the standpoint of

23. Ibid., 56. Citing Ignacio Ellacuría, "Discernir el 'signo' de los tiempos," *Diakonía* 17 (1981): 58.
24. Ibid., 60. Citing Ellacuría, "Discernir el 'signo' de los tiempos," 58.
25. Ibid., 58.
26. For a detailed account of the identification of the oppressed masses as the "Crucified People" and the "Suffering Servant of Yahweh" and how it is that they are a "light for the nations," see the following: Ignacio Ellacuría, "The Crucified People," in *Mysterium Liberationis: Fundamental Concepts of Liberation Theology*, ed. Ignacio Ellacuría and Jon Sobrino (Maryknoll, NY: Orbis, 1993): 580–603; Jon Sobrino, *Jesus the Liberator: A Historical Theological View* (Maryknoll, NY: Orbis, 1993), 254–71; Jon Sobrino, *Witnesses to the Kingdom: The Martyrs of El Salvador and the Crucified Peoples* (Maryknoll, NY: Orbis, 2003), 155–66; and Kevin Burke, "The Crucified People as 'Light for the Nations': A Reflection on Ignacio Ellacuría," in *Rethinking Martyrdom*, ed. Teresa Okure et al. (London: SCM, 2003): 120–30.
27. Kevin Burke, *The Ground Beneath the Cross: The Theology of Ignacio Ellacuría* (Washington, DC: Georgetown University Press, 2000), 8.

maternal suffering, can yield theological knowledge that contributes to a better understanding of the nature of reality than the prevailing monarchial/patriarchal models of Christian theology and practice. In fact, maternal vulnerability and suffering represents doubly subjugated knowledge and thus yields doubly authoritative insights into reality, human and divine. In terms more grounded in the substance of my own project, the suffering and *violation* of vulnerable human beings offers an illuminating perspective on vulnerability as a basic feature of human reality and on the nature of divine residence in and redemptive response to reality. Suffering produced by both "natural" forms of vulnerability and the violation of vulnerability—in this book, maternal suffering—can thus help us discern an appropriate place for vulnerability in our visions of human wholeness and redemption.

The Place of Practice

Practices play an important role in the theological method of this theological anthropology. Both practical theologians in the North American context and liberation theologians in the Latin American context argue that the practices of the Christian faith provide a privileged epistemological *locus* for theological reflection because practices are productive of knowledge. According to practical theologian Craig Dykstra, the practices of faith "bear epistemological weight" because they bring us to "awareness of certain realities that outside of these practices are beyond our ken. Engagement in certain practices may give rise to new knowledge."[28] Engagement in practice is a precondition for knowledge of realities central to the faith and, therefore, it is not simply an outcome of the faith or an ethical application thereof. As such, attention to practice is necessary in

28. Craig Dykstra, "Reconceiving Practice," in *Shifting Boundaries*, ed. Barbara Wheeler and Edward Farley (Louisville: Westminster John Knox, 1991), 45–46.

theology as critical reflection on faith. Christian theology must be grounded in Christian practice because it is only in and through that practice that we have access to the realities of faith. Latin American liberation theologians make similar epistemological and methodological claims. According to Gustavo Gutiérrez, all solid theology must be grounded in spirituality, or following Jesus in the world today.[29] The praxis of this discipleship is important for theology, not only because it is an outcome or ethical consequence of the Christian message, but because it constitutes the act of faith that illuminates the very content of the faith itself. In other words, following Jesus and building the kingdom shed light on who Jesus is and what God's kingdom is all about. For liberation theologians, praxis in which God is present and active represents the first moment of theology (*theologia prima*); only from within this praxis does the second moment of reflection (*theologia secunda*) become possible.[30]

While I am indebted to the theological method of practical and liberation theologies, Dykstra's and Gutiérrez's interests lies primarily in practices of the Christian faith. I make both broader and narrower use of practice. I broaden the place of practice to include not only Christian, but also more vaguely "spiritual" and more mundanely "secular" practices. At the same time, I narrow my engagement with practice to include only mothers as the individuals whose personal and communal practices inform my constructive theological account of vulnerable humanity and divinely empowered human flourishing. As I have sought to demonstrate above, tending to the narratives and experiences of mothers is itself fruitful for coming to a better

---

29. Gustavo Gutiérrez, *We Drink from Our Own Wells* (Maryknoll, NY: Orbis, 1984), 1.

30. See Gustavo Gutiérrez, *A Theology of Liberation* (Maryknoll, NY: Orbis, 1988), xxxiv and 5–11 and Gutiérrez, "Reflections from a Latin American Perspective: Finding Our Way to Talk about God," in *Irruption of the Third World: Challenge to Theology,* ed. Sergio Torres and Virginia Fabella. Papers from the Fifth International Conference of the Ecumenical Association of Third World Theologians, August 17–29, 1981, New Delhi, India (Maryknoll, NY: Orbis, 1983), 223–26.

understanding of the human condition, what ails it, and how divine power responds in love. Practices performed by mothers—both as mothers and as women defined by much more than mothering—are central to these narratives and experiences. Like the Christian practices highlighted in practical and liberation theologies, maternal labors are revelatory—they point to something larger than themselves. These practices "give rise to thought."[31] For example, in chapter 2, I relate how Louise Erdrich places strands of her young daughters' hair in the forest so that a bird might build a nest with them. The practice of offering these strands and collecting the nest as a keepsake give rise to theoretical reflections on the fleeting nature of human existence and the vulnerability to which temporal perishing subjects us. This is merely one example of how practices play a key role in opening up theoretical spaces for reflection on the vulnerable nature of human existence and the role of divine love in responding to human vulnerability.[32]

Just as practices give rise to thought, so too does thought return to practice. This dynamic relationship that moves from practice to theory and back to practice is characteristic of practical and liberationist theological method and is very influential in this theological anthropology. Therefore, an entire chapter is devoted to identifying three specific families of practice that have proven themselves to empower both resilience and resistance in the narratives of memoirist Mary Karr and Liberian peacemaker Leymah Gbowee. I suggest that these practices have the potential (not the guarantee!) to offer human beings a means of managing human vulnerability

---

31. Cf. Paul Ricoeur, *The Symbolism of Evil* (Boston: Beacon, 1967).

32. I do not seek to lay out a system of "maternal thinking" based on maternal practice, as Sara Ruddick does in her *Maternal Thinking*. It would be impossible to systematize mothers' collective ways of thinking on questions of theological anthropology and divine redemption. Rather, I seek to tease out elements of mothers' narratives, experiences, and practices that point to larger truths about humanity and divinity.

with the courage, peace, and compassion offered by divine love. Practices thus have the final word in this theological anthropology, but they also provide an open door for continuing the dialectic interplay between experience, practice, and theoretical models for human existence and divine redemption thereof.

What Lies Ahead

This book is divided into three parts. Part 1, "The Vulnerability of the Human Condition," begins with a maternal argument for the vulnerability of human existence in chapter 1, "The Fundamentals of Human Vulnerability: Embodiment and Interrelationality," and chapter 2, "The Complexity of Human Vulnerability: Perishing, Conflict, and Ambiguity." These chapters, which should be read as a pair, draw on women's diverse experiences of maternity and natality in order to describe the inevitability and universality of human vulnerability, defined as the ever-present possibility of harm, pain, and suffering. Mothers' lives have historically, empirically, been so vulnerable—due to the interaction of biology and social imposition—that their own varied experiences of suffering and their diverse perspectives on the vulnerability of maternal and natal life can provide us with privileged clues regarding the universality of vulnerability in the human condition as a whole. In these chapters, I highlight women's diverse experiences of motherhood as icons of human embodiment, relationality, perishing, and ambiguity—all of which are inherent features of human existence that render us vulnerable to suffering. Grounded in these contours of human vulnerability, I argue that vulnerability is an inherent and unavoidable feature of the human condition. Vulnerability takes many and varied forms, but there is a certain inevitability to the fact of our underlying vulnerability and I am presenting that as the root human "problem." Employing the ethical insights of Aristotle and

Martha Nussbaum, however, I conclude that, as unattractive as our exposure to harm may be, vulnerability is also the condition for the possibility of existence itself, along with the possibility of goodness and flourishing. Human life and happiness are only achievable within the contours of our fragile, finite existence.

Chapter 3, "The Violation of Human Vulnerability: Anxiety, Egocentrism, and Violence," and chapter 4, "Violated Vulnerability and the Violence of Privilege," should also be read together. These chapters explore the link between vulnerability and violence and assert that human beings respond to our vulnerable condition in unhealthy, unjust, and violent ways. I argue that vulnerability—and the anxiety surrounding the suffering that vulnerability causes and/ or threatens—is what ultimately precedes both egocentrism and the resultant communal and individual violation of other vulnerable beings through structural and personal violence. I make this argument by placing maternal experiences of both suffering and perpetrating harm within the social context of privilege. Expanding on Martha Fineman's vulnerability-based understanding of privilege, I interpret privilege as communal mismanagement of vulnerability in which certain groups and individuals have disproportionate access to assets that capacitate them for self-protection and resilience in the face of harm. Drawing on maternal narratives and analyses, I argue that the mismanagement of vulnerability in privilege does violence to human persons and actually exacerbates the problem of human vulnerability for both the powerless and the privileged by engendering both personal suffering and the perpetration of further individual and communal violence. Both privileged mothers and mothers on the underside of privilege are caught up in this vicious cycle, and their narratives and analyses of both maternal suffering and maternal perpetration of violence provide a contextual window into the origins of violence more generally in the vulnerable human condition as a whole. This analysis of the origins of violation in vulnerability sets the stage for parts 2 and 3, which offer theological and practical assets for interrupting this vicious cycle and managing personal and communal vulnerability in more courageous, peaceful, and compassionate ways.

Part 2, "The Trinitarian Dynamics of Divine Love and Human Redemption," offers theological resources for meeting human vulnerability with resilience in the face of harm and resistance to violence and oppression. This is the theological heart of the book, in which I construct an account of human redemption directly informed by a Trinitarian understanding of God. Here I explore both the divine and the human sides of the following questions: What resources does humanity require to interrupt the vicious cycle of vulnerability and violation described in part 1? And what does humanity look like when it encounters the redemptive power of divine love? In response to these questions, I uncover three fundamental dimensions of God's redemptive response to the basic human problem of vulnerability. Each chapter begins with a Marian vignette surrounding Christ's Nativity, and proceeds to offer a theological account of each dimension of divine love and human redemption, drawing on sources in both historical theology and contemporary feminist and womanist theologies. I conclude each chapter with a "virtue" offered by divine love as an empowering resource for coping with and managing vulnerability in courageous, peaceful, and compassionate ways.

Starting off part 2 is chapter 5, "Do Not Be Afraid: The Invulnerability of the *Imago Dei*," which posits that there is an invulnerable dimension to divinity that preserves human dignity in the face of vulnerability, and even in the midst of radical suffering. Beginning with the Annunciation and Visitation narratives and drawing on maternal thinkers such as Julian of Norwich and Delores

Williams, I argue that feminist dis-ease with divine invulnerability eclipses this fundamental human experience of divine love, which is grounded in the inviolability of human creation in the *imago dei*. Mary's experience of divine favor, Williams's analysis of Hagar's and African American mothers' God-dependency, and Julian's own experience and theology all suggest that that which is invulnerable in God—namely, divine love—is what grants vulnerable human beings the strength and courage for survival, resilience, and resistance in the midst of the most destructive forms of violence and suffering.

In chapter 6, "And She Gave Birth: The Vulnerability of the *Imago*'s Incarnation," I explore the meaning underlying the foundational Christian claim that the invulnerable power of divine love enters into solidarity with suffering humanity as a vulnerable and dependent baby. After sustained reflection on the Nativity of Christ, I place the invulnerable divinity of Greek philosophy in dialogue with both feminist theology/philosophy of religion and premodern Christian voices such as Origen of Alexandria, Gregory of Nyssa, Nicholas of Cusa, and Mechthild of Magdeburg. This dialogue culminates in an argument for recovering the natality of the divine as a central icon of redemption in theological anthropology (and Christology/soteriology). I conclude that the divine vulnerability manifested in the Incarnation and Nativity is a powerful resource for both making inner peace with the vulnerability of human existence and making outer peace with vulnerable others (including enemies).

In chapter 7, "Rachel's Lament and Mary's Flight: Love's Longing for Abundant Life," I consider a third dimension of divine love and human redemption: the indwelling presence of divine longing for abundant life. Beginning with the massacre of the Holy Innocents, I take Rachel's lament and Mary's flight into Egypt as icons of how the Spirit of Divine Eros cries out in human beings for survival and flourishing against all odds. Drawing on the medieval writings of Catherine of Siena and the postmodern womanist theology of Monica Coleman, I argue that this spirit, at work in maternal lament and tenacity, is present in all human mourning of life lost and all human celebration of life preserved and protected. Unlike the desirous dynamics of human anxiety, however, the desire of divine love is abundant life for all. Therefore, its power is to infuse human beings with this same desire, which becomes present and active in human life as the virtue of compassion.

Part 3 of the book is titled "To Suckle God with Exercises of Love," a phrase borrowed from Hadewijch of Brabant. The redemptive virtues offered by the Trinitarian dynamics of divine love are not magically made present in human beings without some human cooperation. This section describes and analyzes practices that cultivate the human capacity to cope with and collectively manage vulnerability with courage, peace, and compassion. Chapter 8, "Practices of Resilience and Resistance: Memory, Contemplation, and Solidarity," analyzes practical assets for coping with vulnerability, with the anxiety that vulnerability begets, and with the damage done by the violation of vulnerability. Drawing on the narratives of memoirist Mary Karr and Liberian peacemaker Leymah Gbowee (both mothers), I propose three families of practices (memory of suffering, contemplative kenosis, and solidarity) that have the potential to empower human beings with the redemptive resources of divine love. These practices are themselves grace-filled resources that foster existential resilience and social resistance by both a) opening up psychic space for accessing and embodying the power-in-vulnerability of divine love described in part 2, and b) empowering practitioners to respond to their own vulnerability and that of others with life-giving, compassionate, and just (rather than violent) means.

Finally, in chapter 9, I conclude with a brief meditation on "Contemplating Vulnerability," in which I draw my arguments to a close with a caveat and a final suggestion for practice. My caveat is that the theological and practical resources offered in parts 2 and 3 of this book ought not be understood as a "solution" to the problem of vulnerability or a panacea for the pain, suffering, and utter destruction of lives caused by violence. Furthermore, I note that the redemption offered by divine love within the vulnerability of this world is fragmentary and fragile. As long as radical suffering, injustice, oppression, and violence remain, redemption is incomplete. In an effort to further the cause of divine love in the world, I end by once again suggesting that the practice of contemplating Christ's Nativity as a symbol of the simultaneous power and vulnerability of all human beings has the potential to deepen our awareness of suffering and expand the capacity to respond with ever-widening, radical compassion.

****

While a cure-all for human vulnerability is neither possible nor desirable, it is imperative that we bring an honest account of vulnerability into our discussions of the major moral and practical dilemmas regarding injustice, violence, and aggression in our world today. Like all human beings, Christians must find healthy ways to cope with the reality of vulnerability, and the anxiety and suffering it induces in the midst of everyday life. This book brings the Christian faith into conversation with the vulnerability and anxiety experienced in the daily life of mothers. I have orchestrated this conversation in order to explore some pressing existential, moral, and practical questions: How can we move beyond the anxiety surrounding personal, familial, and national vulnerabilities to respond nonviolently to our own vulnerabilities and to care about and respond with compassion to the vulnerabilities of other human beings, all of whom are "some mother's child"?[33] When our own vulnerable lives and dignity have been harmed by injustice, violence, and aggression, how can we move beyond the violation, heal our wounds, and refrain from striking out in violence to wound vulnerable others in return? How can we transform our fear of the "Other" from violent scapegoating into compassionate solidarity with all of vulnerable and suffering humanity? While there is no definitive answer to any of these questions, paying close attention to human vulnerability, along with the assets and liabilities of both motherhood and the Christian tradition, can lead us in fruitful, nonviolent, and life-giving directions.

33. Kittay, *Love's Labor*, 23.

PART I

The Vulnerability of
the Human Condition

1

The Fundamentals of Human Vulnerability

Embodiment and Interrelationality

You never stop feeling sorrow for your children. . . . The one that was most painful was my eight month old girl who was still nursing. I felt my breasts full of milk, and I wept bitterly. . . . Today I can tell the story, but in that moment I was not able to; I had such a knot and a pain in my heart that I couldn't even speak. All I could do was bend over and cry.

~ Rufina Amaya, sole eyewitness survivor of the Salvadoran massacre at El Mozote in which she lost four children[1]

. . . she was so beautiful. . . . Yeah, like, she's very, very, um. She's special. I don't know. She, 'cos because she, she brought out a hell of a lot of love in people. People could look at her and say, oh she's lovely. She brought out a hell of a lot of love out of people.

~ Sam, working-class British mother, commenting on her young daughter[2]

---

1. Rufina Amaya et al., *Luciérnagas en El Mozote* (San Salvador, El Salvador: Ediciones Museo de la Palabra, 1996), 20.
2. Val Gillies, *Marginalized Mothers: Exploring Working-class Experiences of Parenting* (New York: Routledge, 2007), 119.

In all of their diversity, mothers throughout history and across markers of racial, socio-economic, cultural, and sexual difference have experienced and embodied in their very flesh the stark contradictions of the human condition. Existence in this world of ours encompasses life and death, joy and grief, love and loss, harmony and conflict, creativity and confusion. This "coincidence of opposites"[3] endemic to human life is part and parcel of what Wendy Farley calls "the tragic structure" of finite existence, in which "the very structures that make human existence possible make us subject to the destructive power of suffering."[4] Women's diverse experiences of maternity and natality, suffused as they are with painful ambiguities, provide particularly powerful icons[5] of our tragic condition and the inevitability of vulnerability that it entails.

In this chapter and the one that follows, I argue that the dual realities of maternity and natality, the matrix in which we all have our origins, point to several defining characteristics of human existence: finite embodiment, relational interdependence, perishing, and ambiguity. Borrowing a term from Edward Schillebeeckx, I call these dimensions of human life "anthropological constants"—that is, constitutive conditions of human existence across culture, time, and space.[6] Like Schillebeeckx, I argue that there are certain dimensions

---

3. Cf. Nicholas of Cusa, "On the Vision of God," in *Selected Spiritual Writings* (Mahwah, NJ: Paulist, 1997).

4. Wendy Farley, *Tragic Vision and Divine Compassion: A Contemporary Theodicy* (Louisville: Westminster John Knox, 1990), 31.

5. Thanks goes to my colleague Christina Conroy for suggesting this term to describe the work that maternal experience is doing in this chapter (and part 1 as a whole). I am using "icon" analogously, of course, since what I am trying to do is paint pictures of various maternal experiences that point to truths about the human condition (much in the same way that religious icons point to a truth or reality beyond themselves).

6. Edward Schillebeeckx, *Christ: The Experience of Jesus as Lord* (New York: Crossroad, 1980), 733. My anthropological constants are not based on those laid out by Schillebeeckx, but they do overlap with his (cf. 734ff.): 1) corporeality and a relationship with nature and the ecological environment; 2) personal relationality; 3) social and institutional relationality; 4) cultural conditioning; 5) a relationship between theory and practice; 6) religious and "para-religious" consciousness; and 7) the irreducible synthesis of the preceding six dimensions.

of the human condition that are inherent to being human and therefore must be honored as the system of coordinates within which human beings experience redemption. The features of being human that I highlight here make up the conditions for the possibility of life itself, and of experiencing grace as healing, love, and joy in human life. Unlike Schillebeeckx, however, I assert that each of these anthropological constants is also a source of our inherent exposure to the ever-present possibility of harm. I stress that human happiness—understood in the Aristotelian sense of *eudaimonia*, or flourishing—is only possible working within the confines of our vulnerable condition. This renders our earthly *telos* contingent and vulnerable to destruction. In other words, however much Christians hope for healing and fulfillment beyond this veil of tears, human flourishing in the here and now is a fragile and fortunate and limited experience—a "lucky pane of glass"[7] that is all too easily shattered.

An analysis of motherhood and the human condition might begin differently. It might begin by insisting, as liberation and feminist theorists rightly do, that vulnerability—maternal or otherwise—and the suffering it entails are not inevitable features of the human condition. For example, the suffering of a woman like Rufina Amaya, whose maternal grief is highlighted in the epigraph to this chapter, is not an outcome of the universal frailty of human life, but rather the direct result of social and economic structures that privilege an elite minority who will stop at nothing (not even bayoneting babies) to maintain their positions of power. At the same time, the pride and affection with which Sam regards her child is not a "natural" occurrence rooted in biological destiny. Rather, it is a socially constructed phenomenon that can serve to uphold the patriarchal institution of motherhood. Adrienne Rich makes this very objection

---

7. Carol Shields, *Unless: A Novel* (New York: Fourth Estate, 2002), 1.

to understanding maternal affection and affliction as simply part of the human condition:

> But, it will be said, this is the human condition, this interpenetration of pain and pleasure, frustration and fulfillment. I might have told myself the same thing, fifteen or eighteen years ago. But the patriarchal institution of motherhood is not the "human condition" any more than rape, prostitution, and slavery are. (Those who speak largely of the human condition are usually those most exempt from its oppressions—whether of sex, race, or servitude.)[8]

As a feminist theologian whose theological roots run deep in the soil of liberation theology, I share the conviction that forms of vulnerability resulting from oppression, violence, and injustice are by no means a direct or necessary result of universal human vulnerability. The ways in which we have organized social, economic, political, cultural, sexual, and family life are profoundly unjust and should never be justified as a natural outcome of the human condition. To do so, especially in the realm of theology, would be to resacralize an unjust world order that liberationists and feminists have toiled so hard to unmask as an idolatrous and unnecessary social construction. Suffering is not the divine will and the world *need not be* organized according to the laws of raw power, domination, and violence. As human beings we are free, and even obligated, to struggle for a change in the world order.

What liberationist and feminist approaches can tend to overlook, however, is the liberating potential of analyzing the root causes of suffering located deep in the human condition itself. In these first two chapters, I go deeper than a social critique of oppression will allow (however necessary such critique may be), and uncover the structures of human existence—the anthropological constants—that

8. Adrienne Rich, *Of Woman Born: Motherhood as Institution and Experience* (New York: W. W. Norton, 1976), 33.

a priori render us vulnerable to suffering. There are features of our condition that are essential to human being in the world, and indeed are essential to the pursuit of human happiness. But these same dimensions of our existence expose us to a broad spectrum of suffering, from discomfort to pain to horrors, degradation, and ultimately death. In chapters 3 and 4 it will become clear that our inability to cope with our vulnerable condition and the suffering it entails both arises from and exacerbates the problem, since we often violate the vulnerability of others and ourselves in an attempt to deny, scapegoat, project, and protect ourselves from our own vulnerability to suffering.

In what follows, I draw on women's diverse experiences of maternity and natality in order to lay out the anthropological constants that result in human vulnerability, defined here as the ever-present possibility of harm, pain, and suffering. I proceed with trepidation, given the dangers of positing anything universal about human nature. But I also proceed with confidence in the importance of the maternal perspectives that will be my guide and main resource in this anthropological endeavor. The maternal has been simultaneously revered and feared in Western thought and culture due to both its awesome creative power and its perilous proximity to the vulnerability that plagues our condition.[9] I do not intend to reinscribe forms of gender essentialism that identify women's nature with motherhood or motherhood with vulnerability. Rather, I posit that mothers' lives have historically, empirically, been so vulnerable—due to the interaction of biology and social

9. Cf. Julia Kristeva's analysis of maternal abjection in *Powers of Horror: An Essay on Abjection* (New York: Columbia University Press, 1982).Cf. also Adrienne Rich's chapter on "The Domestication of Motherhood," in *Of Woman Born*; Rosemary Radford Ruether, *Sexism and Godtalk: Toward a Feminist Theology* (Boston: Beacon, 1983); Grace Jantzen, *Becoming Divine: Towards a Feminist Philosophy of Religion* (Bloomington: Indiana University Press, 1999); and Catherine Keller, *Face of the Deep: A Theology of Becoming* (New York: Routledge, 2003).

imposition—that their own varied experiences of suffering and their diverse perspectives on the vulnerability of natal life can provide us with privileged clues regarding the universality of vulnerability in the human condition as a whole.

The in-depth description and analysis of human vulnerability that I offer here is more anthropological than theological. That is, I do not use explicitly Christian categories or metaphors such as sin, bondage, or woundedness to describe our condition. Nor do I attempt to rationalize why a benevolent and omnipotent God would choose to create a world in which evil and suffering are not only possibilities but inevitabilities. Rather, I take it for granted, in the words of Marilyn McCord Adams, that *"God has created us radically vulnerable to horrors, by creating us as embodied persons, personal animals, enmattered spirits in a material world of real or apparent scarcity such as this."*[10] In an attempt to unpack the anthropological reality behind this statement, I argue that the anthropological constants of existence in this world inexorably expose us to the unavoidable possibility of harm. This detailed examination of the human condition will lay the necessary groundwork for the theological and practical reflections on suffering and redemption to follow in parts 2 and 3. Taking account of the human condition exposes the problem to which Christianity must respond with theological and practical assets for resilience and resistance. Before we can begin to understand those assets, however, we need a clearer picture of the predicament they are intended to address. It is to that predicament—the fragility of the human condition and, ultimately, of human happiness—that we now turn, with experiences of maternity and natality to light the way.

---

10. Marilyn McCord Adams, *Christ and Horrors: The Coherence of Christology* (Cambridge: Cambridge University Press, 2006), 37. Italics in the original text. See also *Horrendous Evils and the Goodness of God* (Ithaca, NY: Cornell University Press, 1999).

Finite Embodiment: Vulnerability to Physical Harm

It's a personal plague, this illness, this childbearing. . . . I wonder how it will be
for me: if what's inside me is a source of grief and trouble, how will I survive?
What might happen? That's what comes to me now. . . . Maybe I'll die. Or
maybe I'll live. How will it be? What will happen to me? That's what comes
to me now; that's what's in this heart-and-mind of mine. . . . my heart-and-
mind hurts! I hurt and a crying need overcomes me and then I cry. I cry.
~Nepali woman in her ninth month of pregnancy with her third child[11]

The female reproductive system does not destine women to a life of childbearing, but women who desire to bear children ("successful" or not) and women who do bear children (by "choice" or not) are subject to the possibility of unique and frightening forms of suffering, up to and including death. The fetal and natal bodies of their children are also vulnerable to a whole host of possible harms, from genetic disorders to negative effects of environmental toxins to miscarriage, stillbirth, and infant/early childhood death. Focusing our attention on the vulnerability of maternal and natal embodiment reveals the first anthropological constant: embodiment. The embodied nature of maternity and natality reminds us of our own fragile origins, as well as our continued exposure to bodily harm, suffering, and, ultimately, our unavoidable mortality. Engaging maternal and natal embodiment can put us in touch with the fact that, in Farley's words, "[e]mbodiment in a natural, material world may be the most basic feature of human life, but it subjects human beings to an assortment of dangers and suffering."[12] The maternal has been feared and reviled in large part because of its connection with the dangers and suffering of embodiment. The time is ripe to face our anxiety with a realistic

---

11. Kathryn S. March, "Childbirth with Fear," in *Mothers and Children: Feminist Analyses and Personal Narratives*, ed. Susan E. Chase and Mary Frances Rogers (New Brunswick, NJ: Rutgers University Press, 2001), 170.
12. Farley, *Tragic Vision and Divine Compassion*, 33.

account of just how vulnerable we—and all of our fellow human beings—are as finite, embodied creatures.

Kathryn S. March, a feminist anthropologist who studies the lives of rural Nepali women and who herself has suffered infertility and pregnancy loss, writes in her narrative, "Childbirth with Fear," that "[i]n childbearing, whether from the charged perspective of modern professional women or from distant rural lifeways, bad things will happen to many of us, whether or not we are brave."[13] Due to vast social inequalities that result in unequal access to pre- and post-natal care and modern medical technology, many more bad things are likely to happen to most of the world's women than to the minority of us who enjoy the protections of privilege. However, the fact remains that women's pregnant and post-partum bodies expose them (and their babies) to the possibility of a vast array of risks, including severe discomfort, pain, illness, disability, and even death. Even under the best of circumstances, where medical interventions are readily available, it is impossible to fully control the outcome of pregnancy for mothers or their children.

For example, pregnancy renders the maternal body subject to a variety of ailments, from relatively minor discomforts such as morning sickness and exhaustion to life-threatening conditions such as ectopic pregnancy and preeclampsia.[14] The complications involved

---

13. March, "Childbirth with Fear," 173.

14. An ectopic pregnancy (EP) occurs when the embryo implants outside the uterus, usually in the fallopian tubes and, in rare cases, in the abdominal cavity. EP always results in the death of the embryo, and can also cause maternal death without timely surgical intervention. According to the World Health Organization, "During the first three months of pregnancy, EP is the leading cause of maternal death in industrialized countries, and possibly the second most frequent cause in developing countries (after abortion complications)." Patrick Thonneau et al., "Ectopic Pregnancy in Conakry, Guinea," in *Bulletin of the World Health Organization* 80, no. 5 (2002), http://www.scielosp.org/scielo.php?script=sci_arttext&pid=S0042-96862002000500006.
Preeclampsia is a complication occurring in the second half of pregnancy that is characterized by high blood pressure and problems with the kidneys and other organs. Complications of preeclampsia include eclampsia, which involves seizures that, untreated, can lead to coma, brain damage, and maternal and/or fetal death. Eclampsia is the third leading cause of maternal

in childbirth can be even more devastating. There is, of course, a great deal of pain involved in even the most ideal of birthing stories. However, childbirth can also result in deadly complications such as severe bleeding (hemorrhage), infection, and obstructed labor.[15] They do not always end in death, but can result in what some women refer to as a "living death." For example, obstetric fistula is a consequence of obstructed labor that occurs most frequently in young women and girls whose bodies are biologically mature enough to become pregnant, but are still anatomically unsuited to give birth.[16] It is characterized by a tear from the birth canal to the rectum and/or urinary tract, with the tragic result of incontinence.

Consider the testimony of Kenyan woman Kwamboka W., who became pregnant at 13, suffered a prolonged labor, lost her baby during childbirth, and has ever since experienced the living death of fistula:

> When I went home, I was so traumatized. I had never heard of this thing [fistula] before. I thought it was only me with it. I thought I should kill myself. You can't walk with people. They laugh at you. You can't travel, you are constantly in pain. It is so uncomfortable when you sleep. You go near people and they say urine smells and they are looking directly at you and talking in low tones; it hurt so much I thought I should die. You can't work because you are in pain; you are always wet and washing clothes. Your work is just washing pieces of rags. It is difficult to walk. You feel like your thighs are on fire. You cannot eat comfortably because you fear the urine will be too much. I cannot get into a relationship with a man because I feel embarrassed because I have so much urine coming out. My mother tells me, "you can't get married;

---

mortality worldwide. These are just two of many health problems that women can potentially face during pregnancy.

15. Together, these complications cause nearly 50 percent of maternal deaths worldwide. Cf. World Health Organization, "Maternal Mortality," http://www.who.int/making_pregnancy_safer/topics/maternal_mortality/en/.

16. For an excellent theological analysis of fistula, see Colleen Carpenter Cullinan's article, "In Pain and Sorrow: Childbirth, Incarnation, and the Suffering of Women," *Cross Currents* (Spring 2008): 95–107.

how can you go to someone's home when you are like this? They will despise you." I pity myself so much. My biggest fear is that I may never get a child. I look at my age-mates who are married with children and I feel so worthless.[17]

The case of obstetric fistula is a testament to the vulnerable nature of finite human embodiment. Our bodies can cause us immense amounts of physical suffering. Though medical interventions can reduce the incidence and impact of pain and pregnancy/perinatal problems, the pregnant and birthing body—indeed, the human body in general—is impossible to control and its fragility exposes human beings to not only physical, but social and psychological death as well.

A consideration of the risks to the embryonic, fetal, and natal body offers an even more telling account of human vulnerability than the dangers faced by the maternal body. We don't often stop to think that each of us began our lives as a fertilized egg, then an embryo, a fetus, and a newly born infant. Many risks to the pregnant and birthing maternal body listed above are also dangers for the embryonic and fetal body—major complications that threaten the life of the mother often also threaten the life of the child. However, the health and well-being of embryos, fetuses, and newborn babies is even more fragile than that of their mothers due to the extreme biophysical and neurological vulnerability present at the beginnings of life. Several factors contribute to this vulnerability.

First, DNA—the genetic template for life, growth, and functionality—is itself a vulnerable entity. With each new life, there is a small chance that one or more genes or chromosomes might be missing, mutated, or overproduced, either spontaneously or due to genetic inheritance.[18] Second, fetal outcomes are influenced heavily

---

17. Human Rights Watch, "I Am Not Dead, But I Am Not Living: Barriers to Fistula Prevention and Treatment in Kenya," 2010, http://www.hrw.org/node/91514.

by maternal nutrition. Maternal malnutrition can cause low birth weight, which is linked in turn to a weak immune system, slower development, poor vision and coordination, and learning difficulties later in life. The placenta is an amazing organ, but it can only work with what the maternal body offers.[19] Third, certain maternal infections can pass through the placenta to the fetus and can cause fetal complications, including miscarriage or stillbirth.[20] Because of the acute vulnerability present in the developing stages of fetal life, infections that would present very few problems for healthy adults can be devastating and even deadly for unborn children. Fourth, chemicals present in environmental toxins, over-the-counter medications, licit and illicit controlled substances, alcohol, and tobacco products can pass through the placenta and cause harm to the developing fetus.[21] Maternal exposure to mercury, for example, can cause impaired neurological development in the fetus due to the more vulnerable nature of the developing fetal nervous system.[22] Even the

---

18. Some miscarriages in early pregnancy are thought to be caused by genetic anomalies that render the embryo or fetus nonviable. Other genetic mutations (there are millions of possibilities!) may cause physical disabilities, diseases, and disorders either at birth or later in life. Some children born with genetic disorders lead full and healthy lives. Others do not live past infancy and still others remain at the developmental level of an infant (if that). Others suffer pain and illness throughout their lives.

19. Maternal malnutrition also increases the risk of major pregnancy and childbirth complications that can result in premature delivery and birth defects. Even among women whose caloric intake is high, the absence of certain nutrients, such as folic acid, can increase the chances of neural tube defects (e.g., anencephaly).

20. For example, listeriosis, caused by a eating foods contaminated with a bacteria called listeria, can result in miscarriage or stillbirth. Cytomegalovirus, a common virus that is often asymptomatic in children and adults, can cause both temporary problems (e.g., liver, spleen, or lung problems) and/or permanent disabilities (e.g., hearing or vision loss, mental disability, seizures, and even death) when babies are exposed to the virus *in utero*.

21. These substances can also contaminate breast milk and cause adverse effects in nursing babies. In her memoir, *Having Faith: An Ecologist's Journey to Motherhood*, ecologist and mother Sandra Steingraber writes eloquently and devastatingly of the threat posed by environmental toxins at each stage of fetal and infant development. According to Steingraber, the placenta has a remarkable capability for blocking harmful substances, but "small, neutrally charged molecules that readily dissolve in fat are afforded free passage [through the placenta to the fetus] regardless of their capacity for harm." Sandra Steingraber, *Having Faith: An Ecologist's Journey to Motherhood* (Cambridge, MA: Perseus, 2001), 34.

defenses of the miraculous placenta do not offer failsafe protection for fetal life. As Sandra Steingraber observes, "[T]he placenta not only fails to keep the fetus out of harm's way, it cannot even prevent itself from being damaged. Like any other living tissue, it is fragile."[23]

The fragility of new life by no means ends with the fetal period. Childbirth itself is of course perilous for the child, as we saw in the reference to labor complications above. And the natal body of an infant continues to be threatened by genetics, lack of proper nourishment, and exposure to harmful infections and toxins. Take nourishment, for example. We all need food to survive, and infants generally make their desire for milk forcefully and vociferously known, around the clock and with reason—hunger causes infants pain. This is a good thing because, aside from their affective allure, their incessant demand for food is their only means of protecting themselves from death by starvation and other threatening effects of malnourishment. Infants who do not receive proper sustenance suffer from stunted growth, learning problems, and lower IQ levels, poor immunity, and death. As we will see in the next section, the caregiver's (usually the mother's) own vulnerability is heightened by this dependence of the infant on her for nourishment and other aspects of care.

Though maternal, fetal, and natal bodies face heightened and unique risks to their health, well-being, and existence, their vulnerability points to the universal human vulnerability that arises

22. In addition to cognitive impacts, the United States Environmental Protection Agency reports that further effects of fetal mercury exposure can include impairment of "memory, attention, language, and fine motor and visual spatial skills." Many over-the-counter, prescription, and illegal drugs also contain chemicals that can pose similar threats to the developing fetus. Nicotine actually damages the placenta itself, impairing its amino acid transport system and thus resulting in low-birth-weight babies. It also passes into the body of the fetus, causing impairment of mental and physical development, among other harmful effects. U.S. Environmental Protection Agency, "Mercury: Health Effects," http://www.epa.gov/hg/effects.htm.

23. Steingraber, Having Faith, 35.

from the anthropological constant of embodiment. Fetal and natal bodies in particular remind us that we all begin our lives in circumstances of extreme biological, neurological, and physical vulnerability. Our bodily lives are all utterly contingent, reliant on a constellation of luck, genetics, and environmental factors. This is our condition when we enter this world and, though our exposure to harm may lessen as we grow, it continues to be our condition throughout childhood, into adulthood, old age, and death. At any moment, our bodies might fail us due to illness, or they might be attacked by any number of external agents, from bacteria to toxic chemicals to eighteen-wheelers on the interstate to other human beings with murderous intent. Our bodies are vulnerable to all of these factors beyond its control, and more.

The reason that our bodies are so vulnerable is that part of the nature of embodiment is receptivity. No body is an island. All bodies—and here I include molecular, chemical, cellular, biological, animal, and human bodies—are naturally and necessarily receptive to other bodies in some way, shape, or form. This means that all bodies are affected by their interactions with other bodies (either positively or negatively) and this makes all bodies vulnerable to harm or even destruction by other bodies. Human bodies all originate in a relationship of mutual receptivity that takes place within the bodies of our mothers. Without such receptivity, we would not even exist. But our inherent openness to influence by other bodies also means that we are exposed to the bad things that can happen when other bodies conflict in some way with our own. The maternal body is receptive to the embryo and growing fetus and is thus vulnerable to the harmful effects of the child on her body during pregnancy and childbirth. Even more so, the embryonic/fetal body is receptive to the maternal body, along with many other bodies (DNA, viral, bacterial, chemical, and so on) to which the mother herself is receptive. Our inherent openness to other bodies renders us vulnerable, and this is heightened in the ultra-receptive times of conception, gestation, childbirth, and infancy. But this vulnerability continues throughout our lives. All human bodies are receptive to other bodies and thus vulnerable to harm.

What makes matters worse for sentient bodies is pain. Human bodies are endowed with sentience and thus we intimately, vividly, and often painfully feel the effects of other bodies on our own. Kwamboka agonized through two traumatic days of labor. She now suffers so greatly from her fistula and resultant incontinence because tender bodily tissues are exposed and the constant flow of urine burns her genitals and inner thighs. Not only has her body been mutilated; as a sentient being, she feels the pain of the damage that has been done. And pain, especially traumatic pain—either isolated or prolonged—has lasting effects on our bodies and our bodily response to stimuli in the world. Jill Stamm, a mother and expert on infant brain development, relates that her premature daughter had a feeding tube inserted down her throat without anesthetic. Naturally, she worried about the pain but was reassured by doctors that the baby would not remember it. Stamm suspected that they were wrong. Twenty years later, neuroscientists discovered that such experiences of trauma directly affect the formation of early brain structures and do "in fact play a significant role in the later development of all other regions of the brain."[24] Similarly, children who are physically or sexually abused can also suffer long-term neurological consequences due to the bodily harm inflicted on them, even if the abuse ends at an early age.[25] Our bodies are vulnerable to harm, but our nature as

24. Jill Stamm, *Bright from the Start: The Simple, Science-Backed Way to Nurture Your Child's Developing Mind from Birth to Age 3* (New York: Gotham, 2007), 4.
25. According to the U.S. Department of Health and Human Services' Administration for Children and Families, "[C]hildren who experience the stress of abuse will focus their brains' resources on survival and responding to threats in their environment. This chronic stimulation of the

sentient beings means that we are also vulnerable to the pain that harm can cause. And that pain is often not momentary. It can have lasting effects that are devastating to our health and well-being.

As if sentience were not enough, human bodies have evolved to attain consciousness. Not only do we feel physical pain, we are aware of our feeling of pain along with the responses of others to our pain. Kwamboka is not a walking nervous system that is vulnerable only to painful physical stimuli. She is also a reflective human being who worries about the effect of her pain on her prospects in life and her relationships with others. The Nepali woman whose reflections prefaced this section on embodiment has experienced the pain of childbirth before, and she is aware of the terrible things that can happen to her and her baby. Not only her body, but her "heart-and-mind hurts." Such is the nature of this first anthropological constant. Sentient, conscious embodiment in a world composed of other bodies binds us together in relationships of vulnerability and interdependence. It is to the vulnerability brought about by relationships of interdependence that we now turn.

(Inter)dependence: Vulnerability to Relational Suffering

Walking. Walking. Walking. Rocking her while her cries fill me. They rise like water. A part of me has been formed and released and set upon the earth to wail. Her cries are painful to me, physically hard to take. Her cries hurt my temples, my breasts. I often cry along if I cannot comfort her. What else is there to do?

~Louise Erdrich, Native American author and mother[26]

brain's fear response means that the regions of the brain involved in this response are frequently activated. Other regions of the brain, such as those involved in complex thought and abstract cognition, are less frequently activated, and the child becomes less competent at processing this type of information." Child Welfare Information Gateway, "Understanding the Effects of Maltreatment on Brain Development," 2009, http://www.childwelfare.gov/pubs/issue_briefs/brain_development/effects.cfm.

26. Louise Erdrich, *The Blue Jay's Dance: A Birth Year* (New York: HarperCollins, 1995), 63–64.

I have often marveled at the eminently old and wise appearance of newborn babies, especially my own, whom I have had the privilege of studying for hours on end. They are strangely beautiful creatures, not only because of their miniature features, reptile-like movements, and humorous expressions. The wisdom and strange beauty of infants, I have come to believe, lies in their as yet undiluted immersion in the complete and utter oneness and interdependence of all reality. Having recently emerged from his mother's womb, the newborn human being is a distinct individual to be sure, but in the weeks after birth he has very few (if any) pretensions about being or becoming an independent, autonomous individual. His existence, well-being, and developing subjectivity are entirely dependent on the caregivers that surround him. In his dependence, he is utterly vulnerable. There is a certain ancient wisdom in his trusting acceptance of this fact, whether expressed in peaceful slumber or in the raucous lament that he raises so vociferously (and sometimes relentlessly) in order to make his neediness known. The newborn "knows" he is fundamentally relational, dependent, and vulnerable, yet he somehow places his undaunted trust in what Ruddick, drawing on Simone Weil, calls the "promise of birth," the indomitable expectation that "good and not evil will be done to him."[27] The perspective of natality reveals our second anthropological constant: interdependence and relationality. Babies remind us that we all originate in total dependence on other human beings (and our environment), which should spur us to think more deeply and honestly about the continued interdependence of human life and the cosmos in general. It is easy to romanticize this anthropological constant, but the wisdom of the wailing newborn child reminds us

27. Sara Ruddick, *Maternal Thinking: Towards a Politics of Peace* (New York: Ballantine, 1989), 217–18.

that relationships of interdependence also render us all vulnerable to forces beyond our control.

From the perspective of maternal practice, various feminist thinkers observe that the early maternal labors of pregnancy, birth, lactation, and caring for newborn children can also destabilize illusions of autonomy and reveal the original condition of embodied human life to be relational and interdependent. For example, Bonnie Miller-McLemore reflects that pregnancy and lactation subvert "artificial boundaries between self and other, inside and outside."[28] Pregnancy effects a blending of two (or more!) subjectivities, and in the first several weeks of a newborn's life, it still can be difficult for a mother to distinguish between herself and her child. After the birth of my first child, it felt as if the baby were an extension of myself—another person, with a distinct personality of her own to be sure, but also very much a part of me. Louise Erdrich's reflections on her crying infant daughter cited in the epigraph to this section echo this sentiment—she feels as though "a part of her has been formed and released and set upon the earth."[29] Ruddick similarly observes that the experiences of breastfeeding and holding an infant represent "occasions for 'direct sensuous congress' with another in which boundaries of self are temporarily suspended."[30] And Marcia Mount Shoop avers that "[t]he baby's subjectivity is so entangled with the mother's that we cannot always discern where they are differentiated from one another. . . . The self is so entangled with another self that the very fact of some internal, discrete self is exploded by the disappearance of even the perceived barrier of the physical body."[31] Though this experience of nonduality is by no means universal, and though it is important to remember that

28. Bonnie Miller-McLemore, *Also a Mother: Work and Family as a Theological Dilemma* (Nashville: Abingdon, 1994), 147.
29. Erdrich, *The Blue Jay's Dance*, 63.
30. Ruddick, *Maternal Thinking*, 212.

mothers and their infants oscillate between feelings of separateness and fusion,[32] the underlying condition of human personhood is inseparably relational and interdependent. Based on this experience of the self as multiple, divided, and essentially relational, Miller-McLemore asserts that "we should reconsider views of selfhood as an independent, singular, and separate state."[33] In Mount Shoop's words, "We all live in this entangled subjectivity."[34]

Paying attention to the concrete experiences of maternal practice and other caregiving labor has led these maternal thinkers, along with other feminists, to view the human person as relational and interdependent, rather than the independent, unencumbered, autonomous individual assumed by liberal political philosophy and deontological and consequentialist moral theories.[35] While it would

31. Marcia Mount Shoop, *Let the Bones Dance: Embodiment and the Body of Christ* (Louisville: Westminster John Knox, 2010), 79. Mount Shoop draws on the work of Iris Marion Young to make her argument for the entangled subjectivity of pregnancy and motherhood. She notes that Young, in turn, borrows from Julia Kristeva's description of pregnancy as a "splitting of the subject." Cf. Iris Marion Young, "Pregnant Embodiment: Subjectivity and Alienation," reprinted in *On Female Bodily Experience: "Throwing Like a Girl" and Other Essays* (New York: Oxford University Press, 2005), 46–61.

32. Cf. Daphne de Marneffe, *Maternal Desire: On Children, Love, and the Inner Life* (New York: Little, Brown & Co., 2004), 66–67. De Marneffe reviews recent psychological research on the complex interactions between mothers and newborn babies, which shows that infants process internal and external stimuli differently, thus confirming a sense of separateness from birth. According to de Marneffe, "An important theme underscored by this mother-infant research is that human psychological experience does not follow a linear progression from fusion to autonomy; rather feelings of oneness and separateness oscillate throughout life."

33. Miller-McLemore, *Also a Mother*, 143.

34. Mount Shoop, *Let the Bones Dance*, 79.

35. Cf. Virginia Held, *The Ethics of Care: Personal, Political, and Global* (New York: Oxford University Press, 2006), 46. Cf. also Martha Fineman, *The Neutered Mother, the Sexual Family and Other Twentieth Century Tragedies* (New York: Routledge, 1995) and *The Autonomy Myth: Towards a Theory of Dependency* (New York: New Press, 2004); Cynthia Willett, *Maternal Ethics and Other Slave Moralities* (New York: Routledge, 1995); Rita C. Manning, *Speaking from the Heart: A Feminist Perspective on Ethics* (Lanham, MD: Rowman & Littlefield, 1992); and Joan C. Tronto, *Moral Boundaries: A Political Argument for an Ethic of Care* (New York: Routledge, 1993). Held and others also recognize the danger in this relational view of the self, the danger of becoming so entangled in a web of relationships that a distinctive self-identity is lost. Cf. Held, *Ethics of Care*, 50. Eco-feminists and eco-theologians more generally also argue for an anthropological shift from autonomy to interdependency as the defining feature of not only

be easy to sentimentalize interdependence in general or romanticize the mother-child relationship in particular, paying close attention to the suffering that can result from natal and maternal interdependence serves to remind us that the anthropological constant of relationality is not only an asset in human life but a liability that renders mothers, children, and all of us vulnerable to relational suffering. Unpacking both the material and psychological dimensions of maternal and natal (inter)dependency will help us to better understand the full extent of this form of human vulnerability.

Material (Inter)dependency: Inevitable and Derivative

Stories of "women on the line,"[36] mothers living at the margins of existence, even in the midst of cultures and countries of abundance, reveal how relentless the material demands of human dependency can be within the day-to-day relationships between children and the caregivers (usually mothers or "othermothers") responsible for their survival and well-being. Their stories illustrate the universal reality that feminist legal theorist Martha Fineman refers to as "inevitable dependency," the undeniable fact that "all of us were dependent as children, and many of us will be dependent as we age, become ill, or suffer disabilities."[37] Particularly telling are the stories in which the children of marginalized mothers have special needs that make their material dependency all the more urgent and obvious. Take, for example, the experience of Ursula, a British working-class mother on welfare whose husband left her just before the birth of their third child.

human existence, but the cosmos as a whole. See, for example, Sallie McFague, *A New Climate for Theology: God, the World, and Global Warming* (Minneapolis: Fortress Press, 2008).

36. David Zucchino, *Myth of the Welfare Queen: A Pulitzer Prize–Winning Journalist's Portrait of Women on the Line* (New York: Touchstone, 1997).

37. Fineman, *The Autonomy Myth*, 35. See also Fineman, *The Neutered Mother*, 162; and "The Vulnerable Subject and the Responsive State," *Emory Law Journal* 60 (2011): 23.

My daughter had problems when she was first born. She only weighed four pounds, three ounces. I was so afraid I was going to lose her. I had to take care of her, I loved her. It is a gift from God. After she was born I couldn't work anymore. She was sick constantly. She had problems holding down milk. Her motor skills weren't very good. She couldn't use her hands too well. They didn't pick up on her seizures until she was three. All the years she was growing up, I couldn't work. You never knew when she would get sick. If she had a seizure in school someone had to pick her up. I couldn't give that responsibility to someone else. She is my responsibility.[38]

"She is my responsibility." Ursula's daughter had special needs that compelled her mother to respond with daily (and nightly) vigilance and care. All babies and children have needs and make demands. They require material care—nourishment, physical protection, hygiene, and so on—in order to ensure their survival, health, and physical well-being. All the more so if they are sick or have other special needs. These daily demands are made in the context of relationship. Each and every child has material needs that require a response from *somebody*, and this responsibility usually falls to the child's biological mother. Adults and even older children—usually mothers, but often "othermothers" who share or take over the caregiving role[39]—exist in relationships with dependent children whose very existence demands that they do something to meet their needs.

When a biological mother is unable or unwilling to meet the dependency demands of her child, it is usually an "othermother" who assists in or takes over the maternal role of caregiver. This role-sharing and transferal drives home the relentless urgency of

---

38. Gillies, *Marginalized Mothers.*

39. Cf. Patricia Hill Collins, *Black Feminist Thought: Knowledge, Consciousness, and the Politics of Empowerment* (New York: Routledge, 1991), 119ff. Collins argues that othermothers have been central to the institution of black motherhood because the African and African American communities have historically recognized that "vesting one person with full responsibility for mothering a child may not be wise or possible."

inevitable dependency, since *someone* has to care for the dependent child. Stories of women (and networks of women) who take on the role of "othermother" abound, especially in African and African American cultures. Grandmothers, for example, are often the ones who take over the caregiving role when their grandchildren are not directly cared for by their own biological mothers. In *Myth of the Welfare Queen*, journalist David Zucchino shares the story of African American "matriarch" Odessa Williams, who raises six of her grandchildren due to their own mothers' (her daughters') inability to care for them.[40] Other family members (aunts, sisters, cousins) also play this role, as do friends, neighbors, and fictive kin. In another journalistic portrait of women living at the margins of society, Jason DeParle relates the stories of three African American single mothers on welfare, two of whom are cousins (Opal and Jewell) and the other of whom is a close friend/fictive cousin (Angie). Each of the women is struggling to provide for her own children, but when Opal's addiction to crack cocaine makes it impossible for her to care for her kids, Jewell takes them in. When Opal has another baby, Angie takes her in and Angie's teen-aged daughter takes over the role of direct caregiver for the child.[41] The material demands for care and nurture that children make must be met if they are to survive, let alone thrive. While some mothers release their responsibility for care to othermothers relatively passively, due to overwhelming circumstances, illness, or devastating drug addiction, there are also many mothers who actively respond to their children's dependency by making a conscious decision to transfer the caregiving role to an othermother. This is likely the situation of many biological mothers who give their children up for adoption at birth

40. Zucchino, *Myth of the Welfare Queen*.
41. Jason DeParle, *American Dream: Three Women, Ten Kids, and a Nation's Drive to End Welfare* (New York: Penguin, 2004).

or in early infancy. It is also the decision that many women faced with poverty and violence must make in order to keep their children fed and safe from physical harm. The vulnerability of inevitably dependent children demands a response and when biological mothers are not able to respond, it is usually other women, othermothers, who step in and take responsibility. Their actions drive home the urgency and vulnerability of inevitable dependency—children must be cared for and protected by *someone*, even if it is not their own biological mothers (or fathers, for that matter).

Mothers and othermothers who take on the day-to-day responsibility for inevitable dependency are themselves dependent on various resources available to them to perform their caring labor. Fineman calls this situation of caregivers "derivative dependency" because of the need for material resources that their care for inevitable dependents requires.

> Paradoxically, undertaking dependency—caring for an inevitable dependent—generates a different form of dependency in the caretaker. . . . Derivative dependency arises when a person assumes (or is assigned) responsibility for the care of an inevitably dependent person. I refer to this form of dependency as "derivative" to capture the very simple point that those who care for others are themselves dependent on resources in order to undertake that care.[42]

42. Fineman, *The Autonomy Myth*, 35. See also Fineman, *The Neutered Mother*, 162. In her most recent work on vulnerability, "The Vulnerable Subject and the Responsive State," 24, Fineman points out that, unlike inevitable dependency, derivative dependency is not inevitable, nor is it universally experienced. "Rather, it is socially imposed through our construction of institutions such as the family, with roles and relationships traditionally defined along gendered lines." While I absolutely agree that derivative dependency as we know it has been socially imposed, I would also counter Fineman that even in the most utopian and egalitarian of societies, derivative dependency will still exist. It just will not automatically fall on the shoulders of women. Those who care for others inevitably depend on external resources to do their job. Derivative dependency is unjustly and oppressively managed in our patriarchal society, but it is a reality that will inevitably need to be managed in some way under any social arrangement. Far from contradicting Fineman's overall argument, this fact actually bolsters her case for a more responsive state.

Children are vulnerable dependents who demand material care and physical protection. By extension, mothering is a vulnerable endeavor because it renders mothers themselves dependent on the availability of external resources needed to do their job. "Welfare mothers" like Ursula, Odessa, Angie, and Jewell depend—at least in part—on resources provided by the state, which makes their dependency and consequent vulnerability starkly obvious in a culture of affluence that values independence and autonomy. But middle-class stay-at-home and working mothers are also dependent on resources that are, to a certain extent, beyond their control. Stay-at-home mothers are usually dependent on a breadwinner to provide financial means of procuring food, shelter, healthcare, and other material necessities for themselves and their children. Working mothers might seem more autonomous on the surface, but they too rely on the availability of affordable childcare, the goodwill of their bosses when their children are sick, their prior level of education, and often the sheer luck that affords them the ability to find a job outside the home, and so on. As primary caregivers for inevitable dependents, mothers are thus derivatively exposed to suffering and domination that can result from a lack of resources. This is not due to the unique or "essential" weakness of womanhood or motherhood. Men, and women who are not mothers, are also vulnerable creatures. As Fineman's dependency theory indicates, however, mothers and other caregivers (most of whom are women) experience a unique and even heightened form of vulnerability. Like Fineman, Eva Feder Kittay points out that it is in women's assumed and assigned roles as dependency workers that they have been more vulnerable to exploitation, poverty, abuse, and domination.[43]

---

43. Eva Feder Kittay, *Love's Labor: Essays on Women, Equality, and Dependency* (New York: Routledge, 1999), 40–41.

Nonetheless, maternal care of inevitably dependent infants and children reveals the fact of material (inter)dependency as a basic feature of our condition. The work that mothers and othermothers do reminds us that none of us come from nowhere, that none of us would even be here if it were not for the work of our childhood caregiver and the material resources on which she (or, in rare cases, he) relied to get the job done. We all started out as dependents and continue, throughout our lives, to depend on many external factors for our well-being and material "success." Our inevitable dependency and consequent vulnerability extends from childhood, not only to the obviously vulnerable states of disability, illness, and old age, but also to the rest of human life and human relationships. We all have material needs that must be met in order to survive and attain to health and well-being. Though as adults most of us are less directly dependent on others to meet these needs than we were as children, we all inevitably depend on one another (and our environment) for our needs to be met. This interdependence renders us vulnerable to external factors—the whims of other individuals, the weather, economic markets, sheer luck, and so on—which affect our ability to meet our own needs, as well as the needs of others who depend on us. As Fineman argues in her more recent work on vulnerability and the human condition, dependency thus reveals vulnerability to be a universal dimension of human life.[44]

---

44. See Fineman, "The Vulnerable Subject and the Responsive State," 23ff., and "The Vulnerable Subject: Anchoring Equality in the Human Condition," *Yale Journal of Law and Feminism* 20, no. 1 (2008): 9–10. In Fineman's earlier work (e.g., *The Neutered Mother*, *The Autonomy Myth*), dependency is the central category of analysis, as well as the basis for her arguments in favor of social responsibility for dependency. In the more recent work cited here, Fineman builds on her dependency theory to posit the universal vulnerability of the human condition as a basis for a more responsive state.

Psychological (Inter)dependency

Children are not only dependent on adults for their material needs; their dependency also encompasses a reliance on environmental stimuli, along with the attention and affection of primary caregivers, for healthy physical, psychological, emotional, and cognitive development. In the 1940s, psychiatrist René Spitz compared the development of two groups of disadvantaged babies[45]—one group was raised in an orphanage with adequate material resources but little stimulation or human contact and the other group was kept in a nursery close to their imprisoned mothers who cared for them during allotted times with a great deal of attention and affection. The former group suffered grave setbacks to their physical, emotional, and cognitive development; a large number of them did not even survive to see their second birthday and by age three most of those who did survive were withdrawn, apathetic, immobile, and noncommunicative. The latter group, by contrast, developed normally. Spitz's study, along with the research of other behaviorists, demonstrated that "early nurturing and stimulation are essential to child development."[46] Infants and children not only demand physical resources for survival and well-being, but also require attention, affection, bonds of attachment, and the stimuli of social interaction.

---

45. See René Spitz, *Dialogues from Infancy: Selected Papers*, ed. R. N. Emde (New York: International Universities Press, 1983).
46. Lise Eliot, *What's Going On in There? How the Brain and Mind Develop in the First Five Years of Life* (New York: Bantam, 1999), 3. Spitz's study, along with the research of other behaviorists, contributed to widespread recognition of the importance of environment for early childhood development, and thus led to significant progress in adoption policies (now favoring early adoption) and social programs such as Head Start and early intervention. However, the behaviorist school also contributed to a culturally pervasive and scientifically sanctioned "mother-blame," which assigned responsibility for childhood psychogenic disease to openly hostile, passively withdrawn, or "psychotic" maternal attitudes. See Spitz's 1952 motion-picture presentation of his research on "Psychogenic Diseases in Infancy" at http://www.archive.org/details/PsychogenicD.

Although mid-twentieth-century behaviorists may have swung too far to the side of "nurture" in the "nature vs. nurture" debate, more recent discoveries in neurobiology confirm that the brain, especially in infancy and early childhood, is remarkably plastic and thus profoundly dependent on environmental factors for its development. Neurobiologist Lise Eliot describes the essence of neural plasticity in accessible and eloquent terms: "The brain itself is literally molded by experience: every sight, sound and thought leaves an imprint on specific neural circuits, modifying the way future sights, sounds, and thoughts will be registered. Brain hardware is not fixed, but living, dynamic tissue that is constantly updating itself to meet the sensory, motor, emotional, and intellectual demands at hand."[47] As a child's brain is exposed to stimuli in the first years of life, it produces countless new synapses that prepare the brain to encounter such stimuli again in the future. When synapses are unused (or unformed in the first place due to lack of stimuli)—"whether because of languages never heard, music never made, sports never played, mountains never seen, love never felt—[they] will wither and die. Lacking adequate electrical activity, they lose the race, and the circuits they were trying to establish—for flawless Russian, perfect pitch, an exquisite backhand, a deep reverence for nature, healthy self-esteem—never come to be."[48] The reality of neural plasticity described here reveals a profound anthropological constant: all of us natals are born with brains (that is, hearts and minds) that are dependent on environmental and social stimuli not only for the healthy development of our bodies, but also the development of our cognitive functioning, personalities, psychological well-being, and human becoming.

47. Eliot, *What's Going On in There?*, 4.
48. Ibid., 32.

In more philosophical terms, human subjectivity is utterly dependent on relationality with the other. The development of human selfhood is embedded in relationships of interdependence. Or, more simply, human beings are social animals. Cynthia Willett muses that, contrary to Enlightenment thought and psychoanalytic theory, the interaction between mother and infant unveils this essentially social nature of human beings. The infant is only able to flourish in a rich social milieu. He "is neither identified with the Other in an anonymous or collective existence nor alienated from the Other in the abstract constructions of a private subjectivity but is always oriented toward the Other through the kinesthetics (touches, scents, sounds) of an originary social bond."[49] In Willett's view, the origin of the social is touch itself—the most basic social gesture of the caregiver's caress, which empirical evidence indicates is necessary for the infant to survive and thrive. "Even in the womb, the fetus responds to the parent's caress with the fluttering of a kick. Immediately after birth, the infant seeks the voice, smell, and touch of the mother, and not solely to satisfy an appetite. The mother or other caregiver seeks the sounds, touches, and smells of the child."[50] From this maternal standpoint, Willett addresses the possibilities of pro-social desire with a conception of a human self that is not fundamentally independent, narcissistic, or antagonistic. The self emerges not in autonomous violent opposition to the other, but in the dynamics of mutual desire and reciprocal exchange.

This interdependence of human subjectivity that Willett describes so eloquently can be easily sentimentalized, especially when it is anchored in maternal affection. Intersubjectivity sounds quite lovely, and it is powerful, but its power can also be devastating. What happens when natals, born with plastic brains and a developmental

49. Willett, *Maternal Ethics and Other Slave Moralities*, 16.
50. Ibid., 113.

need for environmental stimuli and bonds of social attachment, are deprived of these goods, or worse—are surrounded by harmful stimuli and violent social interactions? Like Spitz's orphans, such infants fail to thrive and some even fail to survive. The natal's need for society—for bonds of affection and attachment—renders human beings highly vulnerable to the effects of social deprivation in infancy and early childhood, when the brain is so remarkably plastic. But our relational vulnerability extends beyond childhood into the rest of our lives. Our brains continue to exhibit plasticity throughout adulthood and we continue to require social interaction and bonds of affection throughout our lifespan.

Whether due to biological imperatives or social role construction or both, most (though certainly not all) mothers and/or othermothers generally respond to their children's need for environmental stimuli, social interaction, and bonds of affection with the caring maternal labors of preservative love, nurturance to maturity, and training for social acceptance.[51] Most infants— even those who are emotionally deprived—receive more than the minimally adequate social resources for physical survival afforded to the unfortunate orphanage children studied by Spitz. And it is mostly (though certainly not always) mothers or othermothers who provide the primary bonds of affection necessary for survival and flourishing in infancy and early childhood. But it is not only the child who is influenced and formed by the bonds of affection forged between maternal caregivers and their charges. The maternal attachment that can evolve out of a child's material and psychological dependency is also (trans)formative of a mother's subjectivity, and consequently of her well-being. Again, this can sound quite lovely. But the bonds of maternal affection

51. Cf. Ruddick, who identifies these three tasks as constitutive of maternal practice in *Maternal Thinking*.

render mothers particularly vulnerable to vicarious or empathetic suffering—a child's suffering can cause a mother great pain.

In *Myth of the Welfare Queen*, Odessa Williams, deeply pained by her daughter's drug addiction and consequent work as a prostitute, is a case in point:

> It was along Kensington Avenue, beneath the black shadows cast by the El gridwork, that Brenda stood and waited for men cruising in cars to stop and negotiate with her for sex. Each time Odessa drove across Kensington Avenue she thought about Brenda. Each time, she became more reconciled to the awful realization that her daughter was lost to her forever, that crack had seized Brenda and would not let go until she was dead. It was no consolation to Odessa that Brenda was joined by dozens of other women of all ages and races, each one strolling under the El, bending low in a miniskirt or tight spandex slacks to solicit men in cars. Odessa wondered if the mothers of the other women felt the same pain and despair that she felt.[52]

On the other end of the socio-economic spectrum, Carol Shields's novel *Unless* relates the story of Reta Winters, a well-educated, upper-middle-class white mother of three daughters who is devastated by the tragic descent of her eldest child.[53] Reta has everything going for her: three beautiful, intelligent, and well-adjusted daughters; a loving husband; a lovely home; a slowly but surely ascending career as a writer. But her happiness comes crashing down in an instant when her daughter Norah drops out of college, goes missing, and is found sitting day after day on a cold Toronto street corner, holding a sign that says "GOODNESS." Before Norah's breakdown, Reta was asked in an interview about the worst thing that had ever happened to her. She knew in an instant that, though nothing truly bad had yet happened to her, when it did it would have something to do with one of her children. When Norah disappears

52. Zucchino, *Myth of the Welfare Queen*, 39. Cf. also 330.
53. Shields, *Unless*.

only to show up on a street corner, Reta moves into unhappiness and pain as a new way of being in the world:

> It happens that I am going through a period of great unhappiness and loss just now. All my life I've heard people speak of finding themselves in acute pain, bankrupt in spirit and body; but I've never understood what they meant. To lose. To have lost. I believed these visitations of darkness lasted only a few minutes or hours and that these saddened people, in between bouts, were occupied, as we all were, with the useful monotony of happiness. But happiness is not what I thought. Happiness is the lucky pane of glass you carry in your head. It takes all your cunning just to hang on to it, and once it's smashed you have to move into a different sort of life.[54]

As a mother who had spent the past nineteen years attempting to draw out and nurture the beauty and goodness in her daughter, Norah's traumatized search for goodness as a panhandler is devastating for Reta. Like many mothers, her own happiness is so intertwined with the well-being of her children that Norah's demise brings about the demise of her own happiness as well.

In his *Nicomachean Ethics*, Aristotle argues that because human beings are social animals, *philia*—which is often translated as "friendship" but includes other significant bonds of human affection as well—is necessary for human life and the human good. Human happiness depends on *philia*. True friends, interestingly exemplified for Aristotle by mothers, relate to the beloved as another self.[55] Again, quite lovely. But when a friend, in this case a mother like Odessa or Reta, feels the pain of the beloved as her own, her chances of misfortune are doubled. Bonds of human affection, though necessary (or perhaps because they are necessary) for human flourishing, render

---

54. Ibid., 1.
55. Aristotle, *Nicomachean Ethics*, second edition, trans. Terence Irwin (Indianapolis: Hackett, 1999). See Books VIII–IX, on "Friendship," especially Book IX, chapter 9, on the question "Why Are Friends Needed?"

human beings profoundly vulnerable. According to Aristotle, this is especially true of mothers, who place so much practical effort into the birth and care of their children.[56] Drawing on maternal experience, the pioneering care ethicist Nel Noddings explains this relational vulnerability involved in caring labor well:

> When I care, when I receive the other in the way we have been discussing, there is more than a feeling; there is also a motivational shift. My motive energy flows toward the other and perhaps, although not necessarily, toward his ends. I do not relinquish myself; I cannot excuse myself for what I do. But I allow my motive energy to be shared; I put it at the service of the other. It is clear that my vulnerability is potentially increased when I care, for I can be hurt through the other as well as through myself.[57]

Relational existence, then, is inherently vulnerable. We can be hurt by those with whom we are in relation, and when we care for and about those with whom we are in relation, we can be hurt by what hurts them. "Might it not be easier to escape to the world of principles and abstractions? These cared-fors under whose gaze I fall—whose real eyes look into mine—are related to me. I can be hurt through them and by them. Intermittently, they are I and I they. The possibilities for both pain and joy are increased in my world, but I need courage to grasp the possibilities."[58]

The greater the investment of motivational and emotional energy in those for whom we care, the greater our vulnerability to harm. In addition to their dependence on material resources necessary for childrearing, this is why practitioners of maternal care can experience a unique and even heightened form of vulnerability. Kittay avers that "because of the significance of both affect and trust in these

---

56. Ibid., IX.7.7.
57. Nel Noddings, *Caring: A Feminine Approach to Ethics and Moral Education* (Berkeley: University of California Press, 1984), 33.
58. Ibid., 39.

relations [between charge and dependency worker], the ties formed by dependency are among the most important ones we experience. It often seems that to infuse caring labor into such a relationship . . . relaxes our boundaries of self, which makes way for an emotional bond that is especially potent."[59] The result for mothers is a greater openness to being harmed by that which harms either the mother-child relationship or the child herself (even once she is no longer dependent on the caregiver). Miller-McLemore observes this phenomenon in her own experience, and as it has been described by other feminist maternal thinkers and writers:

> Serious involvement in child bearing and rearing involves a constraint, an internal and, in some ways, unrelenting tug of attachment, what [Julia] Kristeva calls a pain that "comes from the inside" and "never remains apart": "You may close your eyes . . . teach courses, run errands . . . think about objects, subjects." But a mother is marked by a tenacious link to another that begins at conception and never quite goes away. Some "deep encoded pattern," writes [Mary] Gordon, draws the heroine in *Men and Angels* physically to her two children and makes her encircle them in a way that neither men nor angels seem to understand.[60]

For many mothers, giving birth to a child and raising that child to adulthood induces the sensation of their hearts walking around outside of their bodies. However joyous the experience might be at times, to mother a child is to render oneself exposed to harm and vulnerable to heartbreak and tragedy.

Mothers are by no means alone in their vulnerability to relational suffering. Though Aristotle uses motherhood as a paradigmatic example of the vulnerability that results from bonds of human affection, he rightly maintains that the human condition is characterized by a persistent need for *philia*. Mothers and infants,

---

59. Kittay, *Love's Labor*, 36.
60. Miller-McLemore, *Also a Mother*, 143.

children and adults, men and women, human beings always and everywhere are embodied *and* social animals. As embodied and relational creatures, we need social bonds—political, cultural, economic, personal, and intimate bonds—in order to live a human life and attain to human happiness. Close ties of affection are part of this need. Love, in its many and varied forms, is a part of this need. But love is not something we can control, and the beloved is not someone we can control. Our need for love, and our attachment to our loved ones, renders us intractably vulnerable to anguish and despair. And yet we cannot resist love's power, for it is on love that our happiness depends.

2

The Complexity of Human Vulnerability

Perishing, Conflict, and Ambiguity

Love is an infinite feeling in a finite container, and so upsets the intellect, frustrates the will. An anarchic emotion that transcends the rules of age, race, blood, passionate love has a wild philosophy at base. Because we can't control the fixation of love and desire, we experience emotional mayhem—stories, fiction, works of art result. Love's combination of attraction and despair thrills us.[1]

~Louise Erdrich, *The Blue Jay's Dance*

The basic anthropological constants of embodiment and relationality render human beings vulnerable to the contingencies and vicissitudes of life in a finite, and thus complex and ambiguous, universe. Human beings are dependent on love for physical, psychological, and spiritual flourishing, but Erdrich's poetic words remind us that love is "an anarchic emotion" with "a wild philosophy at base." As embodied and

---

1. Louise Erdrich, *The Blue Jay's Dance: A Birth Year* (New York: HarperCollins, 1995), 106.

relational creatures, we exist in a changing world made up of external forces and factors that lie beyond our immediate control. These forces and the reality of finitude itself complexify human vulnerability. Our bodies and relationships are vulnerable to pain and suffering in the midst of a dynamic and changing, never static, reality. The receptivity of our bodies and the relationality of our material and psycho-spiritual lives place our experiences, choices, and happiness in complex and often chaotic relationships of conflict and ambiguity with the experiences, choices, and happiness of other embodied and relational beings. Just as maternal narratives and analyses function as icons of the fundamentals of human vulnerability in embodiment and relationality, so too can they illuminate our understanding of how complex human life and love can be under the finite conditions of perishing, conflict, and ambiguity. While love is necessary for the survival and flourishing of human beings and their communities, love's complexity renders it (and us) vulnerable to the pain of passing beauty, and the anguish of an existence marked by conflicting and ambiguous goods.

Perishing: Vulnerability to the Pain of Passing Beauty

I could not have been more full; life could not have been more sweet. And at the same time, there was also that ache, at "the rustling of the grains of sand as they slid lightly away," that ache of beauty and longing and time and the unbearable fragility and surpassing preciousness of this moment.[2]
~Daphne de Marneffe, *Maternal Desire*

I would walk through a tunnel of fire if it would save my son. I would take my chances on a stripped battlefield with a sling and a rock à la David and Goliath if it would make a difference. But it won't. I can roar all I want about

2. Daphne de Marneffe, *Maternal Desire: On Children, Love, and the Inner Life* (New York: Little, Brown & Co., 2004), 313.

*the unfairness of this ridiculous disease, but the facts remain. What I can do is
protect my son from as much pain as possible, and then finally do the hardest
thing of all, a thing most parents will thankfully never have to do: I will love
him to the end of his life, and then I will let him go.*[3]
~Emily Rapp, mother of a child with Tay-Sachs

"An infinite feeling in a finite container," human love cannot possibly
hold onto its beloved forever, not least because the beloved—the
person, moment, or feeling, that is object of love's desire—is not a
static, unchanging entity to be grasped and preserved intact for the
lover's enjoyment. There is not one entity within reality that remains
static, unchanged, or unaffected by the passing of time. Mother-child
relationships in pregnancy, infancy, early childhood, and maturation
reveal this third anthropological constant: perishing. The processes
of growth and change are inherent to human existence. We need
to grow and change in order to survive and thrive in the world.
The anthropological constants of embodied relationality and
(inter)dependence are what keep this process moving forward toward
self-transcendence, but growth and change inevitably carry with
them feelings of discord and pain. Even if it is a mere twinge of
simple recognition that this developmental stage or that will never
again take place, the process of growth is one that mothers can find
difficult. And when the beauty of a mother's child, a developmental
stage, or a moment in time does not move forward to new forms of
beauty but is cut off in disability, disease, destruction, or death (the
last of which will one day be the case for all of us natals/mortals), the
loss can produce the deepest sorrow a mother might ever know.

---

3. Emily Rapp, "Notes from a Dragon Mom," *New York Times*, October 15, 2011, online edition,
http://www.nytimes.com/2011/10/16/opinion/sunday/notes-from-a-dragon-
mom.html/?scp=1&sq=notes from a dragon mom&st=Search.

Beginning the Long Good-bye: Mundane Grief

Although most mothers would likely experience progression toward a child's maturity and self-sufficiency as a positive thing, many mothers also feel a simultaneous nostalgic ache accompanying the stages of passing beauty in their children's lives. Erdrich reflects on her own experience of this feeling when she encounters a nest woven of the strands of her daughters' hair that she had strategically offered to the birds in her family's woods:

> It is almost too painful to hold the nest, too rich as life often is with children. I see the bird, quick breathing, small, thrilling like a heart. I hear its song, high and clear, beating in its throat. I see that bird alone in the nest woven from the hair of my daughters, and I cannot hold the nest because longing seizes me. Not only do I feel how quickly they are growing from the curved shape of my arms when holding them, but I want to sit in the presence of my own mother so badly it hurts. Life seems to flood by, taking our loves quickly in its flow. In the growth of children, in the aging of beloved parents, time's chart is magnified, shown in its particularity, focused, so that with each celebration of maturity, there is also a pang of loss. This is our human problem, one common to parents, sons and daughters too—how to let go while holding tight, how to simultaneously cherish the closeness and intricacy of the bond while at the same time letting out the raveling string, the red yarn that ties our hearts.[4]

This feeling of loss, which Miller-McLemore calls "mundane grief,"[5] accompanies the passage of time and the development of natals from birth through childhood to maturity and, eventually to death. Care for another person, in this case of a mother for her children, carries with it vulnerability to suffering not only because of the pain a mother can experience due to her child's misfortune (as was explored

---

4. Erdrich, *The Blue Jay's Dance*, 68–69.
5. Bonnie Miller-McLemore, *In the Midst of Chaos: Care of Children as a Spiritual Practice* (San Francisco: Jossey-Bass, 2006), 176ff.

in the previous chapter), but also because of the daily, monthly, yearly losses that caring for another growing and changing human being entails. Miller-McLemore observes, in fact, that

> the word *care*, according to poet Kathleen Norris, "derives from an Indo-European word meaning to 'cry out,' as in lament." In [Norris's] poem "Ascension," written as she thinks about her birthing sister bearing down in labor on the day commemorating Jesus' rising to heaven, she pictures the "new mother, that leaky vessel," nursing her child, "beginning the long good-bye." Beginning the long good-bye.[6]

In the maternal circles that I inhabit, it is not uncommon for mothers to lament to one another this "long good-bye," commenting with choked-back tears on the process of weaning a nursing infant or toddler, remarking with a twinge of sadness that we can't believe these kids are in pre-school already, confiding in each other our simultaneous pride and sadness at how quickly our children are growing and changing and becoming more and more independent. "Oh, he's getting so big!" we observe with a frown or, "Before we know it, they will be off to college," we lament with lumps in our throats. For Miller-McLemore, this nontragic grief experienced in family life is anticipatory of future losses, of children leaving home, of separation from family, of the painful realities of finitude and, ultimately, mortality. She relates that, soon after she recognized this mode of anticipatory grief in herself, she drove to the airport to pick up her oldest son and, when he appeared, she found herself overwhelmed with emotion: "I found myself surprised by tears, tears that mixed love and loss in equal portions. The more I tried not to cry, the more I did, and the more my son looked at me strangely. I really couldn't explain it to him easily. To stare finitude straight in the face when the face is so beloved . . . how could you *not* cry?"[7]

6. Ibid., 180.
7. Ibid., 198.

In addition to feeling the pain of the passing beauty in the changing lives of their children, some mothers are also pained by the changes in their own lives and bodies as they move into and, later, beyond their childbearing years. Some mothers, especially middle-class women who have built an identity around their careers and adult-centered social lives prior to settling down and having children, experience a profound sense of loss when they become mothers. A new mother might feel faint and intermittent nostalgia for the freedom and independence of her life before children, or she might feel overwhelming despair at the loss of self-identity that has accompanied the transition to her new role in life. On the other hand, mothers can experience a painful tug of nostalgia for their own lost fertility once they have either decided to end their childbearing years, or once their aging bodies make that decision for them. De Marneffe reflects on her own experience of this form of pain at the passing beauty of maternal life:

> Around the age of forty, when I knew we would have no more children, I felt a pang whenever I saw a newborn or heard a friend was having a baby. It was an odd new position; to be no longer in the "before" or the "during," but in the "after." I could think it through rationally—we'd had a good run; we had been so lucky; I wanted to concentrate on being as good a mother as I could be to the ones we had—but there was this pang anyway. I think it is a particularly female window onto mortality. You can only postpone, but never escape, the final reckoning of no more children. . . . As primal as the urge feels, one is wary of its species-serving deceptions. That cute being envelops one's time and energy, wears away ones joints and muscles, and at a certain point, the system just doesn't have that much to give.[8]

No matter how many children a mother has, the last one will be her last. She will move forward to a new phase in her life, a phase beyond her childbearing years—perhaps not less filled with meaning

---

8. De Marneffe, *Maternal Desire*, 278.

or beauty, but different and new. A change of life. Many (perhaps most?) mothers greet the end of pregnancies and intensive infant and toddler care with gratitude and relief. But some mothers can also experience this simultaneous tug of regret that de Marneffe describes so poignantly. Time does not slow down or stop for anyone. It marches on relentlessly, leaving behind forms of beauty that will be missed and thrusting us ever closer to our mortality.

Though the pain of passing beauty described here is a maternal phenomenon, and though not all (perhaps not even most) mothers experience this mundane grief, it is a reality that touches all of human life and points to a truth about reality as a whole and the human condition within reality. As Erdrich's earlier reflections imply, this maternal nostalgia and longing points to our human problem—that "life seems to flood by, taking our loves quickly in its flow."[9] Such is the structure of human existence, indeed of reality itself. Each finite good that is realized and each finite beauty that is experienced, in some sense, excludes other goods and other beauties. Furthermore, the movement from one good to the next and one beauty to the next, always leaves something of value behind. And the loss accompanying this relentless movement can be experienced as painful. The process thought of Alfred North Whitehead describes this phenomenon as "perishing." In his metaphysics, the Universe is teleologically oriented toward the production of Beauty, which is the perfection of Harmony. Reality is a process that moves in this direction by the persuasive power of Divine Eros, "which is the living urge towards all possibilities, claiming the goodness of their realization."[10] Things within reality are to be understood not as static entities, but rather in terms of their becoming and their passing away. Eros urges these things in reality toward the synthesis of past, present, and future.

9. Erdrich, *The Blue Jay's Dance*, 68.
10. Alfred North Whitehead, *Adventures of Ideas* (New York: Macmillan, 1933), 381.

However beautiful this synthesis may be, the beauties of the past still fade away and their passing is often experienced by human beings as painful. In Monica Coleman's words, "The ultimate evil in the temporal world is deeper than any specific evil. It lies in the fact that the past fades, that time is a perpetual perishing. Objectification involves elimination. The present fact has not the past fact with it in any full immediacy. In the temporal world, it is the empirical fact that process entails loss."[11] The losses that accompany the process of passing beauty do not always produce pain; indeed, Whitehead admits that the new synthesis can be experienced by the Soul as good when the feelings involved fortify each other "as they meet in the novel unity." On the other hand, the synthesis can be experienced as evil when it entails a "clash of vivid feelings, denying to each other their proper expansion."[12] This clash may well be what takes place when a mother laments the loss of a particular stage of beauty in her life and/or the lives of her children. When we try to hold on to a moment in time, when it is so good and so beautiful that a part of us desires its infinite expansion, its passing can produce pain.

Early Good-byes and No Good-byes at All: Traumatic Grief

As poignant as it may be, mundane grief is a luxury. It is a luxury enjoyed most fully by those of us mothers who have enjoyed uncomplicated fertility and have, thankfully, not (yet) had to cope with grave misfortune or tragic loss in our lives or in the lives of our children. There are many situations (far too many) in which the passing of beauty does not lead to a positive synthesis, but to a denial of future forms of beauty in cases such as infertility, pregnancy loss, severe childhood disability, disease, violent destruction, and death.

11. Monica Coleman, *Making a Way Out of No Way: A Womanist Theology* (Minneapolis: Fortress Press, 2008), 56.
12. Whitehead, *Adventures of Ideas*, 355.

Perhaps some form of beauty emerges from these traumatic circumstances, and the second part of this theological anthropology explores this possibility further. But the overwhelming sensation experienced by most mothers in these situations can be devastating grief at the evil of a beautiful life denied its proper expansion. As Miller-McLemore observes, "Compared to the death of a child, daily loss is nothing. . . . The death of a child brings one to the nadir of hopelessness. This is an experience no one should have to endure."[13]

An opinion piece in the *New York Times* cuts to the heart of the primal grief experienced by mothers when such a loss of possibility and beauty occurs in the lives of their children. Emily Rapp is an author, professor of creative writing, and mother of Ronan, who was born with Tay-Sachs. In her opinion piece, Rapp shared that this rare genetic disorder would cause Ronan, who was then eighteen months old, to have seizures, become paralyzed, lose all senses, slowly regress into a vegetative state, and likely die before his third birthday. Ronan did in fact pass away in February of 2013, when he was almost three years old. Most parenting advice, remarks Rapp, is oriented toward the future and the projected physical, material, psychological, intellectual, and spiritual "successes" of our children. Most mothers expect their children to have a future, to live past childhood into adulthood and hopefully old age. In the case of children like Ronan, the future is cut off. The beautiful person he might have become will never be. His life is denied its proper expansion. His mother will never have the chance to experience the mundane grief of passing beauty at his first steps, his graduation from kindergarten, his growth to maturity, and so on.

> Ronan won't prosper or succeed in the way we have come to understand this term in our culture; he will never walk or say "Mama." . . . The

---

13. Miller-McLemore, *In the Midst of Chaos*, 179.

mothers and fathers of terminally ill children are something else entirely. Our goals are simple and terrible: to help our children live with minimal discomfort and maximum dignity. We will not launch our children into a bright and promising future, but see them into early graves. We will prepare to lose them and then, impossibly, to live on after that gutting loss.[14]

Rapp's reflections in her article are powerful and point to hard lessons about the human condition, its vulnerability, its fleetingness. She describes her family's story as "[d]epressing? Sure. But not without wisdom, not without a profound understanding of the human experience or without hard-won lessons, forged through grief and helplessness and deeply committed love about how to be not just a mother or a father but how to be human."[15] We will come back to some of these possible "lessons" on "how to be human" in the midst of a vulnerable and suffering world in parts 2 and 3.

While Rapp has experienced the maternal grief that accompanied her young child's disability, disease, and her prior knowledge of his impending death, traumatic loss also haunts mothers whose children die abruptly due to illness, accident, or violent attack. This was certainly the case for Salvadoran peasant woman, Rufina Amaya, the sole eyewitness survivor of the Massacre at El Mozote, which claimed the lives of at least 1,000 victims, including Amaya's husband and four of her children.[16] Her youngest child, an eight-month-old daughter, was literally ripped from her breast by soldiers to be killed with the

---

14. Rapp, "Notes from a Dragon Mom." See also Rapp's subsequent book, *The Still Point of the Turning World* (New York: Penguin, 2013).

15. Ibid.

16. Cf. Rufina Amaya et al., *Luciérnagas en El Mozote* (San Salvador, El Salvador: Ediciones Museo de la Palabra, 1996). For a full account of the massacre, its place in the overall counterinsurgency strategy of the Salvadoran armed forces, and its subsequent cover-up, see the following sources: Leigh Binford, *The El Mozote Massacre: Anthropology and Human Rights* (Tucson: University of Arizona Press, 1996); Mark Danner, *The Massacre at El Mozote: A Parable of the Cold War* (New York: Vintage, 1994); and UN Security Council, *From Madness to Hope: The 12-Year War in El Salvador: Report of the Commission on the Truth for El Salvador*, 1993, http://www.usip.org/files/file/ElSalvador-Report.pdf.

rest of the town's children in the parish rectory. Despite her apparent strength and the peacefulness of her demeanor, Amaya was haunted by the abrupt and traumatic loss of her children every day until she died in 2007. Her words, which comprise the first epigraph to this chapter, are worth repeating:

> You never stop feeling sorrow for your children. . . . The one that was most painful was my eight month old girl who was still nursing. I felt my breasts full of milk, and I wept bitterly. . . . Today I can tell the story, but in that moment I was not able to; I had such a knot and a pain in my heart that I couldn't even speak. All I could do was bend over and cry.[17]

Imagine this young mother wandering through the mountains of Northeastern El Salvador in the days following the massacre. In addition to the physical cold and hunger, her breasts were full of milk to the point of leaking. Such fullness involved a great deal of pain, and this physical pain was nothing but a constant reminder of the immense, irreplaceable, inconceivable loss of her baby girl and three other children. Painful breasts, overflowing with milk that her child would never taste again, point to the stark fact that Amaya's children were abruptly and violently erased from earthly existence. Their future possibilities were destroyed, their nourishment and development denied. The passing of their beautiful lives plagued her with intermittent waves of grief until her own death decades later.

Both Rapp's and Amaya's stories point to the vulnerability involved in the anthropological constant of perishing. The processes of change at work in embodied and interdependent human life can be destructive, rendering human beings vulnerable to traumatic loss. As relational beings, we require *philia* for happiness and meaning in life. But our cherished loves, significant others, beloved family and friends are all embodied creatures who are "corruptible"—that is, vulnerable

---

17. Amaya et al., *Luciérnagas en El Mozote*, 20.

to disease, death, and destruction. The unthinkable could happen to our loved ones at any moment and the slow or abrupt loss of their presence and proper expansion in the world diminishes our own lives. In Miller-McLemore's words, our grief at their passing "involves the real loss of the materiality of ordinary touch, nurture, and affection."[18] The beauty of such meaningful material pleasures, and the potential for their development, can be cut off forever. The beauty of particular lives and loves that are precious to us can be ripped from existence without a moment's notice. The grief that such loss occasions can be primal, unwieldy, and devastating for those who are left behind. Compared with mundane grief, it is voracious in its power. Unlike daily losses that interact with present and future possibilities to create a positive synthesis, such loss has the potential to subject survivors to the affliction of radical suffering, the destruction of all meaning, hope, and even reason for living. But, as Miller-McLemore points out, there is

> a connection between tragic and mundane loss. All parents [indeed, all human beings] stand on an evolving continuum as people vulnerable before the utter precariousness of the created lives dearest to them, whether they live with present loss or contemplating impending loss. In fact, those who have suffered the death of a child are precisely those who are in a good position to remind the rest of us, as pastoral theologian Bruce Vaughn does, that mourning is "an ongoing and fundamental dimension of what it means to be human."[19]

Even with a lifetime of notice, the passing of mortal beauty is a painful process. The mundane grief that mothers often feel in the face of passing beauty is indeed a luxury, but it can also point to this third anthropological constant: our corruptible condition is inevitably marked by embodied, relational development to maturity and,

18. Miller-McLemore, *In the Midst of Chaos*, 184.
19. Ibid., 179.

eventually, death. Maternal experiences of both mundane and traumatic grief, then, remind us that our natality thrusts us toward mortality. The love we have for our children, parents, partners, spouses, families, and friends will not slow down or bring this process to a halt. Nor can it protect our loved ones from premature encounters with mortality due to disease, destruction, and death (accidental or violent). The human condition thus renders us fundamentally vulnerable to the pain of passing beauty, to grief at the mundane and tragic losses that occur throughout and at the end of our long and short good-byes.

Conflict and Ambiguity: Vulnerability to Failure

Whatever is realized in any one occasion of experience necessarily excludes the unbounded welter of contrary possibilities. There are always "others," which might have been and are not.[20]
~Alfred North Whitehead, *Adventures of Ideas*

In addition to pain induced by the process of passing beauty, mothers experience firsthand and on a daily basis the conflictual and ambiguous, and thus painful, nature of reality as embodied, relational process. Mothers certainly experience their fair share of suffering due to interpersonal conflict with their children, their partners, their families, community members, and so on. However, to illustrate the centrality of conflict and ambiguity to maternal experience in particular and to the human condition in general, I will focus on the phenomenon of conflicting and ambiguous goods internal to the experience and practice of mothering. Maternity thus reveals our fourth anthropological constant: conflict and ambiguity. The inevitability of conflict and ambiguity in human existence renders

---

20. Whitehead, *Adventures of Ideas*, 356.

us vulnerable to failure, with the potentially debilitating guilt this entails.

Conflicting Goods: Something's Got to Give

Because maternal labor is an inherently relational endeavor, there are several goods within its scope that often come into conflict: the well-being of the mother herself, the well-being of her children, and the well-being of society as a whole (including other mothers). It would be a rare occurrence in which these goods coexisted harmoniously. In most cases these goods come into some form of conflict with one another, and in many cases one category of good can actually contain conflict within itself. Paying attention to the global chain of caring labor draws these interrelated conflicts into stark relief. Arlie Hochschild first used the term "global care chain" in reference to "a series of personal links between people across the globe based on the paid or unpaid work of caring."[21] A prototypical example of a scenario linking mothers across the globe involves "an older daughter from a poor family who cares for her siblings while her mother works caring for the children of a migrating nanny who, in turn, cares for the child[ren] of a family in a rich country."[22] While the global care chain results from the unjust demands of global capital and is by no means essential to the practice of motherhood, keeping the care chain in mind helps to highlight how complicated and painful the conflicts inherent to motherwork can be.

---

21. Arlie Hochschild, "Global Care Chains and Emotional Surplus Value," in *On the Edge: Living with Global Capitalism*, ed. W. Hutton and A. Giddens (London: Jonathan Cape, 2000), 131. See also Hochschild's article, "The Nanny Chain," *The American Prospect*, December 19, 2001. In both articles, Hochschild draws on the research of Rhacel Salazar Parreñas, later published in *Servant of Globalization: Women, Migration, and Domestic Work* (Stanford: Stanford University Press, 2001).
22. Hochschild, "Global Care Chains," 131.

At a most basic level, motherhood involves an inevitable conflict between two distinct, though interdependent and ambiguous, goods: a mother's physical and psychological well-being on the one hand, and the intensive labor of caring for a child's or children's well-being on the other. Due to this conflict, it is not uncommon for mothers to feel a certain amount of ambivalence toward motherhood. Adrienne Rich explored this experience of maternal ambivalence in her trailblazing work, *Of Woman Born: Motherhood as Experience and Institution*. In the first chapter of this taboo-breaking account of motherhood, Rich reflects on alternating and at times simultaneous feelings of anger and tenderness evoked in her by her children. Her self-disclosure is raw and courageous and unflinchingly honest, admitting to "the suffering of ambivalence: the murderous alternation between bitter resentment and raw-edged nerves, and blissful gratification and tenderness."[23] The lion's share of Rich's frustration was due to the unjust conditions of patriarchal motherhood and the near impossibility of self-determination and self-development for mid-twentieth-century American women in general, and mothers in particular. However, the physical and psychological limits of finitude also played a role in the conflict between Rich's own needs and those of her children. She could remember little of her children's early years but "anxiety, physical weariness, anger, self-blame, boredom, and division within [her]self."[24] The institution of motherhood exacerbates both the anger and the guilt that mothers experience because of their ambivalence, but caring labor is an inherently difficult and painful undertaking, even in the most ideal of conditions. However utopian, egalitarian, and communal our childrearing practices may be, the needs and wants of children often

23. Adrienne Rich, *Of Woman Born: Motherhood as Institution and Experience* (New York: W. W. Norton, 1976), 21–22.
24. Ibid.

conflict with the needs and wants of adults.[25] There are conflicting goods at work here that cannot be eliminated entirely.

Betty Friedan famously described the frustration of middle- to upper-class, white American mothers like Adrienne Rich as the "problem that has no name":

> The problem lay buried, unspoken, for many years in the minds of American women. It was a strange stirring, a sense of dissatisfaction, a yearning that women suffered in the middle of the 20th century in the United States. Each suburban wife struggled with it alone. As she made the beds, shopped for groceries . . . she was afraid to ask even of herself the silent question—Is this all?[26]

From the mid-twentieth century forward, many mothers in this demographic have sought to overcome this nameless problem in part by seeking personal fulfillment in paid work outside of the home. The result, however, has not been perfect happiness, but further conflict due to the impossibility of perfectly balancing maternal well-being (the fulfillment of which involves both familial and professional relationships) with the well-being of children (who stand to benefit not only from the presence of a stay-at-home mother, but also from the example and well-being of a mother engaged in fulfilling work outside the home). Therefore, many mothers who choose to work for reasons of personal fulfillment feel an acutely painful struggle between the often-divergent goods of being present to one's children and employment outside the home. This internal conflict, of course, can be largely attributed to the impossible patriarchal ideals surrounding the institution of motherhood, to the impossible call for autonomy presented more recently by feminists, to the lack of affordable and high-quality childcare, and to the media hype

---

25. For a well-researched, but popularly accessible account of this conflict, see Jennifer Senior, *All Joy and No Fun: The Paradox of Modern Parenthood* (New York: HarperCollins, 2014).

26. Betty Friedan, *The Feminine Mystique* (New York: W. W. Norton, 1963), 15.

surrounding our culture's "mommy wars."[27] But the fact that the work-family conflict is largely a social construction does not make it any less real or painful for women in real life. In fact, the social pressures to work or stay at home are what make an already difficult decision all the more agonizing. As de Marneffe observes, "Even when the work is relatively rewarding, the conflict between doing it and caring for children can be powerful."[28] In her view, contemporary Western, educated, middle-class women have so many choices before them. Thanks to the feminist activism of the mid- to late twentieth century, such women are free to choose from a plethora of opportunities. Most middle-class white girls of my own generation grew up thinking that the sky was the limit. But "[a]t the same time, the proliferation of choices presents new challenges, as it creates expanded arenas for conflict, indecision, and doubt."[29]

While many middle- to upper-class mothers face the painful luxury of choosing between or, more accurately, combining work and motherhood, many other middle-class and working-class mothers have no choice but to work outside the home in order to provide for themselves and their families.[30] The well-being of children is related to the affection and availability of their primary caregivers, but it is also related to the ability of those caregivers to afford shelter, food,

---

27. As it turns out, the dichotomy between stay-at-home and working mothers is largely fictitious, sensationalized by mainstream media and political ideologues interested in dividing women and furthering their respective conservative or liberal political agendas for women and the family. A great deal has been written on the mommy wars for both popular and academic audiences on this conflict. For an excellent introduction, cf. Amber Kinser, *Motherhood and Feminism* (Berkeley: Seal, 2010). Cf. also Miriam Peskowitz, *The Truth Behind the Mommy Wars: Who Decides What Makes a Good Mother?* (Berkeley: Seal, 2005).

28. De Marneffe, *Maternal Desire*, 52. This internal conflict is by no means universal, but rather depends in cultural and social factors. Cf. Susan Chase and Mary Francen Rogers, *Mothers and Children: Feminist Analyses and Personal Narratives* (New Brunswick, NJ: Rutgers University Press, 2001), 74.

29. De Marneffe, *Maternal Desire*, 11.

30. Cf. e.g., Val Gillies, *Marginalised Mothers: Exploring Working Class Experiences of Parenting* (New York: Routledge, 2007), 43ff.

clothing, and opportunities for educational and social enrichment for their children. Two-thirds to three-quarters of mothers in the United States are participants in the paid workforce.[31] Many, if not most, of these mother-workers (wealthy or not) seek employment out of economic necessity—the need to provide for the material needs (and wants!) of their children. The *en masse* entrance of mothers into the paid workforce over the past several decades—whatever their motivation—has in turn created a high demand for paid childcare (and dependency care in general). Many of the childcare workers who meet this demand are mothers themselves, and are only able to provide for their own children with the wages they earn from taking care of other mothers' children. The good of the paid caregiver's children is therefore dependent on their mother leaving them in the care of another person so that she can earn enough money to put bread on the table.

The movement of American mothers into the workforce—either for their own good or for the good of their families, or both—has thus created what Hochschild calls the "global care chain." The most complicated and extensive example of this phenomenon, referenced above, links together several women across the globe in transferals of caregiving labor. An older sister or other family member cares for children in a poor village in a poor country, while their mother goes to work caring for the children of a slightly wealthier woman in the city who, in turn, migrates to the United States (or another wealthy country) to care for the children of a mother who works as a doctor, lawyer, financier, academic, and so on. Each woman along this chain faces a conflict of goods. We have already visited the conflict faced by the mother at the top of the care chain. The conflicting goods faced by the mothers located on the lower rungs of the economic

31. U.S. Department of Labor, Department of Labor Statistics, "Employment Characteristics of Families Summary," April 26, 2012, http://www.bls.gov/news.release/famee.nr0.htm.

ladder are even more anguishing. Many are forced—by economic circumstances, paternal abandonment, or situations of domestic violence—to leave their homes and their own children in order to make enough of a living to provide for them.[32]

In all likelihood, each woman on this chain weighs the pros and cons of her decision and opts for what is best for both her children and herself. But the reality of conflicting goods means that even the "best" decision comes at a cost that "tend[s] to get passed down along the chain."[33] Because the well-being of children involves both material provision and bonds of affection, their mother's absence—even if it is for their own good—can take a toll. As one Filipina mother related to Rhacel Parreñas,

> My children were very sad when I left them. My husband told me that when they came back home from the airport, my children could not touch their food and they wanted to cry. My son, whenever he writes me, always draws the head of Fido the dog with tears on the eyes. Whenever he goes to Mass on Sundays, he tells me that he misses me more because he sees his friends with their mothers. Then he comes home and cries.[34]

Another mother expresses how the cost of her absence is felt by her children, and how her children's experience of loss is painful for her to behold:

> When I saw my children [on a return trip to the Philippines], I thought, "Oh children do grow up even without their mother." I left my youngest when she was only five years old. She was already nine when I

---

32. Of course, this was also the case for domestic workers in the U.S. long before globalization. African American women historically have stepped in as surrogate caregivers for the children of white women during slavery and beyond. Cf. Delores Williams's analysis of black women's surrogacy roles in *Sisters in the Wilderness: The Challenge of Womanist God-Talk* (Maryknoll, NY: Orbis, 1995).
33. Hochschild, "The Nanny Chain."
34. Ibid., citing the dissertation research of Rhacel Parreñas.

saw her again but she still wanted for me to carry her [weeps]. That hurt me because it showed me that my children missed out on a lot.[35]

Hochschild observes that sometimes the toll that leaving home takes on the migrating childcare worker is overwhelming and the mother yearns intensely and painfully for her own children:

> As one woman told Parreñas, "The first two years I felt like I was going crazy. . . . I would catch myself gazing at nothing, thinking about my child. Every moment, every second of the day, I felt like I was thinking about my baby. My youngest, you have to understand, I left when he was only two months old. . . . You know, whenever I receive a letter from my children, I cannot sleep. I cry. It's good that my job is more demanding at night."[36]

The good of a mother and the good of her children are thus bound together in complex and sometimes impossible ways. Generally speaking, each woman and each child located on this chain of care is left wanting. Conflicting goods make our life decisions terribly ambiguous and thus render mothers along the chain of care vulnerable to the pain of sacrificing something, and usually more than one thing.

The "problem that has no name" experienced by mid-twentieth-century privileged mothers was the result of gender injustice. And the experience of Filipina women forced to leave their children behind in search of a better life for them is the result of both sexism and an unjust world economic order. Patriarchy and global capitalism are not natural to the human condition and require too much sacrifice of all of us (some much more than others). However, the incompatible goods at work in the care chain can serve to illustrate how conflict and ambiguity are an anthropological constant—part and parcel of life in a finite and imperfect world. Whitehead's understanding of

35. Ibid.
36. Ibid.

reality as process can once again help us to understand these maternal experiences of conflict and ambiguity as manifestations of the human vulnerability to conflictual suffering in general. In Whitehead's view, the finitude of all things within reality means that reality is inherently conflictive; various finite goods are often mutually opposing. Sometimes the opposition of various goods can lead to a positive synthesis, in which the result is pleasant or even wonderful. But often the conflict of mutually exclusive goods leads to the tragic experience of destruction and, when destruction is the overwhelming experience, evil. In other words, the limitations of finitude (including the finitude of human love) are an unavoidable part of the system. In Whiteheadian terms, the static realization of all possible perfections of Beauty and Harmony is impossible: "All realization is finite, and there is no perfection which is the infinitude of all perfections. Perfections of diverse types are among themselves discordant."[37] The modes of Beauty are finite and various and not always compatible; therefore, Beauty and Discord must necessarily coexist, often with destructive and painful results. "Whatever is realized in any one occasion of experience necessarily excludes the unbounded welter of contrary possibilities. There are always 'others,' which might have been and are not."[38] The limitations of finitude that necessitate this exclusion of contrary possibilities are not in themselves evil or even the result of an imperfection in reality. In fact, Whitehead insists that it is only in and through the conditions of finitude that Divine Eros can do its work of urging all possible ideals toward their seasonable realization. Ultimate reality, then, involves a process whereby infinitude acquires realization only in and through finitude.[39] Since this process produces discord and suffering when the realization of various ideals and

---

37. Whitehead, *Adventures of Ideas*, 330.
38. Ibid., 356.
39. Cf. ibid., 357.

individualities inevitably clash, there is a sense in which suffering is inherent to the workings of embodied, relational reality as process.

In sum, Whitehead argues that Beauty and Evil intermingle based on "the conjoint operations of three metaphysical principles:—(1) That all actualization is finite; (2) That finitude involves the exclusion of alternative possibility; (3) That mental functioning introduces into realization subjective forms conformal to relevant alternatives excluded from the completeness of physical realization."[40] Simply put, the structure of reality is tragic. Coleman encapsulates Whitehead's metaphysics here well: "What may be optimal for the well-being of one aspect of creation may not promote the health and well-being of another aspect of creation. . . . These losses or evils are realities of the system. The ongoing process of becoming entails loss. . . . These are unavoidable evils. . . . Whitehead defines evil as something that is built into the system of the world."[41] The finite nature of reality, and thus the finite nature of the realization of Beauty, makes it such that disharmony, destruction, and suffering are inherent to reality and our experience of it. Though the experiences of conflict and ambiguity described above are expressly maternal in nature, and though they result from injustices that can and should be redressed, they point to this larger truth about human experience in general: the anthropological constant that as finite, embodied, and relational creatures, we are vulnerable to the limitations of finitude and the pain produced by the impossibility of realizing all the goods that we desire.

If we were to translate Whitehead's metaphysical insight here into more pedestrian language, we might say, "You simply can't have it all," or "Something's got to give." When that something "gives," we might experience the result as fresh and hopeful, but it can often be frustrating, painful, horrific, or even downright evil.

40. Ibid., 333.
41. Coleman, *Making a Way Out of No Way*, 57.

Ambiguous Goods:
Lack of Control, Unintended Consequences,
and Impossible Choices

In and throughout life's processes of growth and change, mothers' diverse experiences and practices indicate that the journey toward self-transcendence, goodness, happiness, and virtue is a fragile and ambiguous process and thus vulnerable to limits, indeterminacy, mistakes, misinterpretation, and even devastation. As embodied creatures, infants and children are vulnerable to physical harm, neurological damage, genetic anomalies, disability, disease, destruction, and death. As relational beings, they are dependent on other, older human beings to respond to their vulnerability with physical protection, material provision, emotional nurture, cognitive stimulation, and social integration. In addition to the limitations placed on maternal practice and maternal well-being by the reality of conflicting goods, a mother's attempts to meet her children's needs are limited by the impossibility of total control, the law of unintended consequences, and the imposition of unreasonable choices. Each of these realities renders the "goods" to which maternal practice aspires ambiguous and vulnerable to demise; this in turn renders mothers vulnerable to guilt and anguish over the impossibility of mothering without harm. Imperfection and failure are built into the system.

While there certainly are mothers who are uninterested in the well-being of their children, most mothers, to the best of their abilities, choose their own ways to perform the maternal tasks of preservative love, nurturance to maturity, and training for participation in society. Most mothers hope that their efforts will be successful, but there is no way to guarantee the purity of their goals or the outcome that their labors will produce. In an embodied and relational universe, it is impossible to control the various factors that contribute to the formation and development of a human child, let alone the forces that will affect the trajectory of his life once he moves into adolescence and adulthood. Although we now know with scientific certainty that the development of the fetal and infant human brain is vulnerable to environmental factors and social stimuli, there is only so much that an individual mother can do to control a child's environment and social interactions. Because a mother's own practices of care interact with other factors that she cannot control, her efforts are vulnerable to ambiguity and failure. Not only does the reality of conflicting goods explored above mean that she cannot possibly "do it all," the fact is that no good that she does is entirely self-sufficient or unambiguous.

For example, feminist mothers of the 1960s and 70s struggled to create a world in which their daughters would be free to pursue their dreams without restraint, and their efforts produced many positive results and widened opportunities for my generation of educated, middle-class women. However, the actions of feminist mothers did not necessarily make life easier for their daughters, since their maternal efforts did not exist in a vacuum but interacted with other forces and factors beyond their control. In her personal narrative of feminist mothering, Alix Kates Shulman reflects on the ambiguous outcome of her efforts to create a better world for her daughter:

> The world she inhabits is [still] a hard world because, although more is permitted women now, so much more is expected of them. Which means increased pressure and anxiety. The idea that I could save her along with me was a utopian delusion—the idea, which some of us held for a brief moment, that by making feminist changes we'd somehow make things easy for our children. The big problems—sexism, racism, violence, poverty—are probably as great as before, though different.[42]

---

42. Alix Kates Shulman, "A Mother's Story," in Chase and Rogers, eds., *Mothers and Children*, 25. A further ambiguity of feminist efforts to create a better world lies in the separation from their children that this work often requires. Leymah Gbowee, Liberian peacemaker and 2011 Nobel laureate, writes of the pain that this separation caused both her and her children during the years

Though they struggle to create positive outcomes—individually and/ or collectively, personally and/or politically—the efforts of mothers to guarantee their children's health, happiness, goodness, and success are vulnerable to problems they cannot predict and forces beyond their control.

The vulnerability of maternal efforts is exacerbated by the law of unintended consequences. Since a mother's best intentions interact with forces beyond her control in a complex and interdependent system, her efforts might not only be mitigated but adulterated. The struggle of Shulman and her feminist contemporaries, for example, opened windows of opportunity for the next generation, to be sure. But they also resulted in increased pressure and anxiety for young women now faced with often-impossible expectations of both combining professional success with egalitarian family life, and experiencing personal fulfillment in the balance between the two. Feminist mothers did not intend for their daughters to be overwhelmed and suffer anxiety over the pressures of "doing it all," but it was, at least in part, their efforts to "make things easy" for their daughters that led to this challenge faced by women today.

Feminist mothers who enjoy racial and economic privilege are relatively "free" to make the best choices they possibly can to ensure the health and happiness of their children, even if those choices are vulnerable to lack of control and unintended consequences. However, there are many situations in which mothers are so subject to forces beyond their control that they are not free to make any good choice in order to promote the well-being of their children and themselves. Embeddedness in a violent social system, for example, can severely constrain or even obliterate a mother's ability to act in the

she was intensely involved in the women's peace movement that played an instrumental role in ending Liberia's long and bloody civil war. Cf. Leymah Gbowee, *Mighty Be Our Powers: How Sisterhood, Prayer and Sex Changed a Nation at War* (New York: Beast Books, 2011).

best interest of herself or her children. Sometimes the choices that mothers face in these situations are not really choices at all. Such is the infamous case presented in the novel *Sophie's Choice*, in which a mother is forced at Auschwitz to "choose" which of her children would live and which would die at the hands of the Nazis.[43] Such impossible maternal "choices" are also a recurrent theme in the novels of Toni Morrison. In her most famous novel, *Beloved*, escaped slave woman Sethe "chooses" to murder her own child rather than allow her to be wrested back into slavery.[44] In Morrison's less popularly known, later novel, *A Mercy*, a seventeenth-century African woman who had been captured, ripped from her homeland, and sold into slavery in the Americas was forced to make such an impossible choice as well. The plantation on which she was enslaved was particularly harsh, especially for women. She had experienced rape by her overseers, resulting in two pregnancies thus far, and suffered untold sexual abuse by her master and his wife. She could see that her young daughter, approaching adolescence and eager to become a woman, would face the same fate. She watched over her daughter "like a hawk," but painfully admits in her unspoken confession to her daughter that "it never does any lasting good, my love. There was no protection. None. It was as though you were hurrying up your breasts and hurrying also the lips of an old married couple."[45]

This slave mother (referred to by Morrison throughout the novel as minha mãe, Portuguese for "my mother"), could see the impending harm that would come to her daughter from rape by her overseers and the sexual perversion of her master and his wife. So when she was given a small window to provide her daughter with the possibility of an alternative life, she took it. When a trader who held the plantation

43. William Byron, *Sophie's Choice* (New York: Random House, 1979).
44. Toni Morrison, *Beloved* (New York: Plume, 1987).
45. Toni Morrison, *A Mercy* (New York: Vintage, 2008), 190–91.

owner's debt came to collect, he was given the choice of any slave on the plantation as payment. The minha mãe is standing by the pump when he approaches, singing a maternal song of sorrow about "the green bird fighting then dying when the monkey steals her eggs."[46] When the trader chooses the minha mãe, she gets down on her knees and begs him to take her daughter instead of herself and her still-nursing son. She confesses the impossible choice:

> One chance, I thought. There is no protection but there is difference. You stood there in those shoes and the tall man laughed and said he would take me to close the debt. I knew Senhor would not allow it. I said you. Take you, my daughter. Because I saw the tall man see you as a human child, not pieces of eight. I knelt before him, hoping for a miracle. He said yes.[47]

This mother's daughter, renamed Florens by her new owner, is transferred to a more humane situation in which her new master's Native American servant takes the child under her wing. Although her new situation is far more humane than the one she would have faced had she remained with Senhor and his wife, Florens is unaware of the reasons behind the choice her mother made. She thus sees her mother's actions as a betrayal and she grows up feeling rejected, abandoned, and unloved.

The impossible choices faced by mothers such as Sophie, Sethe, and the minha mãe seem extreme examples, located in the distant, fictitious past. But these are the kinds of choices that many poor, abused, and marginalized mothers are forced to make throughout the world every day. The global care chain described above is a case in point—women in the Global South are forced to leave their children behind and migrate far from home in search of gainful employment. Other historical and contemporary examples abound:

46. Ibid., 195.
47. Ibid.

Chinese mothers who bound their daughters' feet as a status symbol that would enable them to marry well,[48] Indian mothers who sell their daughters into forced labor or prostitution,[49] poor and working-class mothers who remain in situations of domestic violence that are harmful to their children because they lack the resources and self-confidence to escape.[50] These are impossible choices with disastrous consequences for mothers and their children, but they are choices that many mothers nonetheless find it necessary to make in order to promote the well-being of themselves and their families.

These examples of ambiguity in maternal experience point to this fourth anthropological constant, yet another a painful truth about the human condition. As human beings enmeshed in the relational systems of an interdependent universe, we are not in total control of our fate or the fate of our loved ones. Nor can we predict with certainty the outcomes of our choices, regardless of how good our intentions may be. Try as we might, our efforts to do good are always vulnerable to failure, distortion, and demise. In a sense, the good that we do is always affected by, infected by, a certain amount of evil. Brazilian ecofeminist theologian Ivone Gebara refers to this ambiguity in existence as "the transcendence and immanence of evil," arguing that evil is so ingrained in our reality that it is actually impossible to separate out good from evil, or make a purely good moral choice without any hint of evil being a part of it. In her analysis of women's experiences of evil and salvation, Gebara argues that evil is an inevitable part of the human condition: "[I]t is as if

---

48. Cf. Louisa Lim, "Painful Memories for China's Footbinding Survivors," aired on National Public Radio's "Morning Edition," March 19, 2007, http://www.npr.org/templates/story/story.php?storyId=8966942.

49. A recent incident involved a mother who sold her daughter to pay off a fine imposed by a village council for reneging on her child's arranged marriage. Cf. Narayan Bareth, "Indian Mother Arrested for 'Selling 11-Year Old Daughter for ,000," BBC News Service, January 25, 2013, http://www.bbc.co.uk/news/world-asia-india-21191819.

50. Cf. Gbowee, *Mighty Be Our Powers.*

some ingredient has infiltrated everywhere and can be called 'evil.' It has the potential to destroy human relationships, our affinity with the earth, life in all its forms. This is not only a comment on human weakness but an observation of a kind of net that surrounds us in the very air we breath, of a 'sea' in which we move."[51] The maternal experiences of conflicting and ambiguous goods described here lend credence to Gebara's thesis—it may well be impossible to clearly distinguish good from evil in everyday experience. Human agency is vulnerable, then, to failure and participation (however unintended) in the perpetration of harm.

Conclusion: Anthropological Constants and the Vulnerability of the Human *Telos*

The experiences of maternity and natality described in these first two chapters have functioned as icons pointing to anthropological constants that render human beings inherently vulnerable to harm. As human beings, we are embodied, relational, and interdependent creatures who grow and change, age and die, face limits, lack control, commit mistakes, face impossible choices, and fall prey to the large and small failures that can result from these painful dimensions of our finitude. In sum, we are creatures vulnerable to the ever-present possibilities of physical, psychological, and spiritual suffering and destruction. Because of the close proximity of maternity and natality to human vulnerability, experiences of motherhood—along with the window these experiences provide on the natal origins of human life *in utero*, infancy and childhood—force us to be honest about the anthropological constants that make us vulnerable. When we focus on maternity and natality, it is hard to ignore the inevitable vulnerabilities that accompany human embodiment,

---

51. Ivone Gebara, *Out of the Depths: Women's Experience of Evil and Salvation* (Minneapolis: Augsburg Fortress, 2002), 56.

interdependence, perishing, conflict, and ambiguity. But maternal experiences can also serve to remind us that the very dimensions of the human condition that make our lives so precarious are also the conditions for the possibility of existence itself, and of human virtue, happiness, and flourishing. In her groundbreaking ethical work, *The Fragility of Goodness*, Martha Nussbaum argues that, though human life is inherently exposed to harm, there are certain powers (namely, human virtues) that are *only available in this realm of vulnerability.*[52] Drawing on Aristotle's ethics, she posits that the pursuit of human goodness is fundamentally vulnerable, contingent on external goods and ever subject to the possibility of demise. But the features of human life that expose us to misfortune are precisely those dimensions of our condition that *make possible* our experience of love and joy, beauty and truth. Our embodied, relational, (inter)dependent, changing, and ambiguous condition makes us vulnerable, but it also makes available to us a life of great power and possibility. Mothers live this coincidence of power and vulnerability in their very flesh.

Embodiment renders human beings vulnerable to disease, disability, and death. But without our bodies, we would not even exist, let alone aspire to virtue and happiness. In the first chapter, we witnessed that pregnant and birthing bodies are inherently vulnerable, but without taking on the embodied risks of pregnancy and birthing labor, the creative power of producing another human being would be impossible. Bodies are not only vulnerable; they are also powerful bearers of life, pleasure, and possibility. Similarly, our very existence relies on relationships of interdependency. Not only is our embodied life dependent on the creative act of our biological mothers and the caring labor of our childhood caregivers, we also

---

52. Cf. Martha Nussbaum, *The Fragility of Goodness: Luck and Ethics in Greek Tragedy and Philosophy* (Cambridge: Cambridge University Press, 1986), 341–42.

owe our selfhood to relationships of interdependence with these individuals, along with other human beings, our human communities, the earth, and the universe as a whole. The interdependence of human existence renders us vulnerable to be sure, but as the very origin and end of who we are, its realization in relationship is the condition for the possibility of the powers of human virtue, desire, love, and joy. Perhaps this is why, for many mothers, the power of love and joy involved in the interdependent adventure of mothering is well worth the risk of potential pain. Our interdependence makes us vulnerable, but relationships—especially the close ties of *philia*—are what make life worth living.

Furthermore, our condition is marked by the inherent vulnerability to loss brought on by the process of perpetual perishing. But mothers generally know that growth and change are what make it possible for us to mature and move forward to ever-greater transcendence. Natality thrusts us onto the painful path of corruption and mortality, but it is also the foundation of human becoming.[53] Though the reality of perishing in human life means that we need to let go of goods that we sometimes wish would infinitely expand or last forever, perishing is also the condition for the possibility of leaving behind lesser goods for greater goods, or overcoming destructive situations with constructive resolutions. What would human life, or the universe in general, be like without the possibility of becoming? To be blunt (and scientific) about it, nothing would exist at all. Finally, the difficult realities of conflict and ambiguity that characterize the finite nature of human existence as process are frustrating and painful to endure, but without them, we would not

---

53. Hannah Arendt, Sara Ruddick, and Grace Jantzen all explore natality as symbolic not of the dark side of human vulnerability, but of the promise and possibility of becoming. Cf. Arendt, *The Human Condition* (Chicago: University of Chicago Press, 1958); Ruddick, *Maternal Thinking: Towards a Politics of Peace* (New York: Ballantine, 1989);and Jantzen, *Becoming Divine: A Feminist Philosophy of Religion* (Bloomington: Indiana University Press, 1999).

exist either. Nor would we have the opportunity to discover the meaning that can emerge from the mess in the adventure of daily living. In Mount Shoop's words, motherhood's ambiguity

> both points to open spaces and clears them for us. These open spaces invite us to explore how indeterminacy and ambiguity are the mother of adventure and possibility. These spaces are ripe for indeterminacy to nurture a style of life awake to the potency of feeling's inheritance and novelty. These spaces create the conditions we all need to cultivate hope. The maternal body's language is discordant and melodious; it is silent and it is deafening. It is our mother tongue; it is indecipherable. In motherhood we muddle through and search for opportunities to nurture life. These are spaces available for adventure.[54]

It would be blasphemous to interpret the radical suffering that can result from choosing between conflicting and ambiguous goods as part of the "adventure" of life in all its messiness, especially when such choices are made under circumstances of violence and oppression. However, as part of the contours of our vulnerable condition, the conflictual and ambiguous nature of being is the result of human freedom and, in many cases, can be what makes it possible for us to enjoy existence itself, along with the mysterious and adventurous pleasures of life, love, goodness, and happiness.

It would be easy to end these reflections here, on an optimistic note, stressing the powers and possibilities that make our vulnerability "worth it." But to remain "honest with reality,"[55] I must go back to Nussbaum and conclude on a more frightening note: it is precisely because human goodness and happiness are so closely tied to

---

54. Marcia Mount Shoop, *Let the Bones Dance: Embodiment and the Body of Christ* (Louisville: Westminster John Knox, 2010), 98.

55. Cf. Jon Sobrino, *Where Is God: Earthquake, Terrorism, Barbarity, and Hope* (Maryknoll, NY: Orbis, 2004), 29ff.; and *No Salvation Outside the Poor: Prophetic-Utopian Essays* (Maryknoll, NY: Orbis, 2008), 2ff. Sobrino frequently uses this concept, borrowed from the philosophical and theological work of his martyred Jesuit brother, Ignacio Ellacuría. Cf. Ellacuría, "Hacia una fundamentación filosófica del método teológico latinoamericano," *Estudios Centroamericanos* 322, no. 23 (1975): 419.

vulnerability, indeed are only available *in vulnerability*, that the human *telos* is so vulnerable to destruction. Reality as embodied, relational, interdependent, conflictual, and ambiguous process exposes mothers, their children, and all human beings to great harm. The structure of our existence is inevitably tragic, as we are undeniably and unavoidably vulnerable creatures. What is perhaps most tragic in all of this is the vulnerability of human happiness, understood in the Aristotelian sense as the human *telos*—goodness or *eudaimonia*. Nussbaum maps this moral vulnerability brilliantly, positing that human excellence is like a plant: beautiful, but fragile due to its dependence on nourishment by external factors such as upbringing, social circumstances, and exposure to tragedy. Since the human *telos* is so affected by what happens to a person, rather than what a person does (Nussbaum's definition of luck), it ultimately lies out of our control. In Nussbaum's concluding exegesis of Hecuba's dramatic demise, she offers a maternal example of how tragedy can destroy our souls.[56] By their nature, close and affectionate ties of *philia* (exemplified for Aristotle by the mother-child bond) heighten the vulnerability of the good life. With great love comes great vulnerability.

Nussbaum's take on human excellence and its inherent fragility is based on the insights of Aristotle regarding the role of fortune in the pursuit of human happiness.[57] For Aristotle, happiness, or flourishing, is the highest good for human beings because it fulfills the rational function of the soul in accordance with virtue. Virtue is a state of character that, as the result of habituation, acts in the best way concerning the pains and pleasures we experience as embodied and relational human beings. Human flourishing, which depends on

---

56. Cf. Nussbaum, *The Fragility of Goodness*, 379ff.
57. Aristotle, *Nichomachean Ethics*, Second Edition, translated by Terrence Irwin (Indianapolis: Hackett, 1999). Cf. Book I on "Happiness."

virtue, is a "self-sufficient" good, complete and choice-worthy in its own right. But as a human good it is never realized in isolation by a solitary person. Given that human beings are political animals, our flourishing includes family, friends, and fellow citizens. This means that personal happiness is, to a certain extent, dependent on the good of loved ones and the polis as a whole. For Aristotle, the human *telos* is thus vulnerable to external influence. Though happiness is good and pleasant in its own right, it requires external goods to be added to it. It needs resources to do fine actions. In the words of Shields's character Reta Winters, whose own happiness is buffeted by maternal misfortune: "Unless you're lucky, unless you're healthy, fertile, unless you're loved and fed, unless you're clear about your sexual direction, unless you're offered what others are offered, you go down in the darkness, down in despair."[58] We are all vulnerable to fortune and misfortune, then, in the pursuit of our highest good.

There is something sacred about our vulnerability—it is the condition for the possibility of human becoming, for the manifestation of that which is ultimate in human life (which, as we shall see in part 2, ultimately transcends the human). But it is also what makes our attainment and manifestation of the ultimate so fragile, so inevitably exposed to the possibility of destruction. When the vulnerability of human beings is exacerbated, heightened, and manipulated in situations of poverty, violence, and oppression, it is not a simple or natural extension of inevitable human vulnerability. Rather, it is a violation or abuse of our fundamental condition and our sacred dignity as vulnerable beings. More often than not, such abuse is the byproduct of the desperate attempt to eliminate, manipulate, or control vulnerability at the expense of the those who are most exposed to harm. The dehumanization that results—for both the

58. Carol Shields, *Unless: A Novel* (New York: Fourth Estate, 2002), 224.

privileged and the powerless, violator and violated—further illustrates the vulnerability of the human *telos*. When we fear, project, scapegoat, or exact revenge on our vulnerability, we end up further compromising and even destroying our happiness, our goodness, our ultimate *telos*. It is to this violation of human vulnerability, and human dignity, that we now turn.

3

The Violation of Human Vulnerability

Anxiety, Egocentrism, and Violence

[W]hen we are pleased with that line of Maro, "Happy the man who has attained to the knowledge of the causes of things," we should not suppose that it is necessary to happiness to know the causes of the great physical convulsions, causes which lie hidden in the most secret recesses of nature's kingdom. . . . But we ought to know the causes of good and evil as far as man may in this life know them, in order to avoid the mistakes and troubles of which this life is so full. For our aim must always be to reach that state of happiness in which no trouble shall distress us, and no error mislead us.[1]
~Augustine of Hippo

[A]ll human life can be interpreted as a continuous attempt to avoid despair.[2]
~Paul Tillich

Nearly twenty-two thousand children die of poverty-related causes in our world every day. The vast majority of these deaths are easily preventable.[3] This means that, on a daily basis, at least twenty-two

---

1. Augustine, *Enchiridion*, chapter 16, http://www.newadvent.org/fathers/1302.htm.
2. Paul Tillich, *The Courage to Be* (New Haven: Yale University Press, 1952), 56.

thousand mothers, fathers, and other caregivers have lacked the resources necessary to protect their children from early and unjust death.[4] While vulnerability is an inevitable feature of human existence, the extreme vulnerability of these children and their caregivers is not simply a natural extension or obvious outcome of their universal human vulnerability. Rather, in a world of plenty, it is a grave moral evil—an egregious example of violated human dignity. As the above epigraph by Augustine points out, human happiness—understood here as the human *telos* of goodness and flourishing—depends on understanding the causes of good and evil. For Augustine, and for much of the Christian tradition, the cause of evils such as poverty-induced childhood starvation lies in the original and simultaneously personal sin of pride, which eschews love of God and love of neighbor in favor of self-gratification and lust for power.[5] Christian ethicists and liberation theologians have described such injustices in terms of "social sin," and have employed the tools of social analysis to understand the underlying structural causes of poverty, violence, and oppression.[6] Uncovering original,

3. According to UNICEF, "[N]early 8 million children died in 2010 before reaching the age of 5, largely due to pneumonia, diarrhea, and birth complications." This works out to almost twenty-two thousand deaths per day, the vast majority of which are preventable. UNICEF, *State of the World's Children 2012* (New York: United Nations, 2012), 13.

4. Gustavo Gutiérrez defines poverty as "early and unjust death." Cf. *We Drink from Our Own Wells: The Spiritual Journey of a People* (Maryknoll, NY: Orbis, 1992).

5. Cf. e.g., Augustine, *Confessions*, trans. Henry Chadwick (Oxford and New York: Oxford University Press, 1991), II.v.10–14, and *City of God*, trans. Henry Bettenson (New York: Penguin, 1972), XII.6. A full account, critique, and retrieval of Augustine's doctrine of sin far exceeds the scope of this project. It is interesting to note here, however, that for Augustine not only moral evils but also "natural evils" are caused by sin. For him, the latter—up to and including death—are not natural to the human condition at all, but are rather understood to be part of human beings' punishment for original sin. See, e.g., *City of God*, Book XIII. Vulnerability therefore follows from sin, rather than vice-versa. I will be presenting a very different vision—one in which what the Christian tradition calls "sin" is actually an unhealthy and violent reaction to original (and violated) vulnerability.

6. For an overview of social sin, see Derek R. Nelson, *What's Wrong with Sin: Sin in Individual and Social Perspective from Schleiermacher to Theologies of Liberation* (New York: T. & T. Clark, 2009). Catholic social teaching has taken on the language of social sin as an analogue to personal sin, which is seen as the primary cause of evil in both personal and social life. See, e.g., Pope John

personal, and social sin as causes of injustice can be a helpful, even necessary step on the way to uncovering the causes of evil in our world today. However, I contend that we need to go deeper. In order to understand and redress evils of injustice, oppression, and violence, it is essential to explore their deeper anthropological roots. It is imperative to ask: What is it about the human condition that makes us so wont to perpetrate, participate in, and allow egregious violation of other vulnerable beings (and ourselves)? Sin and pride do not go deep enough into the cause of our implication in evil. We must ask, therefore, *why sin* and *why pride*? Why do we allow pride to thwart our natural desire for loving communion with God, humanity, and all of creation? Though it is impossible to formulate a definitive answer to the mystery of human evil, it is possible to uncover a dynamic, causal relationship between general human vulnerability and the violation of vulnerable others. In other words, what the Christian tradition calls sin—original, personal, and social—has its roots in vulnerability.

This chapter, along with the one that follows, explores this dynamic relationship between vulnerability and violation. My thesis is that vulnerability, along with the fear of and inability to cope with the suffering that vulnerability causes and/or threatens, is what ultimately precedes the violation of oneself and other vulnerable beings. I begin my argument here by tracing the pathway from vulnerability to anxiety and from anxiety to egocentrism, parochialism, and violence.

Paul II's 1984 Apostolic Exhortation, *Reconciliation and Penance*, no. 16, http://www.vatican.va/holy_father/john_paul_ii/apost_exhortations/documents/hf_jp-ii_exh_02121984_reconciliatio-et-paenitentia_en.html. "Whenever the church speaks of situations of sin or when she condemns as social sins certain situations or the collective behavior of certain social groups, big or small, or even of whole nations and blocs of nations, she knows and she proclaims that such cases of social sin are the result of the accumulation and concentration of many personal sins."

Vulnerability and Anxiety

Drawing on maternal experience as an anthropological icon, chapters 1 and 2 characterized human beings as inherently and universally vulnerable—not by accident, by a fault in our design, or due to our own failings, but due to the very nature of our existence as embodied and interdependent beings who are exposed to the possibility of physical and relational harm, pained by the processes of perishing, and strained by the conflictual and ambiguous limitations of finitude. These conditions of human life in the world render us vulnerable to physical pain, relational suffering, horrific loss, paralyzing guilt, and ultimately death. Our vulnerability to these painful experiences also renders us vulnerable, in turn, to particular fears and general anxiety.[7] We often fear the particular physical and emotional harms and losses that might come to ourselves or our loved ones from our vulnerabilities. We can also suffer anxiety due to mundane or tragic grief at the transitoriness of life, experienced in its ordinary passage or abrupt destruction. Or we might suffer agonizing guilt over the ambiguities and limitations of finitude that make it impossible for us to control our circumstances or "succeed" at achieving our desired objectives. Our vulnerabilities and the suffering that they can produce threaten not only our actual existence, but also the perceived value and worth of our lives as human beings. Even for a person who has not suffered immediate threats of physical harm, loss, or death, anxiety surrounding these possibilities and their concrete presence elsewhere in the world, is a powerful force in the psychic makeup of human life, both individually and collectively.[8]

---

7. Tillich differentiates between the distinct but inseparable phenomena of fear and anxiety, fear having a particular object and being a symptom of a more general existential anxiety. Cf. *The Courage to Be*, 35.

8. There is a rich body of literature on existential anxiety in nineteenth- to twentieth-century philosophy and theology, of which Tillich is one important example. In philosophy, the principal figure in this regard is Søren Kierkegaard, *The Concept of Anxiety: A Simple*

For Paul Tillich, anxiety conditions every aspect of our existence and, accordingly, "[A]ll of human life is a continuous attempt to avoid despair."[9] He offers an ontology of human anxiety in which he defines anxiety as "the state in which a being is aware of its possible nonbeing . . . the existential awareness of nonbeing."[10] He details three forms of human anxiety that respond to three distinct, though related threats of nonbeing: fate and death, emptiness and meaninglessness, guilt and condemnation. Maternal experience and the centrality of human vulnerability that it highlights can both illuminate and amplify Tillich's analysis of anxiety, which is a helpful theoretical touchstone for the overall aim of this chapter—namely, understanding the origin of human violence in vulnerability.

For Tillich, death is the most basic factor that conditions human anxiety. In his words,

> It is not the realization of universal transitoriness, not even the experience of the death of others, but the impression of these events on the always latent awareness of our own having to die that produces

Psychologically Orienting Deliberation on the Dogmatic Issue of Hereditary Sin (Macon, GA: Mercer University Press, 2008). Martin Heidegger develops his treatment of existential anxiety most fully in sections 40 and 41 of *Being and Time*, trans. Joan Stambaugh (Albany: State University of New York Press, 2010), 178–89. In theology, prominent representatives of this body of thought in addition to Tillich include Reinhold Niebuhr and Karl Rahner. See Reinhold Niebuhr, *The Nature and Destiny of Man* [1941](Louisville: Westminster John Knox, 1996) and Karl Rahner, "Man as a Being Threatened Radically by Guilt," in *Foundations of Christian Faith: An Introduction to the Idea of Christianity* (New York: Seabury, 1978) and "Anxiety and Christian Trust," in *Theological Investigations, Vol. XXIII* (Baltimore: Helicon, 1992). In an attempt to represent women's experiences of sinfulness, Valerie Saiving critiqued Niebuhr's account of anxiety and sin as androcentric. See Saiving, "The Human Situation: A Feminine View," in *The Journal of Religion* 40, no. 2 (April 1960): 100–112. While I do not engage Saiving's argument here directly, I do respond to her critique indirectly by offering an account of the link between anxiety and violence/sinfulness that is drawn directly from women's experiences. Judith Plaskow offers a more extensive feminist critique of both Niebuhr's and Tillich's theologies of sin in *Sex, Sin and Grace: Women's Experience and the Theologies of Reinhold Niebuhr and Paul Tillich* (Lanham, MD: University Press of America, 1979).

9. Tillich, *The Courage to Be*, 56.

10. Ibid., 35. It is interesting to note here that, in *City of God*, Augustine's analysis of the reason for the fall of the wicked angels also points to anxiety. In his view, their defection from the good had its roots in anxiety over the prospect of their bliss coming to an end. See, XI.13.

anxiety. Anxiety is finitude, experienced as one's own finitude. This is the natural anxiety of man as man, and in some ways of all living beings. It is the anxiety of nonbeing, the awareness of one's finitude as finitude.[11]

Interpreted in a Tillichian sense, vulnerability is ultimately the threat of nonbeing, which is experienced most absolutely in the face of personal death. The basic conditions of human existence—embodiment, relationality, process and perishing, conflict and ambiguity—expose human beings to the imminent threat and ultimate inevitability of death. These very same conditions that facilitate our being in the world contain within them the constant risk and eventual certainty of erasure from embodied existence. Relatively speaking, however, Tillich explains that the ontic threat of death is experienced more immediately in terms of fate, or contingency. Our temporal and spatial being is contingent insofar as the circumstances in which we find ourselves are not ultimately necessary—things could easily be different. "Contingently we are put into the whole web of causal relations. Contingently we are determined by them in every moment and thrown out of them in the last moment."[12] Anxiety ensues from this aspect of the human situation because of the dark irrationality behind and in front of contingency. In an interdependent world of causal relations, our very existence (not to mention our health, wealth, and happiness) is ultimately beyond our control to preserve and protect. The human experience of this universal threat of nonbeing, felt absolutely as death and relatively as fate, is a powerful force that threatens our ontic self-affirmation and thus produces terrible anxiety in human beings.

According to Tillich, nonbeing threatens not only the ontic self-affirmation of human beings, but also our spiritual self-affirmation.

11. Tillich, *The Courage to Be*, 35–36.
12. Ibid., 44.

This threat produces anxiety over absolute meaninglessness and relative personal emptiness. In Tillich's analysis, spiritual self-affirmation occurs in human creativity. Using the examples of a poet and a scientist, he explains that spiritual self-affirmation is the fulfillment of the human person; one who lives creatively affirms oneself as a participant in the making and transformation of reality, a pursuit that, for Tillich, manifests ultimate reality. The absolute threat of nonbeing to spiritual self-affirmation is the threat of meaninglessness, which produces anxiety regarding "the loss of an ultimate concern, of a meaning which gives meaning to all meanings. This anxiety is aroused by the loss of a spiritual center, of an answer, however symbolic and indirect, to the question of the meaning of existence."[13] In relative terms, the spiritual threat of nonbeing is felt in the more immediate anxiety of emptiness, which occurs when "one is cut off from creative participation in a sphere of culture, one feels frustrated about something which one had passionately affirmed, . . . and the creative eros is transformed into indifference or aversion."[14] When the creative potentiality of a human person is frustrated, impeded, or damaged, terrible anxiety can result over personal emptiness of unfulfilled possibilities. And this anxiety, according to Tillich, can drive one to the abyss of meaninglessness, in which the ultimate meaning and value of existence comes into doubt.

Tillich's third and final category of human anxiety arises from the threats of guilt and condemnation that nonbeing poses to human beings' moral self-affirmation. In his analysis, the human being is characterized by "finite freedom," which is the freedom to determine oneself through one's own decisions within the contingencies of finitude. Within these limits, every moral act contributes to the self-affirmation of the human person, and thus to "the fulfillment

13. Ibid., 47.
14. Ibid., 47–48.

of his destiny, to the actualization of what he potentially is."[15] In every act, however, human beings also have the power to lose their destiny. And according to Tillich, the estrangement of human beings from themselves makes this an actuality, thus producing the human experience of the anxiety of guilt: "Even in what he considers his best deed nonbeing is present and prevents it from being perfect. A profound ambiguity between good and evil permeates his personal being as such. Nonbeing is mixed with being in his moral self-affirmation as it is in his spiritual and ontic self-affirmation. The awareness of this ambiguity is the feeling of guilt."[16] In a finite world filled with conflicting and ambiguous goods, all human beings are vulnerable to the anxiety of guilt and condemnation. As finite creatures within this world, we are unable to fully control events, our destinies, or the destinies of those whom we love. As finite creatures, none of us possesses the fullness of Being and, as such, none of us is able to act with purity of Being, Goodness, Justice, or Truth. Our actions are always tainted with an admixture of nonbeing, evil, injustice, and falsehood. We are vulnerable to moral failure and thus to the anguish that accompanies our unfulfilled destinies. Both absolute anxiety over ultimate condemnation and relative anxiety over personal guilt are byproducts of the finitude and interdependence of human life. Our finite and interdependent human condition renders us vulnerable to moral failure because of the profound ambiguity that arises therefrom. Nonbeing is present even in our best deeds, and nothing we do in this life can attain to perfection. The awareness of the ambiguity between being and nonbeing, good and evil, in human life produces this anxiety of guilt, which is "present in every moment of moral self-awareness and can drive us toward complete self-rejection, to the feeling of being

15. Ibid., 52.
16. Ibid.

condemned—not to an external punishment, but to the despair of having lost our destiny."[17]

A maternal unveiling of human vulnerability can serve to illuminate, correct, and amplify Tillich's understanding of anxiety. Human beings are vulnerable to physical, psychological, and spiritual suffering and death due to our nature as embodied, relational, perishing, and finite creatures endowed with sentience and consciousness. These same aspects of our existence that make possible our being in the world also contain within them, and render us vulnerable to, the threat of nonbeing. In other words, Tillich's analysis of threats to being coming from death and fate, meaninglessness and emptiness, condemnation and guilt, is arguably an analysis of the vulnerability that arises from our embodied and ambiguous finitude. His reflections on the finite freedom of human beings articulates in philosophical language the anthropological truth to which maternal experiences of finitude, relationality, perishing, and ambiguity point. What he describes as the threat of nonbeing might also be understood as the same vulnerability that the maternal icons that preceded this chapter so vividly illustrate. And the anxiety over the threat of nonbeing that Tillich examines is actually anxiety over human vulnerability to bodily, relational, spiritual, and moral harm.

For example, the Nepali woman quoted in chapter 1 is a maternal icon of this very real threat of nonbeing coming from death and contingency, which produces human anxiety. Pregnant with her third child in a context where maternal, fetal, and infant mortality pervades the everyday awareness of women, she wonders, "What might happen? That's what comes to me now. . . . Maybe I'll die. Or maybe I'll live. How will it be? What will happen to me?" Anxiety over the ontic threats of death and contingency has overcome her.

17. Ibid., 53.

And this causes her great suffering. Her "heart-and-mind hurts."[18] Maternity and natality drive home the utter contingency and vulnerability to nonbeing that characterize all human life. The threat of ontic nonbeing, the awareness of one's own death and contingency, is a fundamental human vulnerability that causes great anxiety. The experiences of this particular mother and of mothers across the world, especially in contexts of poverty and the absence of prenatal and obstetric care, illuminate the harsh reality of vulnerability in human life, along with the anxiety that Tillich so brilliantly pinpoints as the human response to ontic vulnerability.

To further substantiate the confluence between my analysis of maternal vulnerability and Tillich's ontology of anxiety, it might help to take a more in-depth look at how maternal experiences can also illuminate Tillich's anxiety of guilt and condemnation. Since it is impossible for mothers to realize all potential goods for themselves or their children, mothers are vulnerable to suffering anxiety and guilt over the potential or actualized "failure" of their efforts to protect their children and promote their well-being and happiness. In *Perfect Madness: Motherhood in the Age of Anxiety*, Judith Warner observes that feeling a certain amount of apprehensiveness is a common experience of most mothers across time and space:

> Anxiety is—and undoubtedly always has been—a natural part of motherhood. "There is an enlarged sense of *vulnerability*, personal and social, created by becoming a mother—and accepting the intimate mission of keeping a dependent being alive," writes psychologist Janna Malamud Smith. . . . The writer Francine Prose has described a certain kind of visceral fear that shocked her and changed her life when she became a mother: All at once, we realize what hostages to fortune we are, how fragile and precious life is—our own lives, and those of our

18. Kathryn March, "Childbirth with Fear," in *Mothers and Children: Feminist Analyses and Personal Narratives*, ed. Susan E. Chase and Mary Frances Rogers (New Brunswick, NJ: Rutgers University Press, 2001), 170.

children. Even the bravest of us may find ourselves transformed almost beyond recognition into skittish, nervous versions of our former selves.[19]

Because maternal practice does not, indeed cannot, encompass all possible goods for mothers or their children, it is not surprising that mothers are often prone to anxiety over their inability to "do it all," over their lack of control, the unintended consequences of their actions, or the impossibility of the choices they face. When the vulnerable nature of maternal practice leads to "failure"—when a child is unhappy, sick, unintelligent, abused, maimed, or worse—maternal anxiety often transitions to feelings of shame and guilt, even when the constraints of finitude dictate that there is absolutely nothing a mother could have done to prevent the misfortune that has visited her child.

Warner offers an in-depth exploration of this phenomenon in white middle- to upper-middle-class American mothers, who are gripped by a "caught-by-the-throat feeling . . . of *always* doing something wrong."[20] These are mothers who perpetually feel anxiety and anticipatory guilt over the possibility of "failing":

> Because it feels, very often, that if we don't do exactly the right thing, master all the details, control every moment, then our children will be . . . not just shut out from, say, the best ballet class, but . . . cast adrift . . . left behind . . . limited . . . passed over. They will get fat, they will be immature, they will lack muscle tone, and focus, and a competitive edge. . . . They'll end up as losers.[21]

The feeling described by Warner is largely socially constructed, race and class specific, and reinforced by what she calls the "Mommy Mystique," which places all responsibility for childrearing and

---

19. Judith Warner, *Perfect Madness: Motherhood in the Age of Anxiety* (New York: Riverhead, 2005), 191.
20. Ibid., 3.
21. Ibid., 162.

children's success on mothers, as if they have omnipotent control over children's destinies. Because of the nature of the work that they do and the cultural expectations placed on them regarding the success or failure of their labors, mothers are vulnerable to the anxiety and guilt that accompany an endeavor with no guaranteed results. This is why they are vulnerable to the Mommy Mystique in the first place and this is why the incessant social pressure to "do it all" and do it all just "right" for one's children can be so psychologically devastating.

Even more psychologically devastating is the traumatic aftermath of impossible choices faced by mothers in situations of systemic poverty, violence, and oppression. As we have already seen, mothers in these situations are exposed not only to suffering brought on by trauma or violence to themselves or their children. They are also vulnerable to unbearable anguish surrounding their inability to make free and unambiguous choices on behalf of their children's and their own well-being. Sophie, who must "choose" to send one of her children to slaughter, ends up committing suicide. Sethe, of Morrison's *Beloved*, is haunted by the ghost of the daughter who died at her own hands. The slave mother who mercifully sends her daughter away from a life of certain sexual molestation in Morrison's *A Mercy* is forever afflicted by the impossibility of conveying the truth about her "choice" to her daughter. After kneeling down in the dust to beg for her daughter's removal, she confesses, "I stayed on my knees. In the dust where my heart will remain each night and every day until you understand what I know and long to tell you."[22] These mothers are tormented by the impossible choices they were forced to make. Because the forces at work in their lives and the lives of the children were so far beyond their control, these mothers suffer trauma and grief due to the violence and degradation visited on themselves

22. Toni Morrison, *A Mercy* (New York: Vintage, 2008), 195–96.

and their children. But they also suffer the trauma of not being able to do the maternal work of protection and nurture assigned to them with the birth of their children. Though they are not responsible for their children's misfortune and demise, they nonetheless must live with the afflicting consequences of the impossible choices that they were forced to make. Maternal guilt is a cliché with a strong basis in reality. Tillich's account of the anxiety of guilt and condemnation is an uncannily accurate description of the experience of many mothers.

However much a maternal account of vulnerability illuminates and validates Tillich's ontology of anxiety, women's experiences of maternity and natality can also serve to amplify and correct aspects of Tillich's thought that fall short of a more comprehensive, embodied, and relational account of vulnerability and anxiety. The first aspect of human vulnerability that Tillich sidesteps and that maternal experiences drive home with relentless force is the reality of embodiment. By no means does Tillich ignore embodiment; indeed, the threat of death and contingency are largely based in the finite and embodied nature of human beings. What Tillich overlooks and what maternal experience can offer, however, is an appreciation of the extent to which bodily pain conditions human anxiety in all three categories of his ontology. Take obstetric fistula for example. The story of the Kenyan woman Kwamboka W. detailed in chapter 1 can serve to both broaden and deepen Tillich's analysis of the respective anxieties of death and contingency, meaninglessness and emptiness, and condemnation and guilt. The most immediate and obvious threat to Kwamboka W.'s existence and well-being is the physical reality of bodily harm and pain. She has survived the initial occurrence of the fistula, which many women do not, given that obstetric fistula is responsible for 8 percent of maternal deaths worldwide and is one of the four major causes of maternal mortality.[23] Protection from this malady is contingent on multiple factors such as pelvic size, women's status in society, and access to healthcare. One can only imagine the anxiety over the possibility of death due to obstetric fistula experienced by women in contexts where these contingent factors make this condition relatively common and life-threatening. But even once the threat of death (easily acknowledged within Tillich's system) has passed, the threat, the reality, and the consequences of bodily pain remain. Kwamboka K. and other women who suffer from this condition live with intense and constant pain due to skin irritation and internal infections. Tillich lacks an appreciation for the anxiety that accompanies the possibility and the reality of a life marked by such bodily pain, which threatens not only the ontic self-affirmation of the sufferer, but her spiritual and moral self-affirmation as well. Bodily pain threatens not only personal existence, but also personal creativity, self-worth, and moral agency. Combined with other social and cultural factors, the physical pain of fistula can produce the anxiety-imbued experience of a "living death." This is true even after the immediate pain has passed. Amolo A., for example, is a Kenyan woman who attempted suicide several times due to her fistula, and who later had her fistula repaired and now educates her community in Nairobi on the issue. She relates that after the successful surgery, she was still plagued with her prior condition's psychological effects. She returned to inpatient psychiatric care again and remarks that it was then that she realized, "I am not dead, but I am not living."[24] In this maternal example, bodily pain amplifies the ontic anxiety of death and contingency, but it also affects human relationships and conditions anxiety surrounding the worth of existence and the personal value of a human life.

23. See World Health Organization, "10 facts on obstetric fistula," March 2010, http://www.who.int/features/factfiles/obstetric_fistula/en/#.

24. Human Rights Watch, "I Am Not Dead, But I Am Not Living: Barriers to Fistula Prevention and Treatment in Kenya," July 15, 2010, http://www.hrw.org/node/91513/section/1.

The second aspect of human vulnerability and anxiety that Tillich overlooks and that maternal experiences can offer is an appreciation for the fundamentally relational nature of vulnerability and anxiety. Tillich is by no means an individualist,[25] but in his analysis of the threats of nonbeing to ontic, spiritual, and moral self-affirmation, he fails to give sufficient attention to the essentially relational nature of each of these aspects of human existence. As my analysis of relationality in chapter 1 indicated, motherhood can bring the relationality and interdependence of the human condition into sharper focus. Tillich does not deny the importance of relationality, but his account of anxiety is very much an account of individual anxiety regarding individual existence and self-affirmation. His ontology of anxiety fails to account for the radically relational nature of being, and he thus loses sight of both a) the way in which ontic, spiritual, and moral self-affirmation is fundamentally dependent on relationality, and b) the consequent way in which relationality contains within itself vulnerability, or the threat of nonbeing. If being is ultimately relational, then the fulfillment of being in a finite and interdependent world depends upon the fragile and contingent structure of relationships. Tillich at least acknowledges the role of causal relations in his analysis of contingency. However, motherhood can take us one step further toward a more relational ontology of anxiety. The maternal experiences of "entangled subjectivity"[26] and empathetic suffering described in chapter 1 indicate that one's own being, one's own self-affirmation, is inextricably tied up with the being and self-affirmation of others. Motherhood demonstrates that the fulfillment of human life, of flourishing and happiness, is

---

25. See, e.g., chapter 4, "Courage and Participation," in *The Courage to Be*. See also his anthropology in *Systematic Theology, Vol. 1* (Chicago: University of Chicago Press, 1973) and his attention to history and church in *Systematic Theology, Vol. 3* (Chicago: University of Chicago Press, 1976).
26. Marcia Mount Shoop, *Let the Bones Dance: Embodiment and the Body of Christ* (Louisville: Westminster John Knox, 2010).

inherently relational and thus dependent on the quality of one's relationships and the well-being of one's *philia*. By no means does highlighting the relational nature of being invalidate Tillich's ontology of anxiety. On the contrary, correcting Tillich's analysis with a more relational ontology drives home his emphasis on the centrality of anxiety to the human situation. Relationality makes human beings all the more vulnerable to the threats of nonbeing and the resultant anxieties that Tillich so expertly details.

For example, in the realm of ontic anxiety, motherhood demonstrates that it is not only one's own individual death or one's own individual contingency that conditions the experience of anxiety. For many mothers, it is also, and sometimes more so, the death and contingency of cherished others (in this case children) that produces the greater fear when anticipated and the greater anguish when realized. Furthermore, maternal experiences show how human anxiety over spiritual and moral self-fulfillment are complicated by the ambiguous and conflictual terrain of relationality. Motherhood is an anxiety-ridden experience, even under the best of circumstances. This is because motherhood places women within an intense and ambiguous web of relationships that, despite their potential to offer existential fulfillment, can threaten mothers with the relational negation of ontic, spiritual, and moral self-affirmation.[27]

Without using the concept of vulnerability per se, Tillich takes very seriously the inherent threats of nonbeing to human existence and self-affirmation. What motherhood can offer to Tillich's analysis is not only the language of vulnerability, but also the significance of bodily pain and relationality to the phenomenon of human anxiety surrounding the vulnerabilities of human existence under the ever-present threat of nonbeing.

27. There are, of course, many other roles and relationships in human life that might also serve to illuminate the centrality of relationality to human anxiety.

Egological Existence, Vulnerability, and Relational Anxiety

Despite the fundamentally relational nature of existence, human beings generally experience their vulnerabilities, and their anxiety over them, most vividly as individual selves. Eighteenth-century Scottish philosopher David Hume's observations on self-consciousness offer an apt description of this phenomenon. In his view, the self, or "that individual person, of whose actions and sentiments each of us is intimately conscious,"[28] is always and everywhere intimately present to us. In his words, "our consciousness gives us so lively a conception of our own person, that 'tis not possible to imagine, that any thing can in this particular go beyond it."[29] We are always aware of ourselves and our existence such that we are unable to forget or transcend that awareness and are thus unable to totally forget or entirely transcend ourselves. For Hume, the self is so omnipresent because "the imagination can never totally forget the points of space and time, in which we are existent; but receives such frequent advertisements of them from the passions and senses, that however it may turn its attention to foreign and remote objects, it is necessitated every moment to reflect on the present."[30] The senses (and thus the body) keep us grounded in our own personal experience, existence, and consciousness. When we go outside of ourselves to reflect on an external object, we are continually interrupted by a return to consciousness of self: "[W]e are oblig'd not only to reach [the object] at first by passing thro' all the intermediate space betwixt ourselves and the object but also to renew our progress every moment being every moment recalled to ourselves and our present situation."[31] The structure of human

28. David Hume, *A Treatise of Human Nature* (London: Oxford University Press, 1960), 286.
29. Ibid., 317.
30. Ibid., 428.
31. Ibid.

embodiment and consciousness thus makes it difficult for us to focus our attention outside of ourselves with a great deal of intensity or duration. Although a relational account of existence indicates that "external objects" are not actually separate from the self, it is certainly not uncommon to experience them as such. The constant interruption of ourselves due to our location in bodies, space, and time results in an experience of vulnerability and anxiety that is intensely personal and concentrated in the individual experience of oneself as potentially threatened or immediately affected by harm.

For much (though not all) of the Christian tradition, the concern for ourselves and the difficulty we have in transcending ourselves that Hume describes is attributed to the effects of original sin. Wendy Farley, however, emphasizes those strands of the Christian tradition in which this self-regard is acknowledged as a given fact of sentient life and as a good and fruitful aspect of creation. She calls this location of human experience in a particular ego the "egological structure of personhood":

> Our sense of identity, our sense of even existing at all, arises with an awareness of ourselves as a particular self. We might think of this as the egological structure of personhood. That is, our experience is located in a particular ego. Without this centeredness of consciousness, it is hard to see what a person would be. In fact, sentience itself is probably egological.[32]

We experience our pains (and pleasures), and thus our vulnerabilities and anxieties, intensely and vividly as our own. We desire that which is good for us and fear that which is harmful. In Farley's view, it is perfectly natural, normal, and good that I am aware of myself as a particular center of experience and identity, that my body and consciousness are uniquely mine, and that I am most intimately

---

32. Wendy Farley, *The Wounding and Healing of Desire: Weaving Heaven and Earth* (Louisville: Westminster John Knox, 2005), 32.

and vividly present to myself. It is also appropriate that, due to the vividness of my embodiment and consciousness, I seek what I need for survival and avoid what is harmful. My uniqueness is part of my dignity as a person and my drive to survive is "a good thing: hunger makes us feed ourselves, pain makes us remove our hand from the fire. When these responses are damaged by illness of one sort or another, one's very life can be at risk."[33] I seek health and happiness for myself (in other words, I seek to protect myself from my vulnerabilities) not because I am sinful, but because the life I have been given is good. Theologically speaking, all that exists participates in the goodness of Being, and the life that human beings have been given in creation is good; the God of the Christian tradition is a God of *Life*[34] who desires that human beings choose being over nonbeing, life over death, and who becomes incarnate so that humanity might have life in abundance. It is not only legitimate but *good* that we are structured in such a way as to seek such abundance for ourselves and avoid that which threatens it. In fact, according to Farley, our desires to survive and thrive—and our protests when that desire is thwarted—point to the infinite longing that characterizes us as images of the Divine Eros.[35] To seek protection from our vulnerability to harm, then, is not only a natural and good inclination in human life, but is part of the human vocation to mirror the erotic structure of divine being.

Although Hume and Farley are correct to assert the fundamentally egological structure of human personhood, it is also important to reiterate that our vivid experience of our individual selves is formed in relation with others and is conditioned by those relations. True, we generally experience ourselves most vividly and thus seek life,

---

33. Ibid., 33.
34. Cf. Gustavo Gutiérrez, *The God of Life* (Maryknoll, NY: Orbis, 1991).
35. Cf. Farley, *Wounding and Healing of Desire*, 20.

abundance, protection from vulnerability for ourselves. But it is also true that the human person is so utterly relational that the experience of personal well-being is intimately bound up with the well-being of others. The personal ego, the very foundation of egological existence, is constructed in relation and is dependent on relationships for its self-preservation and happiness. Of course, this is not always consciously felt, explicitly acknowledged, or intensely experienced. Maternal experience can once again help to bring to the fore this inherent relationality of both human well-being and human responses to vulnerability as the threat to well-being. It can also highlight how intensely an individual ego can experience the vulnerability and suffering of another person as her own. Farley suggests that the love of a mother for her infant is a paradigmatic example of how human beings are capable of more immediate awareness of the vulnerability and suffering of another human being. According to Farley, a mother's concern for her infant's well-being is visceral, arising out of mutual delight in the other's existence:

> This delight is the basis of the intimacy between mothers and children that makes pain and pleasure, delight and suffering, flow back and forth between them with little regard for the normal boundaries that separate persons. Intimacy arising out of delight allows the infant's pain to impress itself on the mother as if it were her own pain. Mothers do not feed babies because they have a duty to do so but because the desire to ease the infant's suffering springs as spontaneously as the desire to ease the mother's own suffering.[36]

Farley recognizes that, of course, this is not the experience of all mothers. But when mothers do undergo this intense experience of feeling the pain of their children as their own, it points to the inherently relational nature of egological existence. Although our fundamental structure as human beings is based in the ego, as social

---

36. Ibid., 151–52.

beings, we do feel the vulnerability and pain of others as related to our own pain and vulnerability. Aristotle made this point in his definition of friendship as the experience of another person as a second self. Human beings do incorporate the vulnerability of others into their own personal experiences of vulnerability and suffering. In fact, according to Hume, sympathy is as common to the human condition as the vivid experience of the self:

> We have a lively idea of everything related to us. All human creatures are related to us by resemblance. Their persons, therefore, their interests, their passions, their pains and pleasures, must strike upon us in a lively manner, and produce an emotion similar to the original one; since a lively idea is easily converted into an impression. If this be true in general, it must be more so of affliction and sorrow. These have always a stronger and more lasting influence than any pleasure or enjoyment.[37]

To feel the vulnerability and suffering of the other as one's own, then, is not an unusual or uncommon occurrence.

Like the egological structure of individual personhood, this is a good thing. It is good that human beings are capable of self-transcendence, and that we seek to preserve, protect, and sustain the existence of not only ourselves but others as well. However, the anxiety over personal vulnerability that arises from egological existence is heightened by the radical relatedness of our egos to other persons. The scope of anxiety surrounding the possibility or actuality of harm is thus broadened and deepened. The experience of mothers who feel the pain of their children as their own highlights the painful reality of relational anxiety. When it is not only the individual's own ontic, spiritual, and moral self-affirmation at stake, the anxiety felt in the face of perceived and actual vulnerability is all the more overwhelming. Life is scary enough as it is. When you add

---

37. Hume, *A Treatise of Human Nature*, 369.

anxiety over the well-being of loved ones to the mix, it can become absolutely terrifying.

Egocentrism, Vulnerability, and Violence

Although it can produce much anxiety over personal vulnerability, egological existence is good. It protects us from harm and keeps us alive. And the extension of the ego to incorporate others is even better. It can enhance one's own well-being and lead to the protection, preservation, and sustenance of life for not only oneself but for others as well. But here is the problem with egological existence: "It seems nearly impossible to avoid the slide from the particular vividness of my own experience to the feeling that my ego is the center of the cosmos."[38] And, taking into account the relational nature of the ego, it also seems nearly impossible to avoid the slide from legitimate concern for one's intimate relations to viewing those relations as the center of the cosmos. The vividness of the ego and its incorporation of those to whom it is most foundationally and intimately related becomes a problem when we move from healthy regard for ourselves and our relations to the illusions of egocentrism and its relational correlate, parochialism.

How does this happen? According to Farley, though we are rightfully structured to seek life in abundance for ourselves and our loved ones, our experience is imbued with the very pain we aim to avoid. Indeed, Farley indicates that our nature is to suffer and to long for freedom from suffering.[39] Anxiety surrounding vulnerability is both a response to potential or actual suffering and an experience of suffering in itself. As such, vulnerability, suffering, and the anxiety-ridden pursuit of invulnerability define human existence. We respond to the omnipresence of pain with anxiety and thus employ the self-

38. Farley, *The Wounding and Healing of Desire*, 33.
39. Ibid., 21.

defense mechanisms that Farley identifies as the passions—terror, rage, and addiction. In this "tragic alliance" between the ego and the passions, "the natural vividness of the ego slides into the illusion of egocentrism."[40] While we might intellectually know that we are not the center of the universe, and that other persons are of equal dignity and worth, anxiety over our potential and actual vulnerability to pain overrides the possibility of acknowledging this truth in our lived reality. In Farley's words,

> Egocentrism is like the dentist's drill that has slipped past the reach of Novocain. When that happens, our own pain is all we can experience. There is a sense in which this is a dimension of our ordinary experience. Because of the intolerability of ordinary and extraordinary forms of suffering, egocentrism conspires with the passions because they promise to alleviate pain.[41]

The basic stance of egocentrism is not sinful self-inflation, then, but rather the means of self-defense for a "raw nerve exposed to a great deal of mental and physical suffering."[42] Not sin, but suffering distorts our natural desire to survive and thrive. According to Farley, the passions that bind our souls to destructive patterns of behavior are not originally sinful dispositions but the ego's strategic allies in the struggle to keep pain at bay. As Tillich observes, "All human life can be interpreted as a continuous attempt to avoid despair."[43] In other words, we employ various harmful psychological and behavioral strategies to aid our constant attempts at warding off vulnerability and anxiety, suffering and despair. Unfortunately, the pain relief offered by these strategies comes at a steep price—namely, the violation of human dignity in ourselves and others. When egocentric anxiety gets expressed in actions and attitudes of distorted desire,

40. Ibid., 48.
41. Ibid., 50.
42. Ibid., 51.
43. Cf. Tillich, *The Courage to Be*, 56.

anger, and/or passivity, the result is actually heightened ontic, spiritual, and moral vulnerability (and thus heightened anxiety and further violation) for other human beings and for our own selves.

Given the relational nature of the ego, and given the significance of our loved ones' happiness to our own well-being, the problems of egocentrism, anxiety, and pain relief are not only centered around an autonomous, individual ego. The vast majority of human beings are not sociopaths. As noted above, most of us care about and respond to the vulnerability and suffering of persons other than ourselves. However, it is often the case that the scope of care and compassion is limited to those individuals and groups most closely related to us. Even in the act of self-transcendence, of moving beyond the deluded concern for the self as the perceived center of the universe, the ego tends to identify with other selves with whom it shares some form of significant relation. Egocentrism locates ME at center of the universe. Its relational correlates—parochialism, racism, classism, heterosexism, ethnocentrism, and a vast array of other -isms—place individuals and groups with whom we identify some form of relation at the center of the universe with us. It is the vulnerability and pain of *my* self and *my* world that matters, not the pain of those with whom I perceive no relation. My self, my family, my community, my church, my nation, my race, etc., are all that matters. Although I experience anxiety and seek pain relief for suffering other than my own, my anxiety still produces the illusion of egocentrism because I am still placing myself and those who have most obviously contributed to the construction of my ego at the center of the universe and thus at the center of my attempts to seek relief from suffering and despair. But why do we feel sympathy for the vulnerability of some persons and not for others? Why do we focus our anxiety and actions on our own suffering and the suffering of our own group, to the exclusion of others?

Despite Hume's description of human sympathy as potentially extending to all human beings, he explains that sympathy is selective and usually constrained by certain limitations. Hume describes three reasons for this. First, although all human beings bear a relation of resemblance to one another, contiguity is also required for the perfection of sympathy. Some form of contact, and even direct sight of the object, are necessary for the imagination to do its job in the production of sympathy and compassion.[44] The imagination needs such contact in order to have an idea of the other person's suffering; without such an idea, there is nothing for the imagination to work with. Resemblance and proximity are what produce a relation of ideas; without such a relation, ideas can have no influence on each other, regardless of how vivid one's power of imagination might be. Furthermore, when we have fewer steps to take to reflect on an object that is distant from ourselves, the "diminution of vivacity" occasioned by the constant interruption of the self is "less sensibly felt." Accordingly, concludes Hume,

> [W]e find in common life, that men are principally concern'd about those objects, which are not much remov'd either in space or time, enjoying the present, and leaving what is afar off to the care of chance and fortune. . . . The breaking of a mirror gives us more concern when at home, than the burning of a house, when abroad, and some hundred leagues distant.[45]

Distance, then, affects sympathy negatively and can thus place limitations on compassion.

Second, by way of analogy to *distance*, Hume also asserts that sympathy, and thus compassion, is selective of its objects with regard to *difference*: "[A]ny great *difference* in the degrees of any quality is call'd a *distance* by common metaphor, which, however trivial it may

44. Hume, *A Treatise of Human Nature*, 370.
45. Ibid., 428–29.

appear, is founded on natural principles of the imagination. A great difference inclines us to produce a distance."[46] Sympathy is more easily experienced and compassion more easily felt, then, when the relation between ourselves and the other person is made stronger by acquaintance, custom, and similarity of manners, character, country, language, blood relation, education, etc. Just as distance hinders the relation of ideas required for sympathy, any identifiable difference between ourselves and another person can inhibit the ability of the imagination to give rise to sympathy and thus compassion. The greater the difference, the greater this inhibition will be.

Finally, based on Hume's reflections on love and hatred, we can infer that the perceived importance of the other person (or lack of importance) affects the sympathy and compassion we might feel toward her. This is because "[w]hatever has the greatest influence is most taken note of; and whatever is most taken notice of, presents itself most readily to the imagination."[47] Given the pivotal role of the imagination in the production of sympathy and compassion, it is no wonder that "an affection [e.g., compassion] directed to a person, who is considerable in our eyes, fills and possesses the mind much more than one, which has for its object a person we esteem of less consequence."[48] If social conventions deem that a person is of little importance, then she and her suffering will not occupy much of our attention. In our minds, she is not worth taking note of, and is therefore not worthy of our sympathy or compassion.

Each of these phenomena seem "natural" to the human condition, but as a product of his own social location, Hume does not recognize that each of these factors that contribute to parochialism in human affection and behavior are, to varying degrees, actually the product

46. Ibid., 393.
47. Ibid., 342.
48. Ibid., 344.

of social construction. Even distance, which would seem to be the most natural of the three, is socially constructed when it occurs in cases of geographical proximity. For example, poor communities are all but invisible to affluent citizens of the United States due to social, rather than physical, distance. A run-down trailer park can exist less than a mile from a neighborhood of mansions without the residents of the affluent community ever having to come into contact with their neighbors. Human differences in race, gender, and class are even more of a social construct. Critical race theorists point out, for example, that the concept of race has no natural foundations in genetics or biological difference. Rather, racial difference has its origins in the European social imaginary of the Middle Ages, and its perceived status as "natural" serves the ideological purposes of white privilege.[49] Finally, Hume's observation about the social prominence of a person is the most obviously fabricated of the three—we see as important and worthy of our concern those individuals and groups that society tells us to hold in high esteem. There is no "natural" reason why the death of Princess Diana or the birth of her first grandson years later should garner public attention on a global scale any more than the daily deaths of twenty-two thousand poor children and the daily births of hundreds of thousands of others. Celebrity status, material wealth, and social influence are all social factors that contribute to the relative importance of the former vis-à-vis the latter. Neither distance, nor difference, nor social standing are purely "natural" aspects of the human condition that create "natural" preferences in human sympathy. All three are, to varying degrees, social constructs.

49. Cf. Ian F. Haney López, "The Social Construction of Race: Some Observations on Illusion, Fabrication, and Choice," *Harvard Civil Rights-Civil Liberties Law Review* 29, no. 1 (1994): 1–62. In *Race: A Theological Account* (New York: Oxford University Press, 2008), J. Cameron Carter offers an extensive analysis of the theological roots of a racialized world, tracing the transformation of Christian anti-Semitism into the Western racial (and racist) imagination.

Nevertheless, distance, difference, and status are social realities that are deeply embedded in our psyches. As Ian Haney López observes, for example, biological race is an illusion, but social race is not.[50] The anxious attempts of socially powerful groups to ward off vulnerability and create a stable and solid identity for themselves contribute to the creation and perpetuation of these social mythologies of difference and status. And the social imaginary of the privileged (and marginalized, for that matter) can be infected by these mythologies such that Hume's observations, while far from "essential" to the human condition, are not off base. Distance, difference, and social standing generally cause us to have more concern for ourselves and those related to us than for those who are somehow separated, different, at a distance from, or perceived to be unimportant to us. This is the classic problem of parochialism, which gives rise not only to apathy at the vulnerability of different and distant others, but also to dangerous, oppressive, and violent attempts to protect ourselves and our inner circles from vulnerability and suffering even if it comes at the expense of those others. Coupled with Farley's analysis of egocentrism, Hume's observations are thus helpful for understanding why we are so anxious about the vulnerability and suffering of ourselves and those most closely related to us, but have no problem dismissing and even deriding and justifying the vulnerability and suffering of others. We seek to control our worlds so that we might ward off vulnerability and suffering for ourselves and those individuals and groups that we perceive as most closely related to us. Again, the price of such efforts at control is a steep one. We wound others in an attempt to protect ourselves and our relations from being wounded.

If human beings in general find it difficult to step outside of the anxiety surrounding their own vulnerability in order to feel

50. Cf. López, "The Social Construction of Race."

sympathy for distant and different others, mothers in particular can face even greater challenges to the extension of concern for vulnerability and suffering beyond their children, families, and the groups with whom they identify. Maternal experience demonstrates that when it comes to the actual practice of extending concern, we may well be limited by even more than the socially constructed parochialism of our sentiments. Nel Noddings, one of the key thinkers in the early development of feminist care ethics, observes (like Hume) that the intensity of caring sentiment is lessened as one moves further out from one's inner circle. But she also argues that the practice of caring labor is inherently ("naturally") limited to the proximate other, that is, "the one who addresses me, under whose gaze I fall."[51] Based on her commitment to the centrality of concrete relationality in ethics, she argues for recognizing natural limits to the scope of caring:

> Not only are there those for whom I do not naturally care—situations in which engrossment brings revulsion and motivational displacement is unthinkable—but there are, also, many beyond the reach of my caring. I shall reject the notion of universal caring—that is, caring for everyone—on the grounds that it is impossible to actualize and leads us to substitute abstract problem solving and mere talk for actual caring.[52]

---

51. Nel Noddings, *Caring: A Feminine Approach to Ethics and Moral Education* (Berkeley: University of California Press, 1984), 113. The problem of parochialism in caring relations such as motherhood is of central concern to the field of feminist care ethics. In contrast to Noddings, several other care ethicists find the maternal paradigm problematic and, perhaps because of this paradigm shift, are more optimistic and even exhortative about the ability and moral mandate for extending care beyond the family. Much of this subsequent work in care ethics seeks to extend the moral obligation to care beyond the private sphere of the family to distant others and public life. Joan Tronto, for example, critiques the maternal paradigm for romanticizing the mother-child relationship, confining morality to a relationships between individuals, contributing to the false divide between public and private caring, and placing sole responsibility for childcare on the shoulders of the mother. Cf. Joan C. Tronto, *Moral Boundaries: A Political Argument for an Ethic of Care* (New York: Routledge, 1993), 103. In *The Ethics of Care: Personal Political, and Global* (New York: Oxford University Press, 2006), Virginia Held also seeks to extend the scope of caring relations beyond mother-child and family (cf. 31). Rita C. Manning specifically critiques Noddings for her parochialism in *Speaking from the Heart: A Feminist Perspective on Ethics* (Lanham, MD: Rowman & Littlefield, 1992), 70ff.

In this analysis, our obligation to care about the vulnerability of different and distant others is bounded by our finitude, by our "natural" aversions, by our pressing obligations to care for those in our inner circle, by what can be realistically accomplished, and by the possibility of completion in the other's response. A mother's subjectivity and sense of self can be so bound up with her children that the powerful and often-passionate mother-child bond can intensify the parochialism that seems to come so naturally in human sentiment. Moreover, as Noddings points out, the actual ability to extend the practice of care is limited by the all-consuming demands that children make on their caregivers (the vast majority of whom are women—mothers and "othermothers"). The labor that these demands evoke can also serve to heighten the mother-child bond and can thus result in heightened anxiety surrounding the vulnerability of one's own children to the point of aversion, exclusion, and overt violation of others. As such, Sara Ruddick points out that mothers can possess "passionate loyalties to [their] own children, kin and people. Mothering offers distinctive occasions for tribalism and for racism."[53] The revulsion that Noddings sees as a "natural" limitation of caring can originate in (or at least can be heightened by) mothers' loyalty and the perception of threat to their own. The intimacy and delight between a mother and child that Farley evokes as a paradigm of self-transcendence is a hopeful and beautiful example of the compassion of which human beings are capable. But it has a potentially dark side as well, insofar as it can also lead to an even greater and more pernicious form of egocentrism (in the form of parochialism).

Indeed, the passionate loyalties of some mothers to their own children (and, by extension, to other children who bear some form of perceived resemblance to their own) can fuel aversion, hatred,

52. Noddings, *Caring*, 18.
53. Sara Ruddick, *Maternal Thinking: Towards a Politics of Peace* (New York: Ballantine, 1989), 57.

and violence toward those who appear to place their children's lives, morality, well-being, and wealth in danger. Maternal experience, then, can serve to illustrate not only human vulnerability in general, but anxiety-ridden, exclusivist, and violent responses to vulnerability that are destructive to self and others. To further this illustration, we will conclude part 1 with narratives and analyses of maternal responses to vulnerability that illustrate the way in which human vulnerability and the anxiety that surrounds it can lead not only to personal suffering and despair, but to the violation and abuse of other vulnerable beings. First, however, it is important to set maternal experiences of anxiety in their social contexts—namely, systems of power and privilege that are themselves unhealthy, destructive, and violent means of coping with anxiety through the social (mis)management of vulnerability.

4

Violated Vulnerability and the Violence of Privilege

*You were just so precious, I thought I'd kill you before they all got to hurt you.
. . . I just couldn't imagine bringing up two girls in a world where they do such
awful things to women. So I decided to kill you both, to spare you.*[1]
~Charlie Karr, attempting to explain the psychotic break during which
she nearly killed her two daughters

*You thought pit bulls were tough? Well you don't wanna mess with the mama
grizzlies.*[2]
~Sarah Palin

Human beings are social by nature and respond to vulnerability
and the anxiety and suffering it produces not only individually, but
collectively. The pain relief that Farley claims we seek gets expressed
not only in our personal and familial relations, but in the social,
economic, political, and cultural structures of human life.

---

1. Mary Karr, *Lit: A Memoir* (New York: HarperCollins, 2009), 3.
2. Sarah Palin, "Mama Grizzlies," http://www.youtube.com/watch?v=fsUVL6ciK-c.

Vulnerability is experienced vividly not only by individual egos, but also by social groupings and political communities. Just as individuals seek to mitigate the threat and actuality of vulnerability in their private lives, societies respond to vulnerability with social structures designed to manage vulnerability in shared and public ways.[3] Social structures and institutions (economic, political, cultural, and religious systems of human interaction) are constructed, exist, and are upheld in response to human vulnerability for protection from and resilience to vulnerability. According to Martha Fineman,

> Societal institutions are theorized as having grown up around vulnerability. . . . These institutions collectively form systems that play an important role in lessening, ameliorating, and compensating for vulnerability. Together and independently they provide us with resources in the form of advantages or coping mechanisms that cushion us when we are facing misfortune, disaster, and violence. Cumulatively these assets provide individuals with resilience in the face of our shared vulnerability.[4]

As Fineman indicates here, social structures are arguably a means of responding to human vulnerability by controlling the resources needed to cope with and manage vulnerability at the communal level. That these structures exist is a good thing, because human existence is a good thing and ought to be preserved and protected. And, as social beings, we ought to (and, indeed, have no choice but to) deal with our vulnerability in social, communal ways. Unfortunately, these social structures and the institutions built to uphold them are themselves vulnerable to the anxiety-induced corruption of egocentrism and parochialism described in the previous chapter.

---

3. Of course, there is not a clear divide between private and public responses to and management of vulnerability. See Joan C. Tronto, *Moral Boundaries: A Political Argument for an Ethic of Care* (New York: Routledge, 1993).

4. Martha Fineman, "The Vulnerable Subject and the Responsive State," *Emory Law Journal* 60 (2011): 32.

What follows is an analysis of one defining feature of contemporary social structures that characterizes the unhealthy, unjust, and ultimately violent mismanagement of vulnerability in our world today—privilege.

Having traced the dynamic relationship between vulnerability, egocentrism, and violence, we turn now to the social location of this process in systems of privilege, understood here as the social mismanagement of vulnerability. Social structures that grant disproportionate access to assets for coping with vulnerability to privileged populations do violence to bodies, minds, and spirits. These violent structures of privilege, in turn, can exact a steep moral cost from both the privileged and the marginalized. Drawing on maternal narratives and analyses, I argue that privilege exacerbates the problem of human vulnerability for both the privileged and the marginalized because it engenders both personal suffering and, all too often, witting or unwitting participation in the perpetration of further harm. Locating the further perpetration of violence in systems of privilege can grant us greater understanding of the root causes of "sin" in the vulnerable human condition, which has radical implications for how we envision and embody redemption.

Privilege: Socially Mismanaged Vulnerability

A vast amount of literature has been written surrounding the topic of privilege in recent decades.[5] Here I offer a limited analysis of privilege from within the framework of vulnerability. It is helpful to understand privilege both as a social response to vulnerability and as a major factor in the exacerbation and social production of

---

5. See Peggy McIntosh's influential work, Working Paper No. 189: "White Privilege and Male Privilege: A Personal Account of Coming to See the Correspondence Through Work in Women's Studies" (Wellesley, MA: Center for Research on Women, 1988). For a variety of perspectives on the study of privilege, see Michael S. Kimmel and Abby L. Ferber, eds., *Privilege: A Reader* (Boulder, CO: Westview, 2003).

vulnerability. Following Fineman's lead, I define privilege here as the accumulation of both assets for self-protection from vulnerability and resources for resilience in the hands of certain individuals and social groups. These individuals and groups have inherited and either openly defend or unconsciously inhabit positions of power (to differing degrees) that disproportionately benefit themselves, allowing them to preserve and protect their own interests at the expense of others. Privilege, then, can be interpreted as an unjust, unequal, and ultimately violent means of (mis)managing human vulnerability.

In order to understand privilege in terms of vulnerability, it is important to first have a handle on the assets required in order for human beings to adequately cope with and respond to vulnerability. Irish political economist Peadar Kirby argues that resilience vis-à-vis vulnerability is, at least in part, socially produced by the distribution of resources that prepare individuals and communities to ward off, manage, and/or survive threats and situations of harm.[6] Borrowing language used by International Governing Organizations (IGOs) like the World Bank, he identifies five categories of "assets" that individuals and communities need in order to be prepared to cope with risks to their well-being. Fineman borrows these categories from Kirby in her own analysis of and argument for state responsibility for monitoring equitable asset distribution. The first category of assets are *physical assets*, which Fineman describes as "the physical goods or material things that determine our present quality of life, such as housing, food, entertainment, and means of transportation. Physical resources also can provide us with the means for accumulating additional resources when they take the form of savings and investments."[7] Ownership of and/or access to physical

6. Cf. Peadar Kirby, *Vulnerability and Violence: The Impact of Globalisation* (Ann Arbor, MI: Pluto, 2006), 54ff.

assets can go a long way toward protecting people, tiding them over, and/or helping them to recover when their well-being is threatened by personal, economic, or natural disasters. The second category of assets, *human assets*, also affect material well-being by contributing to personal and communal human development, allowing for participation in the workforce, and making possible the accumulation of physical assets needed for meeting vulnerability with resilience.[8] According to Kirby, human assets are akin to what Amartya Sen calls "capabilities, namely people's innate or developed abilities to make the most of a given situation. Chief among such assets are health and education."[9] Fourth are *social assets*, which include social networks "from which we gain support and strength," such as families, communal associations, unions, identity groupings, and so on. As Fineman explains it,

> The family is a major institution providing social resources, particularly for the young or others in need of care. Social assets are conferred through other associations, such as political parties or labor or trade unions, in which individuals bolster their resilience by joining together to address vulnerabilities generated by the market. In recent decades, a sense of community organized around identity characteristics, such as race, ethnicity, and gender, has constituted powerful networks of affiliation and belonging.[10]

These first four categories of assets are all included in the World Bank's analyses and indices of vulnerability and risk. Kirby adds a fourth category of assets, *environmental assets*, which he draws from a World Bank–conducted survey of poor persons around the world regarding their own perceptions of what constitutes poverty. Based on the voices of the poor themselves, Kirby describes environmental

---

7. Fineman, "The Vulnerable Subject and the Responsive State," 33.
8. Ibid.
9. Kirby, *Vulnerability and Violence*, 60.
10. Fineman, "The Vulnerable Subject and the Responsive State," 34.

assets in terms of "ecological resources such as clean air and water, arable soil, trees, biodiversity, food security, etc., which offer resources that help people cope with life's risks."[11]

Finally, Fineman adds to Kirby's four categories a fifth—namely, *existential assets*. In her words, "Existential resources are provided by systems of belief or aesthetics, such as religion, culture, or art, perhaps even politics. These systems can help us to understand our place within the world and allow us to see meaning and beauty in our existence."[12] In the following analysis of privilege and its cost in suffering and human dignity, I will mainly refer to the first four categories of assets, although it will become clear that privileged access to such assets can affect and even destroy existential human flourishing for both the privileged and those on the underside of privilege. Vulnerability and the suffering to which it exposes human beings threaten us to the very core and can call into personal and/ or collective question longstanding systems of religious belief and moral agency.[13] Though there is certainly a productive element to such questioning, the radical suffering that vulnerability can produce, especially in situations of injustice, oppression, and violence (all implicated in privilege), can destroy not only belief systems, but the human spirit itself. Indeed, it is for this reason that addressing the destructive nature of privilege is so very urgent. In part 2, we will mine the Christian tradition for narrative-theological and spiritual-practical resources that have the potential to offer existential assets for coming to terms with, and responding justly and compassionately to the human problem of vulnerability and suffering.

---

11. Kirby, *Vulnerability and Violence*, 55–56.
12. Fineman, "The Vulnerable Subject and the Responsive State," 35.
13. Take, for example, the rupture in Jewish and Christian traditions that has taken place since the Holocaust. See Irving Greenberg, "Cloud of Smoke, Pillar of Fire: Judaism, Christianity, Modernity After the Holocaust," in *Auschwitz: Beginning of a New Era? Reflections on the Holocaust*, ed. Eva Fleischner (New York: Ktav, 1977).

In previous chapters, we have visited and revisited maternal icons of human vulnerability embodied in the form of maternal suffering due to the physical risks of childbearing, the relational risks of loving a child whose destiny lies beyond one's control, the moral risks of making decisions that offer no optimal consequences, and so on. Although the depiction of maternal vulnerability in these examples was intended to offer a window into the inherent vulnerability of the human condition, by no means were these examples intended to be understood as inevitable occurrences of "natural" human vulnerability. Each and every example cited in chapters 1 and 2 is situated within a social context where vulnerability is already met and (mis)managed by societal structures in unhealthy, unjust, unequal, and violent ways. It is my contention that *privilege* is a defining characteristic of the background context for how human beings experience and are affected by vulnerability in the world today. Privilege is the product of human anxiety over vulnerability; it is a collective attempt to alleviate anxiety through control of vulnerability. It is an attempt to control assets for protection from and resilience to vulnerability. But privilege also produces heightened vulnerability and suffering because it robs entire populations of access to the assets needed for coping with both natural and socially produced threats to their well-being. In privilege, one segment of society (men, whites, the wealthy, heterosexuals, and so on)[14] has

---

14. While Fineman would no doubt admit that such identity groupings play a significant role in determining one's place in privilege, she offers a post-identity analysis of privilege in which vulnerability provides a deeper understanding of how privilege can migrate across identity categories. "[W]ith respect to the assets any one person possesses, it is not multiple identities that intersect to produce compounded inequalities, as has been posited by some theorists, but rather systems of power and privilege that interact to produce webs of advantages and disadvantages. Thus where other theorists expand the traditional equal protection analysis to account for multiple intersecting identities, a vulnerability analysis provides a means of interrogating the institutional practices that produce the identities and inequalities in the first place." Martha Fineman, "The Vulnerable Subject: Anchoring Equality in the Human Condition," *Yale Journal of Law and Feminism* 20, no. 1: 16.

control over and/or privileged access to the physical, human, social, environmental, and (sometimes) existential resources described above as necessary for coping with vulnerability. The power of such control of and access to resources allows the privileged to live with a relative buffer between them and vulnerability. Of course, the privileged can never achieve total control. *In*vulnerability is an impossibility, even for the most privileged among us (in fact, privilege may ultimately render the powerful *more* vulnerable to threats of economic collapse, terrorist violence, environmental degradation, and existential despair). But access to resources for resilience does provide some protection, and the unequal distribution of assets results in the disproportionate protection of some alongside the disproportionate exposure of others. In other words, various systems and institutions in society confer assets differently and unequally, "so that some are more privileged, while others are relatively disadvantaged." The systems that confer privilege and produce disadvantage are quite complex. According to Fineman,

> Privileges and disadvantages accumulate across systems and can combine to create effects that are more devastating or more beneficial than the weight of each separate part. Sometimes privileges conferred within certain systems can mediate or even cancel out disadvantages conferred in others. A good early education may trump poverty, particularly when coupled with a supportive family and progressive social network.[15]

Some aspects of privilege are inherited because of one's identity as male, white, able-bodied, middle-class, upper-class, and/or heterosexual. Privilege is usually something that the privileged are born into. But it is also something that the privileged contribute to either openly and aggressively (for example, in nativist attitudes

15. Ibid., 15.

toward immigration) or complicitly, often in unwitting silence (for example, in liberal whites' assertion of colorblindness).

The invisibility of privilege is a key part of its insidious and pernicious nature. The resources that the privileged possess come from somewhere and are very rarely (if ever) earned wholly on one's own. To deny the reality of privilege and the unequal distribution of assets feeds into the American ideology of the autonomous individual, unfettered and invulnerable to external factors. Fineman refers to this ideology as the "autonomy myth," arguing that "[t]he illusion that independence is attainable for some leads to increased resistance to responding to the obvious dependency of others, as the better off taxpayer detaches himself from the poor and struggling in society."[16] Such self-righteous and "justified" detachment hides the reality of universal human vulnerability and thus feeds the systems of power and privilege that provide the powerful and privileged with the assets they need to protect themselves from vulnerability and advance toward as invulnerable a material position as humanly possible. As care ethicist Joan Tronto points out, the attitude "'I made it on my own, you should make it on your own,' appears to have the formal quality of a morally correct and universalizable judgment." But she argues that it can also "serve to disguise the inequality of resources, powers, and privileges that have made it possible for some to 'make it' while others have not."[17]

The privileged too often forget the reality of their own dependency, the fact that their success in life is not deserved in the sense of having been "earned."[18] Maternal practices of care can help

---

16. Martha Fineman, *The Autonomy Myth: Towards a Theory of Dependency* (New York: New Press, 2004), 32.

17. Tronto, *Moral Boundaries*, 147.

18. Recall the vitriolic reaction to then Massachusetts Senate Candidate Elizabeth Warren's 2011 comment, "There is nobody in this country who got rich on their own." For her comment, see "Elizabeth Warren on the Myth of Class Warfare," http://www.youtube.com/

bring to light this fact of privileged dependency. We all started out as vulnerable dependents and continue, throughout our lives, to depend on access to resources for our well-being and material "success." The ideology of the autonomous individual masks this basic fact about human existence, to the benefit of those privileged individuals who are not responsible for dependency. According to Eva Feder Kittay, the experiences of women (for example, mothers) engaged in dependency work "highlight the ways in which members of human communities are engaged in interdependencies. They emphasize the fact that the independent individual is always a fictive creation of those men sufficiently privileged to shift the concern for dependence onto others."[19] Tronto similarly posits that the powerful in our present culture have much to gain from keeping the fundamental nature of care out of focus:

> By not noticing how pervasive and central care is to human life, those who are in positions of power and privilege can continue to ignore and to degrade the activities of care and those who give care. . . . These "self-made" figures would not only find it difficult to admit the degree to which care has made their lives possible, but such an admission would undermine the legitimacy of the inequitable distribution of power, resources, and privilege of which they are beneficiaries.[20]

Privilege thus masks the dependency of the privileged on the contingent assets that have made possible their protection from and potential for resilience to vulnerability and harm.

Societal systems of power and privilege employ various economic, political, cultural, and even religious means of maintaining control over the various resources needed for coping with vulnerability.

---

watch?v=XcFDF87-SdQ. For samples of the vitriolic reaction, simply scroll down through the comments below the video.

19. Eva Fedder Kittay, *Love's Labor: Essays on Women, Equality, and Dependency* (New York: Routledge, 1999), 17.

20. Tronto, *Moral Boundaries*, 111. Cf. also 162 and 177.

An analysis of such means of social control exceeds the scope of this project. However, it is important to note that when relatively noncoercive means of control fail to maintain systems of power and privilege, the response of the powerful and privileged is all too often one of outright violence. Examples of such violence employed in the defense of privilege are all too numerous to count: male privilege defended with domestic violence; white privilege defended with lynching in the past and massive incarceration of African Americans in the present; class privilege defended with the breaking of strikes and violent dispersion of public protest of inequality; heterosexual privilege defended with murderous hate crimes and bullying; U.S. imperial privilege defended with militarist foreign policy. Even prior to overt physical violence, however, the presence and defense of privilege is violent, since it robs human beings of the assets and resources that would otherwise afford them the ability to live their lives with dignity and respect in the face of vulnerability and suffering. As an unhealthy, unjust, and ultimately violent way of managing vulnerability, privilege comes at a cost to both the marginalized and the privileged themselves. It is to the costs of privilege that we now turn.

The Costs of Privilege: Suffering and Perpetration of Harm

Privilege is an anxiety-ridden social response to human vulnerability that produces heightened vulnerability, greater suffering, and overt or complicit participation in the perpetration of harm. On the surface, privilege most obviously disadvantages the marginalized by denying them access to basic social goods that are needed for protection from vulnerability, resilience to harm, and the pursuit of basic human happiness. Those individuals and groups who are disadvantaged by privilege are therefore disproportionately vulnerable to kinds of suffering from which the privileged are generally shielded. When the powerful must resort to violence to protect their hold on privilege, the suffering of the marginalized can become downright horrific. This is the first and most obvious cost of privilege: the suffering of those on its underside. A second, perhaps even more perplexing cost of privilege is the way in which the heightened vulnerability and suffering it produces can lead the marginalized to perpetrate ordinary and extreme forms of violence toward themselves, toward other marginalized individuals around them, and/or toward the powerful. Not only do the marginalized suffer because of privilege, they can also be so affected by their suffering that they, in turn, participate in harming themselves and others.[21] And their perpetration of such harm induces even greater suffering, guilt, and anxiety, which can in turn exacerbate the perpetration of violence. Those who benefit from privilege enjoy a greater level of protection from vulnerability than those who are unlucky enough to be born on the underside of privilege. However, the privileged themselves are not immune to suffering; they cannot achieve total *in*vulnerability. Indeed, their place of privilege and power also comes with a cost to themselves: it renders them more vulnerable to certain forms of suffering—often less material, but no less real than the suffering of the marginalized. Furthermore, participation in systems of privilege also comes at a moral cost: it entrenches and implicates the privileged in global and local structures of dominance, oppression, and violence. The privileged are thus unavoidably witting or unwitting participants in the usurpation of resources from and perpetration of violence toward the marginalized. The human *telos* is thus rendered even more vulnerable to compromise at best, or demise at worst.

In what follows, I once again draw on maternal witnesses to illustrate that the relative protection from vulnerability afforded to

---

21. Christina Conroy has encountered this phenomenon, called "lateral violence," in her research on Canadian Residential Schools.

the privileged comes at a steep cost in both personal suffering and perpetration of harm by both the marginalized and the privileged. In other words, the costs of privilege are refracted in the diverse experiences of mothers on both ends of the spectrum. Maternal narratives and analyses of suffering and perpetrating harm therefore serve here as icons of human vulnerability and its potentially destructive moral outcomes. These icons in turn drive this chapter, and part 1 as a whole, home to the conclusion of its argument: that the perpetration of harm, the violation of self and other is, in the final analysis, a result of the prior anxiety and suffering that stems from the vulnerability of the human condition.

The Price of Privilege for the Marginalized: The Case of Charlie Karr

The cost of privilege to mothers on the underside of power relations illustrates how relative powerlessness in the face of vulnerability produces not only personal suffering, but also can lead to the infliction of suffering on vulnerable others, especially children. In other words, systems of privilege not only cause personal pain and suffering for the marginalized, they can also exact a moral cost—inducing perpetration of harm by the marginalized themselves. For example, economic disadvantage and lack of social programs designed to mitigate disadvantage increase the risk of child abuse.[22] The exacerbated vulnerability of mothers (and fathers) on the underside of privilege is linked to disadvantaged children's greater vulnerability to maternal (and paternal) neglect, mistreatment, and even death. Of course, it is not always and not even often the case

---

22. See the October 2011 report by BBC News, "America's child death shame," for an indication of the link between systems of privilege and violence against children, http://www.bbc.co.uk/news/magazine-15193530. See also the U.S. Department of Health and Human Services' 2009 Report on Child Maltreatment, December 31, 2009, http://www.acf.hhs.gov/programs/cb/pubs/cm09/cm09.pdf.

that mothers who suffer marginalization pass their suffering onto their children. Not every victim of abuse becomes an abuser. By no means am I suggesting that all or even most women on the underside of privilege are abusers. Nor is it the case that abusive mothers are only victims, lacking agency and determined by their tragic circumstances. But their actions and orientation in the world are located in a context of social oppression and personal pain. The systems of privilege that have contributed to their personal suffering also play a role in the causal chain of events and relationships leading to their perpetration of harm toward vulnerable others, especially children.

In what follows, I relate a narrative of maternal abuse to illustrate the cost of privilege to the marginalized. In my analysis, I hope to avoid both moralistic blame and liberal exoneration. What I seek is understanding—that is, a general understanding of maternal suffering and perpetration of harm within social systems that deny mothers various resources for self-protection and resilience. I intend to arrive at this general understanding in and through the particular understanding of the story behind one abusive mother's personal guilt and moral failing—namely, the story of Charlie Karr, mother of memoirist Mary Karr. I have selected this particular narrative to serve as an icon of what the violation of human dignity within a system of privilege can do to a person, to her moral agency, to her relationships, and to vulnerable others in her care. The narrative structure of how this mother's story is told by her daughter highlights the nature of how prior vulnerability and resultant suffering due to lack of assets for self-protection and resilience can lead to further violation of vulnerable others. The narrative is related nonlinearly, beginning with the mother's perpetration of harm and ending with her own backstory of suffering. This literary structure both a) drives home the damaging nature of the abuse, and b) brings the reader to an understanding of the painful origins of the abusive mother's actions. The narrative also highlights the fact that a mother's abuse of her child is also a violation of her own self, bringing about paralyzing guilt, self-hatred, shame, and loss of self, happiness, and human fulfillment.

In her first memoir, *The Liars' Club*, Mary Karr relates with humor and grace the story of her turbulent childhood, marked by the sometimes horrific, often absent presence of her mother Charlie. The memoir begins with Karr's sharpest memory: seven years old, in the dark on a mattress, being asked by her family doctor to show him where she was hurt. Neighbors and family helped her fill out the memory, which she had long repressed. Her sister in the doorframe, held by the sheriff, feigning sleep. Firemen moving through the house. Red lights flashing on the walls from an ambulance outside. And, "in the window, through a web of honeysuckle, [in her] own backyard flames like those of a football bonfire."[23]

It took Karr thirty years to paste together what happened on that night, when her mother was taken "Away" for being "Nervous." Only after drawing her readers into the dreary and hardscrabble world of Leechfield, East Texas, and only after introducing us to her mother's caustic personality and depressive alcoholism, does Karr fill in the details of this her clearest memory of childhood: her mother's near homicidal nervous-breakdown. Clearly suffering from some form of mental illness, Karr's mother had displayed hints of a "Nervous"-ness that threatened the well-being of her two daughters long prior to the night she was "hauled away in leather four-point restraints."[24] Though she was never physically abusive, her anger, depression, and alcoholism took an emotional and psychological toll

---

23. Mary Karr, *The Liars' Club: A Memoir* (New York: Penguin, 1995), 5.
24. Ibid., 125.

on her daughters. For example, rather than beating her children, she threatened them with homicide. Karr recalls that

> some kind of serious fury must have been roiling around inside her. Sometimes, instead of spanking us, she would stand in the kitchen with her fists all white-knuckled and scream up at the light fixture that she wasn't whipping us, because she knew if she got started she'd kill us. This worked way better than any spanking could have. Your mother's threat of homicide—however unlikely she tries to make it sound—will flat dampen down your spirits.[25]

The alternative to Charlie's whippings and murderous threats was her silent, drunken withdrawal. Karr relates that her mother once took to her bed for over a month, during which Karr sat around "watching cobwebs grow between [her] mother's fingers while she [lay] in bed wishing herself dead."[26] Worse than the neglect that Mary and her sister Lecia experienced during these periods of their mother's absence was their constant fear of her committing suicide, which she threatened on more than one occasion. While Lecia expertly counted the number of drinks their mother had imbibed, Mary "zeroed in on the lines of Mother's face and the timbre of her voice in hopes of divining the degree of Nervous she might get to."[27] Once, the degree of Nervous reached such maniacal heights that, during a violent hurricane, Charlie nearly drove her family off the bridge on which they were evacuating to higher ground. Karr remembers that, just as they began to mount the bridge, her mother was singing the scariest part of "Mack the Knife"—"*When the shark bites with his teeth, dear, / Scarlet billows start to spread.*" She then remembers her mother turning the wheel sharply to the left, sending their car into a 360-degree spin.[28] Karr also recalls repeating the same terrifying experience on

25. Ibid., 71.
26. Ibid., 119.
27. Ibid., 128.
28. Ibid., 90–92.

her birthday, as their family returned home from dinner at a bayou café over that same bridge. On that night, her mother, shouting at her husband that he was a "great Nothing," grabbed the steering wheel and once again tried to take the whole family over the edge of the bridge.

And then there was that fateful night, the night that holds the prized place of Karr's sharpest childhood memory. On that night, Mary arrived home to an empty house and encountered all of the mirrors scribbled dark with lipstick, the last one (hers and Lecia's) shattered to pieces. When she finally found her mother, she saw that Charlie's own face was also scribbled up with lipstick. In that moment, Mary realized that her mother "was trying to scrub herself out."[29] Karr's memory then shifts to her mother tearing apart the girls' bedroom, throwing everything into boxes while muttering, "*I want to be a good hausfrau. . . . That's my job. That's what I am—the wife of this fucking crackerbox house.*"[30] Charlie hauls everything—toys, books, clothing, furniture—out to the yard where she ignites all of the girls' belongings in a giant bonfire. Karr recalls,

> At some point the fire fades to orange background, and I stare only at Mother's face. It's all streaked up with lipstick and soot, so she looks like a bona fide maniac. Her lips move in a muttery way, but I can't make out the words. . . . Mother's voice rises, so I can make out what she's saying over the fire and the whimpering dog: *Rotten cocksucking motherfucking hausfrau.*[31]

Next thing Karr remembers, she and her sister followed their mother into the house, then hid in what they thought might be the safety of their bedroom, where they lay frozen in fear, eyes squeezed shut, listening to their mother crash around the cutlery drawers in the

---

29. Ibid., 149.
30. Ibid.
31. Ibid., 152.

kitchen. Karr recounts that, when she opened her eyes, her mother was standing in the light of the doorframe wielding a butcher knife.

> A long rectangle of light spills over us from the open door. Then a dark shape comes to occupy that light, a figure in the shape of my mom with a wild corona of hair and no face but a shadow. She has lifted her arms and broadened the stance of her feet, so her shadow turns from being a long thin line into a giant X. And swooping down from one hand is the twelve-inch shine of a butcher knife, not unlike the knife that crazy guy had in *Psycho* for the shower scene, a stretched-out triangle of a knife that Daddy sharpens by hand on his whetstone before he dismantles a squirrel or a chicken, though it is also big enough to have hacked through the hip joint of a buck.

Mary detaches herself from the scene by turning her mother into a stick figure cartoon, and after lying still in this cartoon moment for what seemed to Mary like forever, her mother roars "No!" and sets the knife down to dial the phone.

> I count the seven turns of the dial, feel it unwind under her stick figure. She's crying, the stick mommy, with sucking sobs. A whole fountain of blue tears pours from both pin-dot eyes. I guess it's Dr. Boudreaux who answers on the other end, because she says, "Forest, it's Charlie Marie. Get over here. I just killed them both. Both of them. I've stabbed them both to death."[32]

By some miracle, or some restraint on the part of her unconscious mind, Charlie Karr did not kill her daughters that night, though she hallucinated that she had. And young Mary was left with the aftermath of this trauma as the sharpest of her childhood memories.

Karr's memoir goes on to recount other childhood traumas (for example, rape by a teen-aged neighbor and sexual molestation by one of her mother's boyfriends), along with other incidents of Charlie's maternal neglect and/or endangerment. But the narrative begins with

---

32. Ibid., 157.

this snapshot of terror, fills out its details, and returns to it in the memoir's final pages, which recount the grown-up Karr's later attempts both to solve the mysteries surrounding her mother's life before Leechfield, and to understand the origins of her mother's misery. Given an ultimatum by her therapist, Karr finally confronts her mother about her past. Over two pitchers of margaritas, Charlie tells her daughter the truth about her life before coming to Leechfield. What emerges is a tragic backstory that helps Mary (and her readers) to understand why her mother became an alcoholic and finally lost her mind to the point of nearly killing her own daughters.

This is what happened: Charlie Moore was married off by her own mother at the age of fifteen, a few years after which she gave birth to a baby boy. In an attempt to escape her overbearing mother-in-law—"a broomstick-wielding German housewife with a gaze merciless as the sun's"[33]—Charlie convinced her young husband to take a job in New York City, where they moved from Lubbock, Texas, in 1942. An aspiring artist, Charlie wished to study and paint the human form, to which her husband objected and which was put on hold once she gave birth to a new baby girl. What follows this second child's birth is the key to Charlie's ensuing demise. Karr relates:

> After the birth of [the baby girl], the wicked mother-in-law flew north on her leathery wings and assumed control over the household. The young wife responded with an act shameless enough to border on scandal: she took a job, full-time, doing mechanical drawing for Bell Labs. . . . And it was from that job that Mother returned home one evening to find her entire house empty, her family gone.[34]

Charlie's children were taken from her. Gone. Without a trace. And this is when she took her first real drink, when she began to drink until blacking out each night. Charlie searched for her

33. Ibid., 312.
34. Ibid., 313.

children to no avail, until she discovered their whereabouts years later. She immediately boarded a plane, custody papers in hand, with the intention of bringing her children home. But when she arrived, her mere presence caused her daughter to wail and her son to cling to his grandmother's skirts. And then, for the first time, she thought about her own situation in New York, and realized that her studio apartment was no place for children. Charlie remembers, "I knew then that they were better off there. . . . With their Daddy, I mean, and whoever the woman [his new wife] was. I didn't have anybody to watch them while I was at work. I hadn't *thought*, just hadn't *thought* about any of that."[35] So Charlie returned to New York and began her long search for a husband who could support her and help her to get back her children. Four husbands later, she wound up in Leechfield with Mary and Lecia's father, who was the only one who would have taken her children in, but by then it was too late. They were too big and wanted to stay with their father. And the effect on Charlie was devastating: "They didn't want to come. . . . Then it was like a big black hole just swallowed me up all those years without my even noticing. I just collapsed into it. What's the word the physicists use? Imploded. I imploded."[36] Her lost kids haunted her, she blamed herself. Her own mother even blamed her.[37]

Upon hearing her mother's story of loss and shame and self-destruction, Mary Karr began understand the origins of her mother's behavior. She began to understand that "[t]hose were [her] mother's demons, then, two small children, whom she longed for and felt ashamed for having lost."[38] Her mother helped her to understand what had happened that night she had "drunk herself to the bottom of despair" and nearly killed her and Lecia with a butcher knife: "All the

35. Ibid., 317.
36. Ibid., 318.
37. Karr, *Lit*, 65.
38. Karr, *The Liars' Club*, 318.

time I'd wasted, marrying fellows. And still I lost those kids. And you and Lecia couldn't change that. And I'd wound up just as miserable as I started at fifteen." In her third memoir, *Lit*, Karr documents her mother's later musings on what she had been thinking on that night: "*You were just so precious, I thought I'd kill you before they all got to hurt you. . . .* I just couldn't imagine bringing up two girls in a world where they do such awful things to women. So I decided to kill you both, to spare you."[39] In Karr's estimation, "Killing us had come to seem merciful."[40] It was not antipathy or malice toward her children that led Charlie Karr to nearly murder them. Rather, as Karr observes in *Lit*, "An old spark had already been burning down the fuse toward her explosion."[41] Whatever Charlie's merciful or explosive motivation was in the moment of her psychotic break, the nearly homicidal actions she took that night were, at least in part, precipitated by the traumatic experience of having her first two children taken from her. In fact, her entire struggle with alcoholism and mental illness, along with the apathetic and sometimes even vicious nature of her relationship with her daughters, was all somehow, at least in part, related to the loss of those children. Whatever kind of mother she was to them, their disappearance wreaked havoc on Charlie's psyche, and on all of her subsequent relationships. Haunted by the pain of that loss, she began to drink, and she became severely depressed, angry, hardened, and even suicidal and homicidal. She spiraled down into despair, taking those around her—especially her vulnerable daughters—down with her. The violation of Charlie's relational vulnerability—that is, the severing of her bonds of attachment with her first two children—had the effect of bringing about not only her

---

39. Karr, *Lit*, 3.
40. Ibid.
41. Ibid.

own private pain and suffering, but also her moral (and relational) demise.

In Tillichian terms, the anxiety that ensues from personal loss and perceived failure can do this to a person. The destruction of relationships that play a defining role in the constitution of one's own being brings about acute anxiety surrounding the threat of nonbeing. The denial of human creativity results in the anxiety of meaninglessness. And the experience of failure and self-blame leads to the anxiety of guilt and condemnation. When an individual is, for whatever reason, unable to overcome these forms of anxiety with courage, the result can be destructive of both self and other. This was certainly the case with Charlie Karr. The loss of her children seems to have resulted, at least in part, from her scandalous act of taking a full-time job in an era when such a move marked a middle-class mother as cold and heartless. In one fell swoop, then, Charlie's husband's removal of their children from her life destroyed both her relationship with them as a mother, and the perceived legitimacy of her desire for self-expression and creativity as an artist. The contradiction between these two goods (and their mutual destruction) led her to self-blame and overwhelming anxiety over her sense of guilt for having lost her children. She lived her life ashamed of what had happened to her and her children, despite (or perhaps because of) her inability to stop it. The anger and depression that grew from her anxiety surrounding this event consumed her and the new family she created in Leechfield. The violation of this mother's vulnerability ultimately led her to violate the vulnerability of her precious daughters.

How is this the cost of privilege? The removal of Charlie Karr's children did not take place within a vacuum. It was not simply the random or malicious act of an atomistic individual. Rather, it took place within a certain system of privilege (in this case male privilege) that granted disproportionate assets to Charlie's husband (and men in general) that she was denied. At least two aspects of male privilege in 1942 allowed Charlie's husband the motivation and the freedom to disappear with their children forever. The lack of these privileges contributed to Charlie's inability to recover, psychologically and materially, from the loss. First, there was the privilege of working in the public sphere outside the home without having one's motives questioned, or identity as a man threatened. This privilege not only grants its male beneficiaries the physical assets necessary for material survival and for resilience in the face of harm, it also can contribute to a sense of meaning and purpose in life, through the sense of fulfillment and creativity it can provide. In other words, a professional vocation can contribute to the existential assets an individual needs in order to psychologically cope with vulnerability and disaster. The domestic duties of motherhood can certainly contribute to a woman's sense of self, creativity, and fulfillment. Indeed, mothering provides great meaning and purpose for many women. But there are also many mothers who experience a dual vocation, to both motherhood and professional self-development outside the home. Charlie Karr was a case in point. Though she loved her children, she also sought fulfillment in art. While there were no questions surrounding the legitimacy of Charlie's first husband working outside the home, her pursuit of employment was considered scandalous and appears to have precipitated, at least in part, her husband's disappearance with their two children. Charlie was discouraged in her pursuit of painting and punished severely for her decision to take a job using her artistic ability in mechanical drawing. When her children were taken from her, she lost not only her precious loved ones and her own identity as a mother, but also her sense of legitimacy as a woman working outside the home. The development of her artistic talent became riddled with anxiety for her. On the night of her psychotic break, she burned not only her children's belongings, but also many of her own paintings. She never fully developed the artistic side of her personality because she was never able to reconcile her identity as a mother with her identity as an artist and professional woman in her own right. In her mind, she was a failure at both motherhood and art. She was denied the privilege of artistic self-development in her youth, was then punished for seeking it with the removal of her children, and was thus unable to fall back on it as an asset for resilience in the wake of tragedy.

Second, related to his privilege of professional employment, Charlie's husband enjoyed the privilege of earning a wage that provided adequate resources to meet the material needs of his dependent children. Although Charlie had a job at the time, the wage gap between men and women during World War II[42] did not work in her favor and she was left with next to nothing when her husband disappeared. She took a studio apartment, which she later realized upon finding her lost children was not adequate to meet their needs. She did not even have beds for them, nor someone to care for them while she worked. Meanwhile, her (ex-)husband was able to provide not only for his and Charlie's children, but for his mother and his new family as well. Once Charlie realized she lacked the ability to provide for her children, she tore up the custody papers she had acquired, and returned to New York in search of a new husband who could provide the physical assets necessary to get her kids back. Charlie knew that it was only with the help of a man, privileged as he would hopefully be with gainful employment, that she would be able to properly care for her children. And this despite her own employment as a skilled professional. What followed was a series of toxic and failed relationships, which further contributed

---

42. I was unable to find statistics on the wage gap during the 1940s. Most statistics seem to go back only as far as the early 1960s, when women earned about 60% of men's salaries. See National Committee on Pay Equity, "The Wage Gap over Time: In Real Dollars, Women See a Continuing Gap," http://www.pay-equity.org/info-time.html.

to the ongoing demise of Charlie's mental health and moral agency. Lacking the privilege of a living wage, then, Charlie was not only unable to recover her lost children on her own, she was put in the vulnerable position of depending on a man's income to pursue happiness. While other factors (a family history of mental illness, perhaps) no doubt contributed to Charlie's destructive path in life, her location on the underside of male privilege certainly played a role in violating her vulnerability and leading to her own violation of the vulnerable others in her care.

Charlie Karr's story is just one example of the cost of male privilege. There are countless other ways in which male privilege can and has destroyed the lives of women through the infliction of suffering that has the potential to destroy not only the sufferer's personal sense of well-being, but her moral agency as well. This is also true of other forms of privilege such as white privilege, class privilege, heterosexual privilege, and imperial privilege. It would take volumes to adequately investigate instances and analyses of these pernicious forms of privilege that order society today. However, my objective is not social criticism of privilege per se (however important such criticism may be), but anthropological understanding of the social and personal dynamics that link vulnerability, anxiety, privilege, and violence together in a causal network of events and relationships. Where and whenever there are certain individuals and groups who are disproportionately advantaged with assets for self-protection and resilience in the face of vulnerability, there are others who are disproportionately denied advantages that would otherwise help them to cope with their vulnerability. Those who reside on the underside of privilege thus face heightened forms of vulnerability because they are systematically denied the resources needed to ward off or recover from harm. Since vulnerability begets anxiety, the marginalized are also faced with heightened and even horrific forms of anxiety due to their lack of assets to cope with vulnerability. In cases like Charlie Karr's, the anxiety produced by the violation of vulnerability in privilege can result in the downward moral spiral toward violation of and even violence toward vulnerable others. Privilege thus exacts not only the real cost of suffering pain and relative powerlessness, but also the potential moral price of participation in the commission of harm. Privilege causes the marginalized pain, and it also (therefore) can cause the perpetration of further pain by the powerless.

The Price of Privilege for the Privileged:
Of Hockey Moms and Soccer Moms

Given their identity as women, all mothers are located on the underside of male privilege; even as much as this form of privilege has been mitigated in recent decades, it still exists. Charlie Karr was a white, middle-class working woman when her life was destroyed by the removal of her two children, but the privilege of her race and economic class did not protect her from the vulnerability of her status as a woman and mother in a society dominated by male privilege. As long as male privilege persists, mothers will be at a disadvantage in their access to assets that would help them to cope with human vulnerability and recover from harm. However, white middle- to upper-middle and upper-class mothers in the United States do enjoy significant racial, economic, and imperial privileges that provide them with disproportionate access to the physical, human, social, and environmental assets necessary for coping with vulnerability. The top-heavy possession of these resources renders privileged mothers complicit with unjust systems of race and class privilege that deny entire populations access to the basic goods required for protection from and resilience to physical, material, relational, and even psychological and spiritual harm. While the privileged possession of assets for protection from and resilience to vulnerability does provide a certain level of comfort and security, it does not come without a price in both personal suffering and moral degradation. A brief consideration of privileged mothers can help us to understand how privilege is a means of (mis)managing human vulnerability that not only produces personal and moral harm in the marginalized, but also backfires in its effects on the privileged themselves. There is a cost associated with enjoying protection from vulnerability within a system that denies a majority (or minority) of other human beings the ability to protect themselves. While the cost may not be measurable in material currency, it has a very real effect on the pursuit of human happiness and spiritual fulfillment. When it comes to the cost of privilege to the privileged themselves, it is our moral, spiritual, psychic vulnerability that is at stake. Here it becomes clear that the violation of the other is also a violation of one's own self.

We turn now, then, to both the cost of privilege to privileged mothers' moral agency, and the cost to privileged mothers' personal sense of happiness and well-being. In making my case, I focus on the phenomenon of collective complicity with injustice and violence by privileged mothers, rather than individual cases of child abuse, neglect, and so on. This is not because privileged mothers are immune from abusing vulnerable others in their care. Indeed, privileged mothers can and do commit child abuse, and their actions are also situated within and, to a certain extent, conditioned by their privileged context. However, my objective here is to account for the more public moral cost of privilege, and to suggest a relationship between this public cost and the effect of privilege on mothers' personal happiness.

The most obvious price of privilege for privileged mothers themselves is the moral cost of participation in an unjust social system that violates the vulnerability and dignity of other human beings. This participation in the perpetration of suffering in the lives of the marginalized takes two main forms: conservative defense of and liberal blindness to the injustice of privilege and its oppressive and sometimes even horrific effects on the marginalized. Although labels and stereotypes that dichotomize women in general and mothers in particular are usually unhelpful and never fully capture the complexity of women's lives and political commitments, women often use such labels in public discourse to identify themselves with (or distance themselves from) a certain lifestyle and set of principles. For this reason, I draw on recent forms of public discourse that have referred to conservative mothers as "Hockey Moms" and privileged liberal mothers as "Soccer Moms." I employ this admittedly inaccurate dichotomy as a heuristic device designed to explore the social phenomenon of privilege as it plays out in mothers' lives.

During her landmark acceptance speech at the 2008 Republican National Convention, former Alaska governor and soon-to-be Vice-Presidential candidate Sarah Palin remarked that she had the privilege of living her life in a small town, "just your average hockey mom and signed up for the PTA." Her self-identification as a hockey mom clearly resonated with the crowd, some of whom held signs scrawled with "Hockey Moms for McCain." To the raucous applause, she responded with an impromptu joke: "I love those hockey moms. You know they say the difference between a hockey mom and a pit bull? . . . Lipstick."[43] Two years later, during the summer of 2010, Palin's political action committee aired a commercial to garner support for conservative political candidates running in the upcoming midterm elections.[44] In the video, Ms. Palin touts a new movement of women

43. Cf. National Public Radio, "Transcript: Gov. Sarah Palin at the RNC," http://www.npr.org/templates/story/story.php?storyId=94258995; and "Remarks by Sarah Palin," http://www.youtube.com/watch?v=vKgNrb3baNM.

coming together to run a Pink Elephant stampede on Washington politics out of concern for their children's and grandchildren's future. She calls this movement a "mom-awakening . . . 'cause moms kind of just know when something is wrong." Like the mama grizzlies in her home state of Alaska, these moms are rising up to strike out against enemies and protect their young from that which threatens them. These are strong women, ready to do whatever it takes to keep their children safe from danger: "You thought pit bulls were tough, well you don't wanna mess with the mama grizzlies."

While Palin never explicitly incites or condones violence in these examples of conservative maternal discourse, she uses images with violent connotations to define conservative mothers and call them to action. Hockey moms, pit bulls, and mama grizzlies—Palin calls on conservative women to be intense and relentless, willing to take down anything or anyone that threatens the "American way of life" for their children. One can infer from conservative political discourse that what Palin and her supporters perceive to be threatened is actually white, middle-class, heterosexual privilege. While the SarahPAC ad itself does not explicitly mention who or what it is that poses such a grave danger to this privileged way of life, one can also infer from the conservative political agenda that the perceived threats to America and its children come from dangerous others—namely, people of color, Muslims, immigrants, homosexuals, feminists, welfare recipients, and secularists, to name a few. Mama grizzlies are standing up to these groups to say, in Palin's words, "Enough is enough. We are taking our country back." On a maternal mission to "protect" the vulnerable, the mama grizzly movement represents a maternal parochialism intent on protecting privilege and fueled by fear of and hostility toward the dangerous other. The resulting

44. The video was all over the Internet. One site at which to view it is "Mama Grizzlies," http://www.youtube.com/watch?v=fsUVL6ciK-c.

political policies further disadvantage and even legitimize violence toward the dangerous others (including other women and mothers) whose mere presence threatens the maintenance of privilege. Even outside of partisan politics, this maternal crusade against the dangerous other can get very ugly. There are mothers who teach their children to hate those whose difference threatens their perceived identity, security, and privilege as white, heterosexual, middle-class Americans.

When maternal loyalties do not lead to outright revulsion and hostility, liberal sentimentalization of the mother-child relationship can render middle-class white children's privilege invisible and the needs of other, less-privileged children insignificant. For example, moderate to liberal middle-class mothers' passionate interest in their own children's well-being can often conceal a disinterest in the well-being of other children, especially those who are economically disadvantaged. Here we might call to mind the stereotypical "soccer mom"—the mother whose daily, weekly, monthly, and yearly schedule revolves around her children's entertainment and social, physical, and academic enrichment. Such mothers can get so wrapped up in their own children's lives that they simply do not see the privilege of their own lifestyle as unearned or the disadvantage of other people's children as their responsibility. Bonnie Miller-McLemore argues that hypervigilance about privileged children's success limits parents' concern for other people's children and, in fact sees them as "competitors for limited goods."[45] In her words,

> The private sentimentalization of children and child rearing, it seems, has been inversely related to a collective indifference toward other people's children. The heightened pace of middle-class children's extracurricular activities and the billions of dollars in available

45. Bonnie Miller-McLemore, *Let the Children Come: Reimagining Childhood from a Christian Perspective* (San Francisco: Jossey-Bass, 2003), 89.

discretionary income, so sought by market specialists, contrasts sharply with the lack of opportunities and resources for the large number of U.S. children living in poverty.[46]

According to Miller-McLemore, privileged parents' obsession with their children's success "is not unrelated to the neglect of children with fewer resources in the United States and around the world. Although some people lack the economic and social means to attend to their children's pressing needs, those with greater assets are literally obsessed with their own individual children."[47] The more obsessed mothers (and fathers) become with the advancement of their own offspring, the dimmer the view of other children, especially poor children, becomes. This is a less overtly hostile position than the aggressive stance of mama grizzlies who strike out against the dangerous other with vitriol and violence. But the result is arguably no less damaging for the well-being of poor mothers and their children. Whether overtly derisive or blissfully ignorant and apathetic, maternal parochialism is no myth. It is a default position for mothers who (understandably and laudably) love their children and want what is best for them. But its damaging consequences for the "dangerous" or disadvantaged other are very real.

Participation in social, racial, sexual, and economic systems of privilege comes with a cost to privileged mothers themselves—this moral cost of directly and/or indirectly violating the vulnerability of other human beings. Although they are privileged, and thus protected from a great deal of vulnerability and afforded the resources needed for resilience, privileged mothers are also vulnerable to personal suffering as a cost of privilege. In fact, it seems that participation in privilege might not be a recipe for happiness, but for misery. Privileged mothers face a level of guilt and anxiety

46. Ibid., 12.
47. Ibid., 89–90.

surrounding vulnerability that ironically comes out of their participation in privilege, but that also results in their further clinging to privilege for protection and control. In our earlier analysis of maternal anxiety, we witnessed what Judith Warner describes as "that caught-by-the-throat feeling so many mothers have today of *always* doing something wrong."[48] The "new kind of soul-draining perfectionism," resulting from what Warner calls the "Mommy Mystique,"[49] is in part a mechanism of male privilege, which places responsibility for care and vulnerability—and for children's success and happiness—in the hands of women. But for privileged mothers, this form of maternal anxiety is also a means of defending the great machine of racial, social, economic, and heterosexual privilege.

When a person, family, or community benefits from privilege, certain anxiety-filled needs occur: 1) the need to defend privilege as earned or merited, not inherited; and 2) the need to stave off vulnerability and pass on the benefits of privilege to the next generation. If, as the autonomy myth supposes, privilege is earned, then its benefits lie within our control. If we are able to control our own access and our children's access to privilege, if we are capable of staving off vulnerability with privilege, then we should do everything in our power to do so. As Warner observes:

> The mommy mystique tells us that we are the luckiest women in the world—the freest, with the most choices, the broadest horizons, the best luck, and the most health. It says we have the knowledge and the know-how to make "informed decisions" that will guarantee the successful course of our children's lives. It tells us that if we choose badly our children will fall prey to countless dangers—from insecure attachment to drugs to kidnapping to a third-rate college. And if this happens, if our children stray from the path toward happiness and success, we will have no one but ourselves to blame.[50]

48. Judith Warner, *Perfect Madness: Motherhood in the Age of Anxiety* (New York: Riverhead, 2005), 3.
49. Ibid., 13.

In today's economic climate, fierce competition for employment, prestige, and power impels parents in general and mothers in particular to spend unparalleled time, energy, and financial resources on grooming their children for success. This "parenting pressure cooker" results not only in the aforementioned eclipse of marginalized mothers and their families, but also in tremendous levels of stress, anxiety, and guilt.[51] In Warner's research with privileged mothers in the Washington, D.C., area, she found that "[t]he more women bought into the crazy competitiveness of our time, the more they tended to suffer as mothers. . . . [Their] anxiety was palpable. The desire to contain it with magical acts of control was so clear."[52] The failure of maternal magic to produce happy and successful children is indeed soul-draining. But even when mothers enjoy "success," the interruption of privilege by the ever-present threat of vulnerability can induce that "caught-by-the-throat feeling" of relentless anxiety as a way of inhabiting the world. Furthermore, the deep-seated individualism that underlies the autonomy myth and the Mommy Mystique—and the systems of privilege that these myths uphold—induces in the privileged a vast internal emptiness, a spiritual lack that inevitably results from cutting off connection with others. This privilege-induced anxiety and emptiness surrounding vulnerability and privilege leads to further participation in the

50. Ibid., 32. For a similar analysis, see Andrea O'Reilly, Marie Porter, and Patricia Short, eds., *Motherhood: Power and Oppression* (Toronto: Women's Press, 2005), 98.
51. Political economist Peadar Kirby pinpoints such anxiety as an impact of neoliberal globalization. See his "Theorising Globalisation's Social Impact: Proposing the Concept of Vulnerability," *Review of International Political Economy* 13, no. 4 (October 2006): 638. "[L]ife is experienced as a daily struggle constantly accompanied by the awareness that, no matter how much is achieved, one's life is also under threat. 'Even behind the facades of security and prosperity,' [. . .] 'the possibilities of biographical slippage and collapse are ever present. Hence the clinging and the fear, even in the externally wealthy middle layers of society.'" Citing Ulrich Beck, "Living Your Own Life in a Runaway World: Individualisation, Globalisation and Politics," in *On the Edge: Living with Global Capitalism*, ed. Will Hutton and Anthony Giddens (London: Vintage, 2001), 167.
52. Warner, *Perfect Madness*, 23–24.

violation of vulnerable others, either directly and intentionally or indirectly and unwittingly.

Here this chapter, and part 1 as a whole, has finally arrived at the conclusion of its argument: Vulnerability begets anxiety, which begets the violation of vulnerable others. Violation begets greater vulnerability and even greater anxiety (for both the violator and violated). Further vulnerability and anxiety in turn beget further violation. Both privileged and marginalized mothers are caught up in this cycle. As icons of the human condition, the maternal examples I have described in this these pages point to the reality of this dynamic of vulnerability and violation at work in the human community as a whole.

Conclusion: Theological Implications of the Dynamic of Vulnerability and Violation

In the first chapter of her memoir *Lit*, Mary Karr addresses an open letter to her teen-aged son to help him understand how she came to peace with the horrific events of her childhood and how she came to understand that her mother wound up as blameless in her story as her son was in his youth and innocence. Though the wounds of her childhood might never fully heal, Karr's ultimate stance toward her mother in her memoirs is one of compassion. How is it possible to attribute blamelessness and extend compassion to a woman whose alcoholism, neglect, and psychological abuse nearly cost Karr her own life? The answer to this question lies somewhere in the theological implications of the complex and dynamic relationship between vulnerability and violation.

Vulnerability is an ever-present, governing force in our lives. The ways in which we inhabit our world—our habits, our lifestyles, our interactions with other people, our joys and hopes and sorrows—are in large part determined by our exposure and response to vulnerability. In the foregoing analyses, mothers have functioned as icons of how human vulnerability precedes the violation of vulnerable others. The maternal witnesses in this chapter have shown how prior anxiety surrounding vulnerability and the suffering produced by the violation of vulnerability are root causes of both personal suffering and the violation of vulnerable others. Vulnerability produces anxiety, which in turn leads to social systems of privilege designed to mitigate vulnerability for some, while amplifying vulnerability for others. The social mismanagement of vulnerability in privilege is rooted in anxiety surrounding human vulnerability. The violation of vulnerability in systems of privilege produces suffering and further anxiety for both the privileged and those on the underside of privilege. And the cycle continues. We are all born into and located within these contexts of mismanaged and violated vulnerability. This is as true in personal or familial relationships as it is in the public realm of politics and economics. When we wittingly or unwittingly participate in the perpetration of harm toward vulnerable others, we are acting out of our own experiences of vulnerability, our own fears and experiences of harm. The thrust of this argument implicitly critiques and presents an alternative to Christian language of sin and guilt.

In the Christian tradition, the violation of other human beings has been interpreted as a result of human sinfulness. As fallen creatures, our wills are corrupted and thus incapable of choosing to recognize and respect the fundamental dignity of other persons. Despite this incapacitation, we are capable of accepting the transformative power of grace and, as such, are still responsible for our actions and attitudes in the world. When we violate others, especially vulnerable others, we sin. The injustice, violence, and oppression that beget and uphold privilege are sinful. Our personal participation in these evils, even if unwitting, is sinful. When we harm God's creation, we are guilty and worthy of blame and punishment. From the prophets of Israel to Augustine to liberation theology, this dynamic of sin and guilt pervades the Christian imagination. This imagination can produce powerful and prophetic critiques of injustice, violence, and oppression. Such critiques of personal and social sin are undoubtedly necessary in the struggle for a more just and peaceful world. However, employing the language of sin in the struggle for justice can also lead to a rather simplistic and dualistic understanding of the anthropological roots of injustice, violence, and oppression. Sin language easily plays into other-directed, fearful, and self-righteous attacks on "the enemy," whoever that may be—militant Islamists (or all Muslims), radical feminists, homosexuals, addicts, capitalists, Republicans, the wealthy, the poor. In Farley's words,

> We seem justified not only in our anger and pain and in our efforts to change institutions and political systems. We seem justified also in our hatred of the oppressor and in our judgment that oppressors are beyond the pale of divine or human reconciliation. The temptation to condemn utterly offers a dangerous spiritual practice. It nourishes our incapacities to love and is therefore harmful to ourselves. It also hides the wounds hidden in those who exercise their power in obviously harmful and destructive ways.[53]

The dualistic thinking often spawned by sin language can kill the cultivation of compassion toward others. Turned in on the self, sin language also plays into destructive internal dynamics of self-loathing and paralyzing guilt for the marginalized—for women, LGBTQ persons, people of color, the poor, those who suffer mental illness. Healthy, life-giving retrievals of sin language are by no means impossible. However, such retrievals would benefit from both a robust understanding of vulnerability and suffering as defining

---

53. Wendy Farley, *The Wounding and Healing: Weaving Heaven and Earth* (Louisville: Westminster John Knox, 2005), 23.

features of the human condition and a complex acknowledgment of the roots of sin in suffering and vulnerability.

Reaching behind and beneath sin to vulnerability can help us to better comprehend the human condition, its vulnerability, and its propensity to violation. Such is the task I have sought to accomplish in these pages. A robust understanding of the dynamic of vulnerability and violation offers not only an alternative to sin as the root problem of the human condition. It also calls for an alternative understanding of *what human beings need* in order to experience wholeness, flourishing, and life in abundance. The human *telos*, *eudaimonia*, is a fragile endeavor. This is not simply because we are sinful creatures with corrupted wills, but because we are fundamentally *vulnerable* creatures. Focusing on vulnerability changes the picture, the narrative, of what we need as human beings to solve or address our problem. The antidote to the human problem is not simply divine forgiveness of sin in the hopes of eternal *in*vulnerability. What is needed—more deeply—is a divine response appropriate to the persistent reality of vulnerability and the anxiety and suffering it produces in earthly human life.

As vulnerable, suffering creatures, human beings are like the servant in Julian of Norwich's parable of the lord and servant. In her retelling of creation and the fall, the noble lord sends the servant out to do his will. The servant runs off eagerly, but quickly falls into a dell and is injured. In his suffering state, "he groans and moans and tosses about and writhes, but he cannot rise and help himself in any way." Ever compassionate, Julian does not blame the servant for his fall or for his inability to rise, but comes to understand that, in all of his pain, "the greatest hurt which I saw him in was lack of consolation, for he could not turn his face to look on his loving lord, who was very close to him, in whom is all consolation; but like a man who was for the time extremely feeble and foolish, he paid heed to his feelings and his continuing distress."[54] What the servant needed in order to rise from the dell was not a reprimand or punishment, perhaps not even forgiveness (though there may be a rightful place for such helps on the road to redemption). The servant was consumed and blinded by his pain such that he was feebly and foolishly unable to understand or recognize what he needed to overcome in his suffering. What the servant needed, most deeply, was to feel the lord's consolation in his distress. What he needed to rise from the dell was a set of assets for resilience: comfort, strength, wisdom, and the wider vision that only the lord's loving countenance could provide. But this love is precisely what he could not see.

Julian's servant, like Mary Karr's "blameless" mother, represents the human condition: natal and mortal, eager to flourish but vulnerable to suffering. The treasure of doing the lord's will (love) is the greatest possibility of human becoming as natals, but our natality carries with it vulnerability to pain and suffering (not to mention mortality). This vulnerability trips us up and sends us flailing into the dell. There we suffer—pains of the body and soul, of hunger and thirst, of relationships, growth, rejection, aging, illness, death, and so on. There we are consumed and blinded by our suffering and by the anxiety produced by both our suffering and our fear of suffering. In our blindness, we fail to experience the consolation of divine love and, in our thrashing about, in our raging attempts to escape our vulnerability, we hurt vulnerable others around us. Like the servant, and like Karr's mother, we need assets for resilience in our state of vulnerability, pain, and suffering. We need resources to soothe our pains, recover from harm, and cope more peacefully with our vulnerability. We need comfort, compassion, and solidarity. We need empowerment to live life abundantly, even in the face of our

54. Julian of Norwich, *Showings*, trans. Edmund Colledge and James Walsh (Mahwah, NJ: Paulist, 1978), 267.

vulnerability. We need the courage to feel the warmth of divine love, overcome our anxiety, resist the injustice and violence of privilege, and reach out in compassion and solidarity to vulnerable others (including our enemies). And so we now shift from a purely anthropological focus to an anthropology informed by resources in the Christian tradition—in Fineman's words, "existential assets"—that offer access to the divine love that consoles and empowers human beings for resilience and resistance in the face of our vulnerable existence. Because of their proximity to vulnerability and because of their powerful experiences of divine love, maternal witnesses will once again light the way.

PART II

The Trinitarian Dynamics of Divine Love and Human Redemption: A Theological Anthropology of Resilience and Resistance

Theological Interlude
and Introduction to Part Two

On the final page of *The Liars' Club*, Mary Karr recalls a moment
of puzzlement on the car ride home from the diner at which her
mother revealed the painful secrets of her past, the deep wounds that
festered and had such a toxic effect on Charlie and, in turn, on her
daughters. Passing by a landscape dominated by East Texas refineries,
Karr observes the flickering of fireflies in a field of wild flowers and
wonders how it is that such tiny creatures could survive the noxious
environment of the oil fields:

> Here and there in the flowers you could make out small gatherings of
> fireflies. How odd, I thought, that those bugs lived through the refinery
> poisons. Beyond Mother's tired profile the fireflies blinked in batches
> under spreading mist like little birthday cakes lighting up and getting
> blown out.[1]

The second and third parts of this theological anthropology contain
exploratory analyses of how human beings, like Karr's fireflies, are
able to survive and even thrive in the midst of a vulnerable existence
marked by suffering, anxiety, and violation. Part 2 mines the

---

1. Mary Karr, *The Liars' Club: A Memoir* (New York: Viking, 1995), 320.

Christian tradition for theological resources that empower both resilience and resistance. My thesis is that the Trinitarian depths of divinity respond to the needs and violations of vulnerable humanity with invulnerable love, incarnation, and empowerment for creative transformation. Divine love can thus empower human beings to live with courage, peace, and compassion even in the midst of the "refinery poisons" that threaten vulnerable human existence.

Thus far we have seen that vulnerability and the suffering it threatens and/or inflicts can destroy a person's ability to find life meaningful and maintain a moral center to existence. Existential anxiety is a common human response to vulnerability, and living passively or violently out of this anxiety is a cause of great harm to self and others. However, what will emerge in the following pages is a hopeful witness (though not a guarantee) that it is possible to inhabit vulnerability differently. As Karr observes, "Sure the world breeds monsters, but kindness grows just as wild, elsewise every raped baby would grow up to rape."[2] In other words, it is possible to respond to vulnerability, pain, and suffering not with passivity or violence, but with courage, peace, and compassion. But how? How is it possible for human beings to live as vulnerable creatures without succumbing to the anger and paralysis that anxiety over vulnerability can so easily induce? How is it possible to break the vicious cycle that moves us from vulnerability to anxiety to violation of ourselves and other vulnerable beings? How is it possible to stabilize our fragile *telos*, to prevent its monstrous distortion? How can we live with courage, peace, and compassion when such virtues can lead not to less vulnerability but more?[3]

---

2. Ibid., 261.

3. Nussbaum observes that, for Aristotle, the virtuous person is more vulnerable. See Martha Nussbaum, *The Fragility of Goodness: Luck and Ethics in Greek Tragedy and Philosophy* (Cambridge: Cambridge University Press, 1986), 336.

There is no escaping vulnerability. Indeed, the relentless and blind pursuit of invulnerability destroys human bodies and spirits. What human beings need in order to inhabit vulnerability constructively and nonviolently are spiritual resources that capacitate us for dealing with anxiety differently—in other words, existential assets for facing vulnerability with courage, peace, and compassion, rather than aggression, passivity, and insularity.[4] We need assets that empower wounded human beings for resilience—the ability to recover from harm when it occurs.[5] When disaster strikes, or the threat of harm is overwhelming, these assets can keep human beings going; they stave off total despair and make life worth living. Such resources can

4. Chapter 4 drew on Peadar Kirby and Martha Fineman to lay out five sets of "assets" that enable human communities to cope with social, economic, material, and ecological risks to their well-being. According to Fineman, existential assets are systems of belief that "can help us to understand our place within the world and allow us to see meaning and beauty in our existence." See Martha Fineman, "The Vulnerable Subject and the Responsive State," *Emory Law Journal* 60 (2001): 35. Other scholars in the interdisciplinary field of vulnerability studies alternatively refer to such assets as socially produced "capacities" and "adaptive measures" that allow for resilience. See the work of Amartya Sen on capacities, cited by Peadar Kirby, "Theorising Globalisation's Social Impact: Proposing the Concept of Vulnerability," *Review of International Political Economy* 13, no. 4 (October 2006): 646.

5. Kirby notes that, according to the UN Economic Commission for Latin America and the Caribbean, resilience is "a critical factor in enabling units such as individuals, households, communities and nations to withstand internal and external shocks." Cited in Kirby, "Theorising Globalisation's Social Impact," 646. To further the secular parallels, it is illuminating to examine the definitions of resilience in a variety of disciplines. Geographer Gabi Hufschmidt lays out several understandings of resilience in her article, "A comparative analysis of several vulnerability concepts," *Nat Hazards* 58 (2011): 621–43 [quotations below are from page 626]. Hufschmidt argues that resilience depends in great deal on "adaptive capacities" that allow for anticipation and reduction of further harm. Originally a psychological term referring to an individual's ability to "bounce back" from stressors, it is described in mechanical engineering as "the ability to deflect under pressure without breaking," and is understood in ecology as "a measure of the persistence of systems and of their ability to absorb change and disturbance and still maintain the same relationships between populations or state variables. . . . This understanding implies that resilience can be assessed by the magnitude of disturbance a system can absorb until its fundamental structure is altered." It is interesting to note here that in both ecological and social systems resilience is directly linked to diversity: "examples illustrate that resilience is fostered if the level of biodiversity is high. High biodiversity is an insurance mechanism. Similar to ecological systems, manifold (seemingly redundant) adaptive options within social systems are related to a high level of resilience." It would be fascinating to explore religious diversity as an asset for resilience in the face of vulnerability rather than a liability that leads to greater violence.

provide not only wellsprings of resilience, but also motivation and empowerment for resistance to the unjust violation of vulnerability in systems of privilege, injustice, and oppression.

The Christian tradition offers a system of existential assets (narratives, beliefs, practices, spiritualities, etc.) that help people to find meaning and beauty in life, despite suffering and the toxic environment created by violent responses to suffering and vulnerability. Unfortunately, this tradition has often favored doctrines and disciplines that a) relativize vulnerability in this lifetime by focusing on invulnerability in the next,[6] and/or b) privilege the insecurities and perceived vulnerabilities of dominant groups over the vulnerability and suffering of all "others." In other words, the existential assets available in Christianity are often biased in favor of responding to the vulnerability of the privileged at the cost of increased social and spiritual vulnerability for the marginalized. For example, in the past, white European male anxiety may have been assuaged by not only the social benefits but also the existential assurances offered by theological arguments for their divine right to ownership of women and slaves as property. Exclusive male language for God, interventionist doctrines of divine omnipotence, the identification of women with sinfulness, the division of humanity into the saved and the damned, the glorification of self-sacrifice, theological anthropologies of gender complementarity, world-denying eschatologies—such distortions of the tradition's wisdom function to shore up not only social and material privilege, but also *existential* privilege, understood as the inequitable distribution of existential assets for coping with vulnerability. A tradition rich

---

6. See, e.g., Grace Jantzen's critique of Christianity's necrophilic imaginary in *Becoming Divine: A Feminist Philosophy of Religion* (Bloomington: Indiana University Press, 1999). See also Carter Heyward's critique of Augustinian and Irenaean eschatologies in *The Redemption of God: A Theology of Mutual Relation* (Lanham, MD: University Press of America, 1982).

in wisdom for living courageously, peacefully, and compassionately with vulnerability is thus drawn into the vicious cycle of vulnerability, anxiety, and violation that we have just witnessed. Like other forms of privilege, the existential privileges afforded by patriarchal Christianity exact a cost in both suffering and moral integrity for both the privileged and the marginalized.[7] Feminist, womanist, and liberationist theologians, therefore, have condemned these and other aspects of the Christian tradition as idolatrous instruments of oppression.

But there is another way. The following three chapters form the theological heart of this anthropology. Here I construct a theology of human redemption in which divine love responds to vulnerability with existential resources for courageous, peaceful, and compassionate resilience and resistance. The alternative understanding of the human situation set forth in part 1 calls for an alternative understanding of what we need and how God responds. The *root* human problem is not sin; sin is not the *root* cause of vulnerability and suffering, but vice-versa. Christians place their hope and trust in a God who saves human beings from that which ails us. If vulnerability is the root cause of violations of human dignity (in self and others), then a Christian understanding of God as redeemer ought to correspond to the human problem with an appropriate response. Human vulnerability and its anxiety-filled devolution into violation cry out for redemption. In what follows, I mine the Christian tradition for significant threads in the tapestry of divine love's redemptive response to human vulnerability and suffering. In Trinitarian fashion,[8] I lay out three dimensions of divine love

---

7. A full-blown critique of privilege in Christian tradition far exceeds the scope of this project. I suggest this critique here as a counterpoint to what follows: a constructive theology that responds to vulnerability in healthy, life-giving, nonviolent, privilege-deconstructing ways.

8. The Trinitarian influence on my theological anthropology here is admittedly limited in scope, and has emerged not from a full-blown Trinitarian theology, but from noticing the ways

and human redemption—invulnerability, incarnation, and creative lament—each of which grants human beings the courage, peace, and compassion necessary for flourishing even in the midst of our vulnerable existence. Meditations on the maternal narrative of Mary of Nazareth will introduce and illustrate each dimension of divine love at work in her experience of the nativity of her divine, yet vulnerable, human son. I draw on a variety of sources—early Christian theologians, medieval contemplatives, contemporary feminist theologians, and maternal narratives of suffering and grace—to fill out the content of each dimension of divine love's redemptive response to human vulnerability. What emerges is a theological anthropology in which human flourishing is experienced not in flight from vulnerability, but in empowerment for resilience and resistance.

in which redemption is variously experienced in human life as a triune offering of resources for personal and political empowerment in the face of vulnerability, suffering, and violence. My work thus hints at a Trinitarian theology "from below," but a project of that scope will have to wait for a future volume. Relatively recent works that offer theological anthropologies rooted in Trinitarian theology proper include: Leonardo Boff, *Trinity and Society* (Maryknoll, NY: Orbis, 1988) and *Holy Trinity, Perfect Community* (Maryknoll, NY: Orbis, 2000); Stanley Grenz, *The Social God and the Relational Self: A Trinitarian Theology of the Imago Dei* (Louisville: Westminster John Knox, 2001); Catherine LaCugna, *God for Us: The Trinity and Christian Life* (New York: HarperCollins, 1991); Thomas Norris, *The Trinity: Life of God, Hope for Humanity* (New York: New City Press, 2009);Kathryn Tanner, *Jesus, Humanity and the Trinity: A Brief Systematic Theology* (Minneapolis: Fortress Press, 2001); and John D. Zizioulas, *Being as Communion: Studies in Personhood and the Church* (Crestwood, NY: St. Vladimir's Seminary Press, 1997).

5

Do Not Be Afraid

The Invulnerability of the Imago Dei

Anyone who has thus waded through love's depths,
Now with deep hunger, now with satiety,
Neither withering nor blossoming can harm,
And no season can help:
In the deepest waters, on the highest gradients,
Love's being remains unalterable.[1]
~Hadewijch of Brabant

Can a mother forget the baby at her breast
and have no compassion on the child she has borne?
Though she may forget, I will not forget you!
~Isaiah 49:15

The Annunciation is a story of maternal vulnerability met with steadfast divine love that inspires courage in a fearful and humiliated mother-to-be. I imagine Mary of Nazareth as a young woman living

---

1. Hadewijch, *The Complete Works*, trans. Mother Columba Hart (Mahwah, NJ: Paulist, 1980), 165.

in a time of great political and economic vulnerability for her people, along with great social and physical vulnerability for her sex. She had not been socialized to think of herself as anyone special. In all likelihood, she embodied a way of being in the world that is similar to the young peasant women I have met in the countryside of El Salvador—humble and shy, self-conscious and fearful of asserting themselves in bodily presence, conversation, or action. I wonder if, despite scriptural evidence to the contrary, this unmarried woman already suspected that she was pregnant at the time of Gabriel's appearance.[2] I picture her engaged in some domestic task—sweeping dusty floors, kneading bread, or pulling water from a well—all the while ruminating with fear over the shameful and potentially deadly consequences of her situation. Through the thick fog of her anxiety, Mary receives an angelic message from beyond: "'Greetings, you who are highly favored! The Lord is with you'" (Luke 1:28). Far from assuring her that all would be well, she was distressed by this greeting, this strange interruption of her worry and self-doubt: "Mary was greatly troubled at his words and wondered what kind of greeting this might be" (Luke 1:29). She must have been thinking, "Who am I that an angel of God would come to me? What, me, highly favored?

2. In no way do I mean to suggest, let alone argue, that this version of events might be historically accurate. It is simply an imaginary device, designed to invite the reader into the anxiety Mary must have been feeling at the prospect of an unplanned, "illegitimate" pregnancy in a social context where such a scandal would have been terrifying. For a historical argument that would support the story as I have imagined it here, see Marianne Sawicki's in-depth analysis of the Galilean social and cultural context at the time of Mary's pregnancy, *Crossing Galilee: Architectures of Contact in the Occupied Land of Jesus* (New York: Continuum, 2000). Sawicki agrees with Jane Schaberg that Jesus was conceived as result of Mary's rape during the Roman siege of Sepphoris in 4 BCE. See Schaberg, *The Illegitimacy of Jesus: A Feminist Theological Interpretation of the Infancy Narratives, Expanded 20th Anniversary Edition* (Sheffield, UK: Sheffield Phoenix, 2006). Sawicki argues that this interpretation of events would not overturn "Christian belief in Mary's free assent to a divine invitation (Luke 1:26-38)." Rather, the disastrous social consequences of such a conception would redirect Christian belief "to a much more courageous decision on her part. . . . The assent that the Almighty asked of Mary was her decision to go on living, to survive rather than take her own life after realizing that she had lost eligibility to become a mother in a legitimate Israelite lineage" (*Crossing Galilee*, 192).

No, not me. Who am I that God would be with me? Is this visit motivated by judgment? Am I to be punished?" Gabriel sees that she is frightened, and quells her doubts with a second assurance of divine favor: "But the angel said to her, 'Do not be afraid, Mary; you have found favor with God'" (Luke 1:30-33). What!? Favor with God? How can this be? And then her fears are confirmed: she will bear a son. But not just any son! A savior. Of course, this does not change the danger that Mary will face once her pregnancy is revealed to her betrothed, or once it becomes obvious to others.

Although Luke tells us that she trusts in God and gives her free consent, Mary must have been terrified by this strange and perilous announcement of divine favor. As Denise Levertov observes in her poem, "Annunciation," "we are told of meek obedience" but "no one mentions [the] courage" that such a momentous decision required on Mary's part.[3] Elizabeth Johnson points out that, prior to Joseph's dream and acceptance of her condition (Matt. 1:18-25), Mary is in grave danger: "[N]othing but public disgrace, endless shame, perhaps a life of begging, perhaps even death loomed before her."[4] In Johnson's view, "The terror of her situation should be allowed once again to fertilize the Christian imagination, which has tended to 'wrap Mary in an aura of romantic joy' at finding herself pregnant."[5] Mary's fear could not have evaporated in the instant Gabriel declared divine favor and she verbally accepted God's will. Her rapid flight to "the hill country of Judea" (Luke 1:39) seems to indicate otherwise. Perhaps her journey was filled with mixed emotions—excitement at the prospect of welcoming new life into the world; wonder at the strange knowledge of her unborn son's unique identity; fear of

3. Denise Levertov, "Annunciation," in *Door in the Hive* (New York: New Directions Books, 1989), 86–88.
4. Elizabeth Johnson, *Truly Our Sister: A Theology of Mary in the Communion of Saints* (New York: Continuum, 2004), 230.
5. Ibid.

childbirth; and certainly terror at what this all might mean for her reputation, her relationship with Joseph, and even her own physical safety. I imagine that this journey was a meditative one, filled with doubts and fears, but filled also with a deeper and deeper sense of courage and acceptance. Gabriel's reassurance must have come to Mary over and over again: "Do not be afraid, Mary," but it is in the familial embrace of solidarity with Elizabeth that Mary overcomes her fear, as

> [t]oward each other they swayingly stepped
> and caressed the dress and the hair.
> Each woman was filled with sacred life
> and safe and at ease with the relative.[6]

Over time, and then in sisterly solidarity with her cousin Elizabeth, this insignificant Jewish girl comes to a deep knowledge of divine protection and favor, so deep that she speaks with the voice of a prophet and is able to courageously declare:

> My soul glorifies the Lord
> and my spirit rejoices in God my Savior,
> for he has been mindful
> of the humble state of his servant.
> From now on all generations will call me blessed,
> for the Mighty One has done great things for me—
> holy is his name. (Luke 1:46-49)

Mary's song of praise defies the vulnerability of her situation. Despite the precariousness of her pregnancy, she experiences the God of her ancestors to be trustworthy—a steadfast, loyal, and redemptive presence who looks with favor on even (or especially?) the lowliest and most vulnerable people of the earth. This God is Mighty and can do great things. This God is holy, the One from whom "no word

---

6. Rainer Maria Rilke, "Visitation," in *Pictures of God: Rilke's Religious Poetry* (Livonia, MI: First Page, 2005), 38–40.

. . . will ever fail" (Luke 1:37). The God Mary encounters and relies on in her doubt and fear is a God who meets human vulnerability and anxiety with the strength and protection of invulnerable love. Without knowing what lies ahead, without even knowing that Joseph would spare her life, Mary knows herself to be full of grace, lifted by divine love, and capable of mediating God's prophetic and redemptive action in the world. From the love of the Mighty One, Mary draws the strength to inhabit her vulnerability with the indomitable courage of a luminous image of God, a bearer of God's steadfast love for human beings and all of creation. Her witness points to a theological anthropology dependent on the invulnerability of divine love as a source of strength and courage, as a power that preserves the inviolable dignity of the divine image in vulnerable, violated, and suffering humanity.

Feminist Dis-Ease with Divine Invulnerability

Divine invulnerability has been professed and theologized throughout the Christian tradition in terms of the metaphysical attributes of immutability and impassibility. Divine omnipotence also indicates a supreme degree of invulnerability. Even in relation to an intractably vulnerable creation, the divine essence does not change, suffer, or lack the power to accomplish the divine will. Feminist theologians, along with others who are horrified by the accumulation of barbarous suffering throughout history, have rightly questioned the invulnerability of God.[7] An immutable God lacks reciprocity with the creation to which God has granted freedom. An impassible God removed from the suffering of creation is a monstrosity. An

---

7. William Placher offers a helpful overview of both classical notions of divine invulnerability and twentieth-century theologies in which God is vulnerable to suffering in *Narratives of a Vulnerable God: Christ, Theology, and Scripture* (Louisville: Westminster John Knox, 1994), 3–7. Grace Jantzen gives an extensive critique of these divine attributes in *God's World, God's Body* (Philadelphia: Westminster, 1984).

omnipotent God who controls the universe, yet allows the suffering of the innocent belies the very goodness of God. As Irving Greenberg would ask, do any of these divine attributes make sense in the presence of burning children?[8]

Feminist theological discourse on God is not always explicitly couched in terms of vulnerability and invulnerability, but feminist theologians are especially wary of these divine attributes, which are all characterized by invulnerability. Elizabeth Johnson, for example, offers a feminist deconstruction of the classical doctrines of divine impassibility and omnipotence, replacing these doctrines with an emphasis on the vulnerability of divine love. In her view, the barbarous excess of suffering in human history calls these classical doctrines into question:

> The idea of God cannot simply remain unaffected by the basic datum of so much suffering and death. Nor can it tolerate the kind of divine complicity in evil that happens when divine power is conceived as the force that could stop all of this but simply chooses not to, for whatever reason. A God who is not some way affected by such pain is not really worthy of human love and praise [and] is morally intolerable.[9]

Johnson asks, how can a loving God remain unaffected by or invulnerably controlling of a history in which so much suffering and death has destroyed so many human beings, along with creation? With other liberation, feminist, political, and process theologians, she proposes that we begin to think about God primarily as a suffering God and divine power as characteristically manifested in and through solidarity with human suffering. The merits of Johnson's emphasis on divine vulnerability will become clear in chapter 6, which explores the vulnerable dimension of divine love vis-à-vis human

---

8. Irving Greenberg, "Cloud of Smoke, Pillar of Fire," in *Auschwitz: Beginning of a New Era? Reflections on the Holocaust*, ed. Eva Fleischner (New York: Ktav, 1977), 23.

9. Elizabeth Johnson, *She Who Is: The Mystery of God in Feminist Theological Discourse* (New York: Crossroad, 1992), 249.

vulnerability. Here, however, I pause to contrast her emphasis with my own and with that of the women who inform these reflections on divine invulnerability as the ground and source of human courage in the face of vulnerability, suffering, and violence. While Johnson's vulnerable God does not lack the power to offer redemption to human beings in their vulnerable condition, her emphasis on divine vulnerability does overlook the foundational strength and stability that a theological anthropology grounded in a feminist retrieval of divine invulnerability can offer.

In the final analysis, nothing makes much sense in the presence of burning children, but in these pages I seek to demonstrate that it is possible to reinterpret divine invulnerability without casting God as a distant monarch whose providence cares little for collateral damage. Divine invulnerability is not the invulnerability of an almighty tyrant who lacks compassion for His subjects, their pain, and suffering. It is not the invulnerability of an unchanging divine entity that remains unaffected by the unfolding of the cosmos and vicissitudes of the human heart. Rather, invulnerability is that dimension of divinity that offers vulnerable human beings stability of identity as *imago dei* and an unchanging love on which to draw for courage, resilience, and resistance, even in the face of horrors. From what we know of her story, Mary of Nazareth's primary experience of grace in the midst of her vulnerable situation was a deep grounding in the unfailing favor of a mighty God who does great things for those who are vulnerable. Without a strong theological sense of divine invulnerability (reinterpreted as the invulnerability of love), it is difficult to imagine a conceptual (let alone ontological) ground for that which is inviolable in the human person—that is, the image of God. This image is vulnerable insofar as it can be violated; it can be and is all too often diminished or marred in the most heinous and horrific ways, but ultimately it cannot be destroyed. Although we may not be able to experience the illuminating and emboldening power of our innermost divine nature, the Christian tradition holds that nothing—not anything we have done or anything that has been done to us—can keep God from loving us (Rom. 8:39). It is in this deep and broad, invulnerable love that the divine image within human beings is preserved and protected. In contrast with Johnson, Delores Williams emphasizes this invulnerable dimension of divine love that is present in the stories of biblical and African American mothers to whom God offers stability of identity and courage for survival in the midst of vulnerability, suffering, and violence.

Delores Williams: "Nobody in the wide world to look to but God"

Williams does not use the language of invulnerability (let alone impassibility, immutability, or omnipotence), nor does she employ the concept of *imago dei* in her groundbreaking work, *Sisters in the Wilderness*. Her theological task in that volume is not to construct a theological anthropology or theology of God. Rather, she engages in the first theological task of womanist theology: to create a mosaic of black women's experiences by retrieving "from the underside of the underside partial facts about [black women] and partial visions of missing parts of [their] experience." This mosaic is intended to provide a lens through which later to view and formulate the questions and content of womanist theological reflection on "God's relation to black American life and to the world in general."[10] My project here is a constructive one that stands to benefit from Williams's analysis of both the biblical story of Hagar and the narratives of African American women. Their stories (read through her analysis) reveal a God who is a stable, salvific, and empowering presence for violated human beings in the midst of the vulnerability

---

10. Delores Williams, *Sisters in the Wilderness: The Challenge of Womanist God-Talk* (Maryknoll, NY: Orbis, 1995), 12.

violently imposed by slavery and subsequent racial and sexual oppression.

According to Williams, Hagar's story is a mirror in which many African Americans, especially African American women and mothers, can and have seen their own stories. Both are closely associated with motherhood and the oppressed mother's reliance on divine grace for survival:

> Hagar's heritage was African as was black women's. Hagar was a slave. Black American women had emerged from a slave heritage and still lived in light of it. Hagar was brutalized by her slave owner, the Hebrew woman Sarah. The slave narratives of African American women and some of the narratives of contemporary day-workers tell of the brutal or cruel treatment black women have received from the wives of slave masters and from contemporary white female employers. Hagar had no control over her body. It belonged to her slave owner, whose husband, Abraham, ravished Hagar. A child Ishmael was born; mother and child were eventually cast out of Abraham and Sarah's home without resources for survival. The bodies of African-American slave women were owned by their masters. Time after time they were raped by their owners and bore children who the masters seldom claimed—children who were slaves—children and their mothers whom slave-master fathers often cast out by selling them to other slave holders. Hagar resisted the brutalities of slavery by running away. Black American women have a long resistance history that includes running away from slavery in the antebellum era. Like Hagar and her child Ishmael, African-American female slaves and their children, after slavery, were expelled from the homes of many slave holders and given no resources for survival. Hagar, like many women throughout African-American women's history, was a single parent. But she had serious personal and salvific encounters with God—encounters which aided Hagar in the survival struggle of herself and her son. Over and over again, black women in the churches have testified about their serious personal and salvific encounters with God, encounters that helped them and their families survive.[11]

---

11. Ibid., 3.

Williams attributes Hagar's resilience and the resilience of African American women to their God-consciousness and God-dependence. "Hagar, like many black women, goes into the wide world to make a living for herself and her child, with only God by her side."[12] Dependence on divine accompaniment functioned for Hagar and for African and African American slaves as a resource for survival. Williams cites church historian Gayraud S. Wilmore on this point:

> "The slave relied upon religion, not primarily because he felt himself to be converted; but because he recognized the power inherent in religious things." That power had to do, first of all, with the necessity of survival—with the creation of an alternative reality system that could keep the slave alive and possessed of some modicum of sanity. The protest and resistance elements we find in early forms of black folk religions in the Caribbean and in the southeastern United States express the determination to survive against all odds.[13]

In Williams's own words, "The slaves' efforts to create an alternative value system represents a struggle to achieve a positive quality of life. . . . [T]hey believed in God's presence with them. This belief, connecting with the survival/quality of life struggle, gave hope to the slaves' daily lives of toil and oppression."[14]

Tracing the theme of motherhood in African American literary history, Williams finds that black mothers in particular "used religion to support themselves emotionally, psychologically and spiritually when they were exploited first by the white world and later by some members of the black community."[15] Slave narratives reveal that the bodies and labor of slave women were ruthlessly abused, especially in the violation of their sexuality as "breeder women"

12. Ibid., 33.
13. Gayraud S. Wilmore, *Black Religion and Black Radicalism*, 2nd ed. (Maryknoll, NY: Orbis, 1984), 223, as cited in Williams, *Sisters in the Wilderness*, 7.
14. Williams, *Sisters in the Wilderness*, 7.
15. Ibid., 35.

forced to bear children for their owners' use or sale. Despite their exploitation, slave mothers were dedicated to the care and nurturing of their children, nursing their babies while working in the fields and mourning their loss when they were sold away. Their violated vulnerability required resources for resilience. The grueling slave labor, relentless mothering functions, and traumatic suffering of slave women required a great deal of strength for survival. According to Williams, "This strength was manifested not only by her ability to perform the difficult tasks associated with her mothering and nurturing roles. Strength was also manifested in her ability to endure and to gain victory over the suffering and pain often accompanying these tasks."[16] Spirituals and slave narratives both attribute the endurance and victory of slave mothers to their faith in and dependence on God:

> My mother died with a staff in her hand,
> She had so much trouble in this land,
> But she held on to God's hand.[17]

Williams is careful to point out that this personal strength did not equal the social power for black women in their families, the slave community, the slavocracy, or society at large. Lacking social power, and subjected to a system that brutalized their vulnerable bodies and spirits, however, many slave mothers exhibited spiritual power. These women embodied

> a vigorous spiritual self-confidence even though their sexuality had been completely brutalized and exploited by white men of every social class. Though they were continuously raped, used as breeder women and made accessible to the sexual appetite of all white males, many slave mothers endured with strength and dignity. They endured because, as

16. Ibid., 37.
17. Ibid.

one slave mother taught her daughter, they believed there was "nobody in the wide world to look to but God."[18]

For many slave women, then, divine strength is what gave them the strength to survive the brutality of their oppression. Vulnerable to the highest degree, the slave women relied on the existential asset of divine strength within them for survival, endurance, and even spiritual empowerment.

Williams notes that black protest writers (such as novelist Richard Wright) have critiqued both ante-bellum and post-bellum black mothers' God-consciousness and God-dependence as problematic for both their own vulnerability vis-à-vis black preachers and for the vulnerability of the black community to the forces of oppression. For Williams, this critique "raises serious theological questions about the Christian religion in relation to black mothers' and black people's experience of racial oppression in America."[19] Nevertheless, Williams finds compelling interpretations of black mothers' God-experience in the work of post-bellum African American women writers. Margaret Walker's *Jubilee*, for example, emphasizes the asset of survival intelligence that slave mothers gained from their religion.

> The concern of many African American mothers has been for the survival of their children, the family and the race. The economic, spiritual and physical assault upon black life in America by white people and white-controlled institutions has caused the African American mother to try to develop survival strategies her family can use. She has not always been successful, but she has depended upon her religion to help her develop these strategies and to muster the courage to survive when survival gave no promise. Often these survival strategies took the form of spiritual values.[20]

18. Ibid., 40.
19. Ibid., 49.
20. Ibid., 50.

In Alice Walker's *The Color Purple*, newly transformed spiritual values are what aided Celie in her growth toward self-discovery and self-love, both of which were essential to her survival *and* her empowerment in the midst of a racially and sexually oppressive situation. In Williams's words,

> when Shug helps Celie begin her process of self-discovery, Celie starts to understand that her notion of God must change, because "you have to git man off your eyeball before you can see anything a'tall." Thus Celie's God becomes an internal experience rather than a physical manifestation to be worshiped like the man Jesus. Her new understanding of God is similar to that expressed by one of the women in a play by black feminist playwriter Ntozake Shange—the woman who testified "I found god in myself and I love her/fiercely."[21]

This transformation of Celie's God-consciousness points toward the ways in which mothers' inner reliance on God for strength, survival, and resilience can actually challenge the traditional nurturing roles that make black mothers vulnerable. Walker thus portrays black women's religiosity in a positive light, as a source of empowerment when it transforms certain oppressive conceptions of God into foundations for their human dignity and self-worth.

Despite their differences, the African American writers Williams surveys "would perhaps agree on at least one point—that black women have been devout in their mothering and nurturing tasks. They have believed God supported them in their struggle. Perhaps these writers would also agree that, more often than not, the rank-and-file black woman believes as Celie believed: 'Long as I can spell G-O-D I got somebody along.'"[22] The God Williams uncovers in African American literary history—from slave narratives to womanist

---

21. Ibid., 55. Williams attributes the two citations in this passage to Alice Walker, *The Color Purple* (New York: Harcourt Brace Jovanovich, 1982), 168, and Ntozake Shange, *For Colored Girls Who Have Considered Suicide When the Rainbow Is Enuf* (New York: Macmillan, 1975), 63.
22. Williams, *Sisters in the Wilderness*, 56, citing Walker, *The Color Purple*, 18.

novels—is a steadfast presence and anchor for the identity, survival, resilience, and resistance of black mothers whose basic human vulnerability has been met with violation after violation throughout the history of this country. Black mothers have turned to the power of God for strength, endurance, and empowerment and, in doing so, the indomitable presence of the divine image shines forth in them with tragic brilliance.

The experience of God at work here is not invulnerable, though, for it is still subject to manipulation, distortion, and despair. The invulnerability of divine love and the grounding of the *imago* in that love is not a guaranteed experience in human life, for its accessibility can be obstructed by various factors due to the intractable reality of human vulnerability, especially in situations of injustice, violence, and oppression. However, I set down Williams's work with a renewed confidence in the invulnerable character of divine power vis-à-vis human vulnerability. While there may be human obstacles to experiencing the staying power of divine love, that love is always and everywhere there offering itself as a resource for inner resilience and resistance. Divine love meets vulnerability with inner stability of identity and the promise of someone to look to, someone to have along, something to hold onto, even in the most horrific of circumstances. Again, the experience of this love is by no means invulnerable. Hence the distress of Julian of Norwich's servant thrashing about in the dell. And surely there are many African American women not featured in Williams's work who have despaired of God's love—who could ever blame them for that? As Julian notes, divine love ascribes no moralistic blame when we despair and suffering blinds us to our true identity as God-bearers. In spite of this vulnerability of human self-understanding and courage, the graced experiences of African American mothers' God-consciousness and God-dependence gives testimony to the presence of a force so powerful and so invulnerable that it is capable of strengthening the divine image in us and offering resilience of spirit and resistance to oppression, even when human vulnerability has been violated in the most heinous ways.

Julian of Norwich: "I protect you most truly"

Although she is located in very different context from African American mothers, Julian of Norwich lived in a time of great turmoil, violence, disease, and suffering. In addition to experiencing the effects of war, the Black Death of 1348–49 (along with subsequent outbreaks) exposed Julian to "the physical horror of death on a large scale at a young age." According to Jane F. Maynard, who views Julian as a survivor of traumatic loss, it is possible to make this assumption based on two facts: "that Julian, who was born in 1342, would have been six or seven when the first plague epidemic arrived in England; and that according to the best estimates available Julian would have experienced the death of roughly half of the people she knew."[23] Furthermore, some scholars have asserted that there is a strong possibility that Julian was married and was a mother who suffered the loss of family members to the plague.[24] John Julian's historical research on the matter has led him to assert the strong possibility that Julian was a twice-widowed, wealthy laywoman who gave birth to three children.[25] Benedicta Ward similarly maintains that Julian was a bereaved mother who lost one or more children to the Black Death before becoming an anchoress.[26] It is certainly true

---

23. Jane F. Maynard, *Transfiguring Loss: Julian of Norwich as a Guide for Survivors of Traumatic Grief* (Cleveland: Pilgrim, 2006), 86. Maynard notes that the extent of this loss is comparable to the loss experienced by the victims of the 2005 tsunami in northern Indonesia.

24. Maynard agrees with this assessment of Julian's biography, but admits that there is no external evidence to support it, nor is there likely to be. Cf. *Transfiguring Loss*, 222–23, fn. 5.

25. Cf. Fr. John Julian, OJN, *The Complete Julian of Norwich* (Brewster, MA: Paraclete, 2001), 21–27.

THE POWER AND VULNERABILITY OF LOVE

that, "if Julian herself had been a mother, many of her comments on the motherhood of Christ and God make more poignant sense in that she would have experienced motherhood first hand."[27] Historical speculation aside, Julian's reflections on divine love fill out the theological content and implications of divine love as the invulnerable foundation and fulfillment of vulnerable human beings. Much of her imagery for God and Christ is deeply and compellingly maternal; here, however, I will focus less on the image of God and Christ as mother and more on Julian's anthropological understanding of the human person as held and protected by the invulnerable power of divine love.

In Julian's *Showings*, God responds to the vulnerability and suffering of human existence with the invulnerable power of divine love. For Julian, this love is manifested most fundamentally as the unfailing power to create, sustain, and protect the godly nature of all things. Just after the appearance of Christ's crown of thorns in Julian's first showing, she reflects on her Lord's familiar love by contemplating an image of this divine power to create and sustain the existence of all that is—even the smallest, most insignificant little thing:

> And in this he showed me something small, no bigger than a hazelnut, lying in the palm of my hand, as it seemed to me, and it was as round as a ball. I looked at it with the eye of my understanding and thought: What can this be? I was amazed that it could last, for I thought that because of its littleness it would suddenly have fallen into nothing. And I was answered in my understanding: It lasts and always will, because God loves it; and thus everything has being through the love of God.[28]

26. Cf. Benedicta Ward, "Julian the Solitary," in Kenneth Leech and Benedicta Ward, SLG, *Julian Reconsidered* (Oxford: Sisters of the Love of God Press, 1988), 17–25.

27. John Julian, *The Complete Julian*, 26.

28. Julian of Norwich, *Showings*, trans. Edmund Colledge and James Walsh (Mahwah, NJ: Paulist, 1978), 183.

Although the minuscule object of Julian's contemplation is vulnerable to the threat of nonbeing, its existence is originated and eternally sustained by divine love. Regardless of what happens to this small thing, regardless of God's inability to control the forces that would destroy it, or that apparently do destroy its material integrity, the protection of divine love ultimately will not ever allow it to fall out of existence. This invulnerable power of God to create and sustain existence is born of divine love and cannot be conceived apart from the power of love. One of the understandings at which Julian arrives by the end of her reflections on this first showing is that God "created everything for love, and by the same love it is preserved, and always will be without end."[29] Key to drawing out the anthropological implications of such a strong theology of divine invulnerability is the utter conviction that all that exists partakes of the unfailing goodness of divine love: "God is everything which is good . . . and the goodness which everything has is God."[30] The love and goodness of God is invulnerable—it cannot be diminished let alone destroyed. Because everything that exists partakes in divine goodness simply by the fact of existence, all of creation is somehow upheld and protected at its core by the invulnerable power of divine love—even if it appears to be destroyed. If this is true of an object as small as a hazelnut, then it is certainly true for human beings, made in the image and likeness of such powerful and invulnerable love.

In Julian's theology, the creation and preservation of the universe is interpreted as the work of the first person of the Trinity, which she calls the "work of nature." In the creation of humanity, God imputes divine goodness to the soul such that the very nature of human beings is united with the divine substance. There is nothing that human beings can do and there is nothing that can be done to human beings

29. Ibid., 190.
30. Ibid.

that can ultimately sever this union. Julian's reflections on the godly will of the soul provide further insight into the immense power and invulnerability of this divine protection. According to Julian, in every soul there is a godly will that "never assents to sin and never will" and that "is so good that it cannot ever will any evil, but always good."[31] Because of this godly will, "there may and will be nothing at all between God and man's soul. And in this endless love man's soul is kept whole."[32] We are held sacred to and undivided from God in this higher part of human nature because it is in this will that we are united to God, "knitted" into God's substance in our making with a "subtle and mighty" knot.[33] While human vulnerability and the horrors it can entail may destroy our bodies, minds, and psyches, God wants us to know, avers Julian, that no matter what happens, no matter what we suffer, no matter what we have done, this inherent dignity as *imago dei*—as reflections of divine light and love—cannot be taken away.

Such is the invulnerable power of God's love to protect us and keep us as the image of that love, even in the face of our vulnerabilities and even in the midst of our sin and suffering. This is not a protection that prevents bad things from happening to good people; indeed, Julian may be off base to insist that divine love keeps us "whole." Rather, it simply *keeps* us, holds us tenderly with a protection that preserves the core of our identity even when it has been shattered by what we have done or by what has been done to us. For Julian, God's love is so powerful, so invulnerable, that nothing can keep God from loving us. There is nothing we can do and nothing we can endure that can

31. Ibid., 241–42. Cf. also 283.
32. Ibid., 284.
33. Ibid. According to Julian, through the Incarnation our entire nature is enclosed in God and the noble dignity of that nature can never be destroyed, "for our nature, which is the higher part, is joined to God in its creation, and God is joined to our nature, which is the lower part in taking flesh" (291).

remove us from the enclosure of God's love. In Julian's words, "God wishes us to know that he keeps us safe all the time, in sorrow and in joy."[34] The invulnerable power of God, then, is to defend human dignity, to protect our innermost selves, our identity as *imago dei*, and to love us even when it seems that we are most wretched and unworthy of love. This is what Julian means when she states that "[o]ur good Lord protects us with the greatest of loving care when it seems to us that we are almost forsaken and abandoned because of our sins and because we see that we have deserved it."[35] Whether we are truly blameworthy or unjustly blamed (or engaged in self-blaming) for our failures, the invulnerability of divine love undergirds an ultimately inviolable dimension of the human person, the divine image that is itself invulnerable.

It would be helpful here to recall Julian's example of the lord and servant, which illustrates the need of human beings for illumination, comfort, and strength in their vulnerability and suffering. According to Julian, the servant's "greatest hurt" is his "lack of consolation," the fulfillment of which is unfailingly offered in the loving countenance of the ever-present lord.[36] This parable reveals to Julian and to her readers that the invulnerability of divine power at work here is not the self-enclosure of an unfeeling monarch. Nor is it the impervious authority of a distant judge who possesses the power to punish or forgive us for our failings. Julian insists that the lord looks on his servant in the dell, not angrily with blame or wrath, but rather lovingly with unfailing pity and compassion. She is most convinced by this example, and by the rest of her visions, that what is invulnerable and almighty in God is love, which cannot be perturbed

---

34. Ibid., 205.
35. Ibid., 244.
36. Ibid., 267.

even by wrath. God's judgment assigns us no blame and that God is never angry and never will be because

> he is God, he is good, he is truth, he is love, he is peace; and his power, his wisdom, his charity and his unity do not allow him to be angry. For I saw truly that it is against the property of his power to be angry, and against the property of his wisdom and against the property of his goodness. God is that goodness which cannot be angry, for God is nothing but goodness. Our soul is united to him who is unchangeable goodness. And between God and our soul there is neither wrath nor forgiveness in his sight. For our soul is so wholly united to God, through his own goodness, that between God and our soul nothing can interpose.[37]

Again, God's invulnerability in the face of human sin and suffering does not consist of the power to mete out suffering as punishment for sin. The servant does not fall into the dell and suffer there because the lord wanted to punish him for something he did wrong. Human vulnerability and suffering is not to be understood as humanity's collective "just deserts" for the fall or as an individual's punishment for past wrongs or failings. God's invulnerability to human vulnerability is not the invulnerability of a cold and distant *deus ex machina*, nor that of an objectively rational penal system. Rather, the lord continues to look on the servant—in both his suffering and his sin—with the unfailing pity and compassion that characterize his abiding love.

That God's love and protection enfolds and protects the divine image even in perpetrators of the worst crimes against humanity is not to treat violence and injustice glibly, as if to say that God does not mind the trampling of God's creation, or that it would be just fine if the wicked preferred to continue their destructive path, causing suffering and violating the human dignity of others. To the contrary, Julian argues that "we must hate sin because of

---

37. Ibid., 259.

love."[38] For Julian, sin means suffering for both the perpetrator and victim of wrongdoing. God looks on both the sinner and the sinned against with loving compassion and the desire to remove the causes of suffering. Therefore, Julian is confident that the more we see and understand the invulnerability of God's love for us, even in our imperfection and vulnerability, the more we too will desire to refrain from perpetuating our own suffering through sin. For Julian, this is the power of persuasion, whereby God inspires and infuses human beings with the power of divine love and teaches us to live into our identity as bearers of the divine image by doing as God does—by loving others even in their wrongdoing, and by doing good in return for evil:

> And God is as willing as he is powerful and wise to save men. And Christ himself is the foundation of all the laws of Christian men, and he taught us to do good in return for evil. Here we may see that he is himself this love, and does to us as he teaches us to do; for he wished us to be like him in undiminished love towards ourselves and our fellow Christians. No more than his love towards us is withdrawn because of our sin does he wish our love to be withdrawn from ourselves or from our fellow Christians; but we must unreservedly hate sin and endlessly love the soul as God loves it. Then we should hate sin just as God hates it, and love the soul as God loves it. For these words which God said are an endless strength: I protect you most truly.[39]

The power of divine invulnerability, then, is God's power to love us and to preserve the oneness of human beings with God as bearers of the *imago dei*, even in the worst of our pain, suffering, sorrow, and wrongdoing. This is just as true of the most reprehensible criminal as it is of the most violated victim of abuse. The divine protection at work here is so invulnerable that nothing can undo the knot that unites us to God and nothing can keep God from enclosing us in

38. Ibid., 247.
39. Ibid.

God's unreserved, unconditional love. By the power of this protective love, we are not coerced, but persuaded and empowered to live in God's love, to realize our sacred identity and calling as conduits of that love, and to love ourselves and others—even our enemies—in return. Such love both requires and provides courage for living with dignity and purpose as witnesses to the invulnerability of the *imago dei* in the face of our vulnerable condition.

Courage

Mary's experience of divine favor, Williams's analysis of Hagar's and African American mothers' God-dependency, and Julian's own experience and theology all suggest that that which is invulnerable in God—namely, divine love—grants vulnerable human beings the strength and courage for survival, resilience, and resistance in the midst of the most destructive forms of violence and suffering. These maternal witnesses offer to theological anthropology a vision of human wholeness in which the invulnerability of divine love upholds, defends, and protects the image of divine love as it exists within each and every vulnerable human being. Existential knowledge of this unfailing love and care is empowering not only for personal resilience but also for active resistance to systems of privilege and violence that impose unjust and horrific forms of vulnerability and suffering on the marginalized.

Mary Karr ends her memoir *Lit* with a compelling image of the courage that knowledge of our true identity as beloved by God can bring. Karr's own experience of divine love is what finally siphons all the old anger out of her "like poison from a snakebite."[40] It is a love that reminds her of her true identity and thus gives her the strength to face her vulnerability with love and courage:

---

40. Mary Karr, *Lit: A Memoir* (New York: HarperCollins, 2009), 384.

Every now and then we enter the presence of the numinous and deduce for an instant how we're formed, in what detail the force that infuses every petal might specifically run through us, wishing only to lure us into our full potential. Usually, the closest we get is when we love, or when someone beloved beams back, which can galvanize you like steel and make resilient what had heretofore only been soft flesh. (Dev [Karr's son], you gave me that.) It can start you singing as the lion pads over to you, its jaws hinging open, its hot breath on you. Even unto death.[41]

Tillich describes the experience of love and acceptance portrayed so poetically by Karr as "the courage to be." In his analysis, such courage is "the self-affirmation of being in spite of the fact of nonbeing." Courage in the face of human vulnerability depends on the transcendent power of being-itself for its manifestation: it "needs the power of being, a power transcending the nonbeing that is experienced in" the various types of anxiety induced by vulnerability.[42] This means that the power of being-itself, recast here in terms of the power of divine love, grants courage—as we have seen above in the witnesses of Mary, Williams, and Julian. It also means that every manifestation of courage in human life, every self-affirmation in the face of human vulnerability, even the weakest self-affirmation expressed in the experience of despair, is rooted in the power of being-itself and thus the power of love. According to Tillich, the courage to be is therefore the key to the question of being-itself: "In the act of the courage to be the power of being is effective in us, whether we recognize it or not. Every act of courage is a manifestation of the ground of being, however questionable the content of the act may be. The content may hide or distort true being, the courage in it reveals true being."[43] The invulnerable power of divine love to uphold the *imago dei* in human beings

41. Ibid., 385.
42. Paul Tillich, *The Courage to Be* (New Haven: Yale University Press, 1952), 155.
43. Ibid., 181.

cannot be proven by means of theological argumentation; rather, it is revealed and it is witnessed in the courage of women like Mary of Nazareth, Hagar, Celie, Julian, and Mary Karr. In their courage to be and to love, they reveal the invulnerable character of God's love for, and union with, human beings as God's own beloved image. This love and union may not be experienced by all or most human beings due to the intractable vulnerability of the human condition; in fact, there are forms of perceived human "courage" that may even distort divine love in their unhealthy or destructive responses to vulnerability. In other words, the human experience of divine love is vulnerable. However, the courageous witness of the vulnerable women in this chapter indicates that divine love itself is invulnerable. There is nothing that can destroy the loving countenance with which the lord looks on the servant in the dell. And there is nothing that can completely extinguish the light of divine love's image that burns within each of us. As Hadewijch so poetically professed,

> In the deepest waters, on the highest gradients,
> Love's being remains unalterable.[44]

44. Hadewijch, *The Complete Works*, 165.

6

And She Gave Birth

The Vulnerability of the Imago's Incarnation

Did the woman say,
When she held him for the first time in the dark of a stable,
After the pain and the bleeding and the crying,
"This is my body, this is my blood"?

Did the woman say,
When she held him for the last time in the dark rain on a hilltop
After the pain and the bleeding and the dying,
"This is my body, this is my blood"?

Well that she said it to him then,
For dry old men, brocaded robes belying barrenness,
Ordain that she not say it for him now.
~Frances Croake Frank[1]

---

1. This poem is unpublished, but is quoted in Susan Ross, "God's Embodiment and Women: Sacraments," in *Freeing Theology: The Essentials of Theology in Feminist Perspective*, ed. Catherine Mowry LaCugna (New York: HarperCollins, 1993), 185–86.

Behold the unalterable power of Love's being: now a single-celled zygote . . . now a free-floating blastocyst . . . now an embryo, fully implanted in the thick and marshy, nutrient-rich endometrial lining of a young peasant woman in ancient Palestine.[2] The fused cells of Love-incarnate "push long, amoeba-like fingers deep into the uterine lining while secreting digestive enzymes that facilitate its burial. In response, the tips of the spiral arteries break open and spurt like geysers. Thus, life begins in a pool of blood."[3] The incarnate life of divine love begins in a pool of blood—life-giving blood that nourishes the progression of Mary's pregnancy through neurogenesis, musculoskeletal somitogenesis, organogenesis, replete with "cellular migrations worthy of Odysseus."[4] The bloodiness of this second Genesis makes the life of Mary's child possible—a re-creation not from nothing, but from *everything*, from the universal stuff of life.[5] But the blood-borne origins of the Incarnation remind us that the invulnerable nature of divine love becomes not only possible, but also *vulnerable* in the crimson waters of Mary's womb. Nearly one in four pregnancies end in miscarriage. So much could have gone wrong . . . Mary did not have to do an anxiety-filled Google search on "miscarriage" to know this. Surely she witnessed or heard tell of the painful passage of bloody tissue by women of her family or community. Perhaps Elizabeth remained childless for so many years due to multiple miscarriages and her younger cousin Mary had been aware of the pain and the shame of that experience.

---

2. Portions of this chapter form the basis for an article in which I argue for retrieving the Nativity as a symbol of redemption in contemporary Christology. Cf. Elizabeth O'Donnell Gandolfo, "A Truly Human Incarnation: Recovering a Place for Nativity in Contemporary Christology," in *Theology Today* 70, no. 4 (2013): 382–93.
3. Sandra Steingraber, *Having Faith: An Ecologist's Journey to Motherhood* (Cambridge, MA: Perseus, 2001), 9–10.
4. Ibid., 14.
5. This calls to mind how Edward Schillebeeckx references Christ as "concentrated creation." See *Interim Report on the Books Jesus and Christ* (New York: Crossroad, 1981), 128.

Did Mary worry about the progression of her pregnancy? That we will never know. What we do know is that the pregnancy progressed, that child in Mary's womb passed through each vulnerable stage of fetal development, growing and changing and, over the course of nine months, becoming a viable baby boy—kicking and moving within her, making known his eagerness to stretch out into a new life potent with possibility.

When Mary neared the end of her pregnancy, she and Joseph were required to travel from Nazareth to Bethlehem in order to comply with the Roman emperor's census decree. This long journey was difficult, uncomfortable, even dangerous for her and the child she cradled within. Whether she walked or rode the fabled donkey, she was likely in danger of pre-term labor from the stress and physical exertion of travel. But these expectant parents made it to Bethlehem, and sought a suitable place for Mary to rest and eventually deliver her baby. Unable to find a guest room, it seems that they took up residence in a cave or a stall where animals were kept. And in this cold, unfamiliar, and uncomfortable setting, the time came for her to give birth. "For nine months Miriam of Nazareth had been knitting her child together in her womb, sheltering a mystery of unfolding genes, developing tissue, growing movement, aiming toward viability. Now came the moment to deliver."[6] Mary and her baby had made it through the pregnancy safely, but childbirth was a very risky endeavor in premodern times (as it continues to be in many places still today). Mary could have died, her baby could have died. Or both. The bloodiness of her labor could have ended differently. Love incarnate did not pass into the world through Mary's womb like a ray of light.[7] Rather, the hard-as-steel muscles

---

6. Elizabeth Johnson, *Truly Our Sister: A Theology of Mary in the Communion of Saints* (New York: Continuum, 2004), 276.

7. Johnson cites the source of this belief in the *Protoevangelium of James*, 17–19, found in *New Testament Apocrypha*, ed. E. Hennecke and Wilhelm Schneemelcher (Louisville: Westminster

of Mary's uterus pressed the baby's head down on her cervix until it slowly, painfully dilated and effaced and made way for the child to gradually inch his way through the birth canal with each grueling push, his bruised and misshapen head finally emerging through the stretching, tearing perineum into the hands of Mary's birthing attendant (if she had one!). What was this experience like for Mary, and for Jesus? When did she begin her labor and how long did it last? Did she push for twenty minutes or two hours? Did she tear? Were there complications? Was the baby breech or backwards, or tangled in the umbilical cord, or stuck on her pelvic bone? As Johnson observes, Luke gives us no details, but Mary's delivery

> recalls women's pain and strength involved in laboring, sweating, counting contractions, breathing deeply, crying out, dilating, pushing hard while riven to the very center of one's being with unimaginable bursts of pain, until slowly, slowly, the baby's head finally appears and with more pushing the little creature slips from the birth canal, to be followed by the discharge of the placenta, with much bleeding, and then deep fatigue . . .[8]

Johnson further describes Jesus' first moments of life: "After wiping mucus from the baby's mouth and nose, allowing it to gasp its first breath, and after tying and cutting the umbilical cord, the midwife

---

John Knox, 1991), 383–85. The belief endured for many centuries, appearing also in the Catechism of the Council of Trent: "Besides, what is admirable beyond the power of thoughts or words to express, He is born of His Mother without any diminution of her maternal virginity, just as He afterwards went forth from the sepulchre while it was closed and sealed, and entered the room in which His disciples were assembled, the doors being shut; or, not to depart from everyday examples, just as the rays of the sun penetrate without breaking or injuring in the least the solid substance of glass, so after a like but more exalted manner did Jesus Christ come forth from His mother's womb without injury to her maternal virginity." See Article III of the Council of Trent, *Catechism for Parish Priests*, http://www.fordham.edu/halsall/mod/romancat.html. While maintaining belief in the perpetual virginity of Mary, the current Catechism of the Roman Catholic Church does not include these direct assertions of a miraculous passage through the walls of Mary's womb. Rahner also has an essay on this—"Virginitas in Partu," *Theological Investigations* 4:134–62.

8. Johnson, *Truly Our Sister*, 277.

would bathe and swaddle the baby from head to toe. Then she would assist in the discharge of the mother's placenta."[9]

This is an especially vulnerable moment in the nativity of Love Incarnate. Delivered from the perilous labor of childbirth, neither mother nor child is out of harm's way. Placed in his mother's arms, Jesus looks up at Mary and hears her voice with cloudy recognition, then remembers that he was born hungry and roots around desperately searching for the colostrum he needs for survival. It would be easy to cast this moment in the romantic glow of new motherhood, but it is a terribly vulnerable time for both Mary and Jesus. Mary's body has just been riven by childbirth: Would she hemorrhage or become eclamptic? Would this needy, dependent child be left without the protection and nourishment offered by his mother? Would the damage done to her perineum leave her debilitated? Would her breasts offer the colostrum her child so desperately needed? Would Jesus latch on to his mother's breast successfully? Would his suckle succeed in drawing forth the liquid that would keep him alive? Even if everything went without a hitch, Jesus' infancy was not bathed in the easy glow of celestial halos and hallelujahs. His parents were far from home, lacking the social supports a close-knit community might have given the new mother and her child. Jesus was laid in a *manger* for goodness sakes—a *feeding* trough. Johnson observes that the manger, mentioned three times in the Lukan birth narrative, "could be a movable wooden container or a low curved depression on a rocky ledge. While it served the purpose of cradling a baby, as do cardboard boxes and other such artifacts creatively appropriated by poor people today, its previous use removes any romantic pretense about the ease of this birthing scene."[10] Like homeless persons on the city streets of the United

9. Ibid., 276.
10. Ibid., 275.

States, like squatters, displaced persons, and refugees around the globe, Jesus' mother improvised to provide for his care. And like babies in all times and places, Jesus was entirely dependent and vulnerable. In this cold stall in Bethlehem, divine love's unalterable being entered the world as the vulnerable human child, the body and blood of a young Galilean woman exhausted from labor and far from home.

Incarnation: A Coincidence of Opposites

How can this be? How can it be that the invulnerable can at once become vulnerable, that the vulnerable can bear the image of invulnerability, that the divine can become human, and that the human is capable of en-fleshing the divine? Vulnerability is a hallmark of human life and our attempts to live it well. We are plagued by suffering in our bodies and our minds from the moment we are born. Our bodies are subject to hunger, cold, sickness, old age, desire, and death. Our goodness depends a great deal on external factors and can be shattered to pieces by one hard blow. Because we see God as a reality that is above all of this, we look to God as a rock to stabilize us and keep us safe from harm—if not in body, then in spirit. In its primordial dimension, divine love is ultimately invulnerable to the pain and suffering that we experience as embodied and relational creatures. There is nothing that can alter or destroy the essential power of divine love. But Nussbaum points out in *The Fragility of Goodness* that there are limits to divine power understood in this way (even when reinterpreted as the invulnerability of love). She argues that, in contrast with Plato, Aristotle held that the unlimited perspective is not necessarily unlimited: "Lack of limit is itself a limit."[11] Far from infinite and

---

11. Martha Nussbaum, *The Fragility of Goodness: Luck and Ethics in Greek Tragedy and Philosophy* (Cambridge: Cambridge University Press, 1986), 342.

boundless, invulnerability cannot encompass all goodness because it lacks the fragility of human goodness. As we have seen, human values are inherently instable, changing, and open to harm. The good life is dependent on external goods and actually leads the virtuous person into situations of increased vulnerability. There is a certain attractiveness to the Platonic attempt to close off ultimate risk in favor of the purity and simplicity of stable value. However, human virtue is risky and whenever its ultimate risk is closed off, a loss of value occurs. Love is inherently unstable. With Aristotle, Nussbaum esteems a life of human goodness that goes out to the world in love and openness. The "safe" life of stable and eternal value is not really a human life, for it lacks the virtues only available in the realm of embodied and relational vulnerability.

Based on Nussbaum's Aristotelian critique, the invulnerability of divine love described above is actually incomplete due to its own invulnerability to harm. The unchanging, stable power of divine love that invulnerably maintains the ultimate dignity of human nature is, in this sense, a limited power. Because it is invulnerable and divine, it does not and, by definition, cannot really participate in the vulnerable power of *human* love and *human* goodness. Deity conceived as only invulnerable and only divine is curtailed in the infinite power and goodness and love that divinity possesses because it is limited to the realm of invulnerable divinity and thus precludes values and powers that are only available in the vulnerable realm of humanity. How can divine redemption—understood here as the empowerment of human flourishing—take place in the vulnerable domain of human love without the power of human love itself? And how can the vulnerability of human love possibly mirror, let alone embody, the invulnerability of divine love? The genius of Christianity is to answer this predicament with the doctrine of the Incarnation.

In the Incarnation, the invulnerability of divine love becomes vulnerable human flesh and the vulnerability of human flesh manifests the invulnerability of divine love. In the vulnerable body and blood of Jesus of Nazareth, Christians experience the fullness of divine love at work for the redemption of the cosmos. God from God, light from light, one in being with the invulnerable essence of divine love—Jesus answers the problem of human vulnerability with living proof of the possibility of bringing together the divine with the human, the infinite with the finite, the impassible with the passible, the immutable with the mutable, the invulnerable with the vulnerable. While it is the unalterable power of love that becomes human in the Incarnation, this "miracle" does not sidestep the reality of truly human vulnerability. The paradoxically perfect union of the invulnerable and vulnerable is not "guaranteed" in the Incarnation, for the human condition assumed therein is intractably and unavoidably vulnerable and contingent. What this realization does for theological anthropology is reinforce our awareness of and sensitivity to the hard and inevitable reality of human vulnerability. If even *God* is vulnerable when taking on human flesh, then it is truly impossible to avoid our own fundamental vulnerability as embodied and relational human beings. This points to a deep need on the part of humanity to come to terms with the fact that our own incarnation as image of God's invulnerable love is also vulnerable. Further reflection on this mysterious paradox of human existence and divine incarnation is in order.

In his contemplation of the divine face, Nicholas of Cusa immerses himself in this paradoxical mystery of love, which he calls "the coincidence of opposites." Addressing God as infinity itself, Nicholas professes that "there is nothing that is other than or different from, or opposite you. For infinity is incompatible with otherness; for since it is infinity, nothing exists outside it." Without being one particular thing, "[a]bsolute infinity includes and embraces all things."[12] Here we find a very different approach to infinity from Aristotle and Nussbaum. If divinity is truly infinity, then it must include the finite and its invulnerability must find a place for vulnerability. This means that vulnerable humanity is capable of receiving divine invulnerability, but not without remaining vulnerable. This seems to make no sense—how can it be possible? In contemplating this coincidence of opposites, Nicholas avers that it is necessary to enter the cloud of impossibility and recognize that the more this cloud seems obscure and impossible, the more truly its necessity shines forth: "Therefore, I thank you, my God, because you make clear to me that there is no other way of approaching you except that which to all humans, even to the most learned philosophers, seems wholly inaccessible and impossible. For you have shown me that you cannot be seen elsewhere than where impossibility confronts and obstructs me."[13] The intellect must become ignorant,[14] abandoning reason in its pursuit of divine truth, which lies in the seemingly impossible coincidence of opposites:

> I have discovered that the place where you are found unveiled is girded about with the coincidence of contradictories. This is the wall of paradise, and it is there in paradise that you reside. The wall's gate is guarded by the highest spirit of reason, and unless it is overpowered, the way in will not lie open. Thus, it is on the other side of the coincidence of contradictories that you will be able to be seen and nowhere on this side.[15]

Within the wall of paradise, where the impossible is possible, Nicholas encounters Jesus—equally divine and human, infinite and

12. Nicholas of Cusa, "On the Vision of God," in *Selected Spiritual Writings*, trans. H. Lawrence Bond (New York: Paulist, 1997), 258.
13. Ibid., 251
14. Cf. ibid., 258. Nicholas's doctrine of "learned ignorance" suggests that the incarnation is best contemplated by way of the *via negativa*.
15. Ibid.

finite, invulnerable and vulnerable: "O Jesus, End of the universe, in whom every creature rests as in the ultimacy of perfection, you are utterly unknown to all the wise of the world, for of you we affirm contradictories as most true, since you are equally creator and creature, equally attracting and attracted, equally finite and infinite."[16] This statement of praise highlights the truth of divine love's confounding capacity for both invulnerability and vulnerability, but it also points to the truth of the divinely bestowed human capacity for bearing the invulnerability of divine love without abandoning the reality of created vulnerability.

Centuries earlier Gregory of Nyssa makes a similar point in *The Great Catechism*. In his view, the loving mystery of divine omnipotence is most visibly and effectively made apparent in the descent of divinity to the "humiliation" of humanity. It is only by entering into the realm of human vulnerability, taking it on and becoming one with it, that divine power manifests itself most fully as love:

> That the omnipotent nature was capable of descending to man's lowly position is a clearer evidence of power than great and supernatural miracles. For it somehow accords with God's nature, and is consistent with it, to do great and sublime things by divine power. It does not startle us to hear it said that the whole creation, including the invisible world, exists by God's power, and is the realization of his will. But descent to man's lowly position is a supreme example of power—of a power which is not bounded by circumstances contrary to its nature.[17]

The grandeur of the heavens and all of the miracles in the world, which usually function to override our vulnerability, are not very impressive at all because they simply show the divine nature to be

---

16. Ibid., 276.
17. Gregory of Nyssa, para. 24 of his "Address on Religious Instruction," in *Christology of the Later Fathers*, ed. Edward Roche Hardy (Philadelphia: Westminster, 1954), 300.

what we think it to be by definition—divine. What is much more impressive is the power of God to become that which we think God is not—human, and thus vulnerable. In this same passage, Gregory uses the analogy of fire to demonstrate his point. When we see a flame burning in an upwards direction, it is lovely, but not very impressive because that is what is naturally in the power of a flame to do. Now imagine seeing a flame burning in the opposite direction, downwards. That would be a marvelous sight to see! That a nature is capable of taking on its opposite is powerful indeed! According to Gregory,

> So it is with the incarnation. God's transcendent power is not so much displayed in the vastness of the heavens, or the luster of the stars, or the orderly arrangement of the universe or his perpetual oversight of it, as in his condescension to our weak nature. We marvel at the way the sublime entered a state of lowliness and, while actually seen in it, did not leave the heights. We marvel at the way the Godhead was entwined in human nature and, while becoming man, did not cease to be God.[18]

In Gregory's view, it is this power (Nicholas of Cusa's coincidence of opposites) that effects our redemption from the devil. In less mythological terms, human beings are freed from the vicious hold that our vulnerabilities have on us by the power of divine compassion for and solidarity with our condition. While human beings may not be free to escape our vulnerability, the Incarnation does offer a divinely empowered anthropological alternative to allowing our vulnerabilities to define us and lock us into destructive patterns of thought and practice. That alternative is to renounce the egocentric and violent pursuit of unilateral power and invulnerability in favor of remaining in compassionate solidarity with the rest of vulnerable and suffering humanity. It is in this vulnerable solidarity that the

18. Ibid., 301.

unalterable nature of divinity is most perfectly incarnated as self-giving, vulnerable love.

For Nussbaum, the problem with divine invulnerability is not a theological or theoretical one concerning the true nature of divinity. Rather, her concern is an ethical critique of human attempts to close off vulnerability and deny their own fragility by aspiring to an invulnerable union with an invulnerable deity. Valuing a human life of goodness that opens the self up to others in vulnerable solidarity, Nussbaum sees the relentless pursuit of invulnerability as an ultimately inhuman pursuit. I couldn't agree more. But for Christians, the impossibility that Nussbaum encounters in invulnerability is answered, is made possible, beyond the wall of paradise in the coincidence of opposites that takes place in the Incarnation. This "answer" is not a logical solution or a theoretical argument. Nor is it an otherworldly flight to invulnerability alone. Rather, it is an *experience* of divine compassion that grants vulnerable and suffering human beings—vulnerable incarnations of the *imago dei*—the power to access the invulnerability of divine love even in the midst of their vulnerability and suffering. It is the *experience* of bearing an image of love that is both unstainable and inviolable, but at the same time vulnerable to the risks of relational human embodiment. This was the experience to which Hadewijch witnessed when she wrote: "But the new power he then gave me, which I did not possess previously, was the strength of his own Being, to be God with my sufferings according to his example and in union with him, as he was for me when he lived for me as man. That was the strength to endure, as long as the fruition of Love was denied me: really to endure the arrows Love shot at me."[19] For Hadewijch, along with many other Christians throughout the ages, the almighty power of Being-itself

19. Hadewijch, *The Complete Works*, trans. Mother Columba Hart (Mahwah, NJ: Paulist, 1980), 302.

is accessed through the Incarnation of invulnerable love in the flesh and blood of a vulnerable human being. In other words, the power of divine love is redemptive, not as a means of escape from human suffering and vulnerability, but rather in and through love's solidarity with the suffering and vulnerability of the human condition. When Christians encounter this divine vulnerability in the Incarnation of Jesus, it has the power to effect a redemptive interruption of our approach to vulnerability as something we must avoid at all costs (to ourselves and others). While sacralizing the unjust exacerbation or violation of human vulnerability is anathema to this vision, the Incarnation does point to the sacredness of our vulnerability—it is the condition for the possibility of God's becoming in the world both in the Incarnation of Jesus and in the everyday incarnations of divine love in the vulnerable flesh of all human beings.

Contemporary Feminist Theology: Only a Vulnerable God Can Help

In the previous chapter's discussion of divine invulnerability, we saw that feminist theologians are wary of invulnerability as an ideological tool at the service of patriarchal privilege. At the same time, wariness of human vulnerability is also present in feminist attempts to critique and reconstruct the place of women in personal and political life. The enshrinement of vulnerability as sacred is dangerous for women and other marginalized persons who have been pressed into ideological corners of submission and passivity for too long. Nevertheless, a common current in feminist theology has been the idea of a vulnerable and suffering God.[20] Elizabeth Johnson is one prominent feminist theological voice who finds the power of divine redemption at work in the suffering God's solidarity with vulnerable creation.[21]

---

20. Dietrich Bonhoeffer famously wrote from his Nazi prison cell that "only a suffering god can help." *Letters and Papers from Prison* (London: SCM, 1967), 361.

Johnson does not limit the suffering of God to the second person of the Trinity or the Incarnation. Rather, she sees vulnerability and suffering as somehow implicated in the very heart of who God is as the mystery of relation itself.

Johnson's *She Who Is* sets forth a constructive theological proposal for understanding God in terms of female imagery and women's experience. The paradigm shift that she offers, however, is far more radical than a simple change in pronoun would entail. Johnson's feminist theology of God is not just about changing names and images for God, but rather recasting our entire outlook on the divine to center on the mystery of relatedness at the heart of all reality. Just as feminist thinkers have moved away from defining the self as an autonomous agent over and against the other and toward defining the self in free relation to the other, Johnson argues that we should no longer think of God as a distant, solitary, and invulnerable monarch ruling over humanity. Rather, God is the mystery of free and mutual relation. In a word, God is love. And the relational mystery of divine love at the heart of all reality suffers along with human beings and creation. In Johnson's analysis, each dimension of the divine life is implicated in this radically relational definition of God, a definition that places divine suffering and thus divine vulnerability at the forefront.

Each person of the Trinity has relationality at the core of its being, and divine activity in the world and each person of the Trinity (not just the second person) is implicated in the vulnerability and suffering that relationality entails. Spirit-Sophia is the relational power that

---

21. Not all feminist theologians argue as Johnson does for divine vulnerability. Sarah Coakley, for example, argues against any concept of divine kenosis that empties God of the power to save. Her argument in favor of vulnerability (carefully conceived) is on the human side of things, recognizing a kenosis of worldly power in the human Jesus and advocating a similar renunciation of worldly power and acceptance of vulnerability in the spiritual life of Christians. See *Powers and Submissions: Spirituality, Philosophy and Gender* (Malden, MA: Blackwell, 2002).

vivifies, connects, and renews all of creation. But her noncoercive way with the world leaves her vulnerable because her power is mediated through human praxis and thus depends on our free response. Bound to compassion for the world, Spirit-Sophia suffers whenever her power is rejected by human beings. Jesus-Sophia explicitly reveals God's character as life-giving and empowering relationality in and through his mission of enacting a new form of human relationship in which compassion and inclusivity hold together a discipleship of equals. His death represents the ultimate parable of divine compassion made manifest in solidarity with all the suffering and the lost. The cross in particular represents the vulnerability effected by the "kenosis of patriarchy": "The crucified Jesus embodies the exact opposite of the patriarchal ideal of the powerful man, and shows the steep price to be paid in the struggle for liberation. The cross thus stands as a poignant symbol of the 'kenosis of patriarchy.'"[22] Jesus' resurrection, however, places divine suffering within the larger paschal mystery of pain generating new life that mothers embody in their birthing labor. Finally, Mother-Sophia, the unoriginate origin of all that is, represents the absolute mystery of love to which we owe our very existence. Thinking about the first person of the Trinity in these relational terms is especially poignant with regard to divine suffering, given doctrinal resistance to talking about the suffering of the Father.[23] Johnson points out that using mother language to speak of our ultimate origin

---

22. Elizabeth Johnson, *She Who Is: The Mystery of God in Feminist Theological Discourse* (New York: Crossroad, 1992), 161. Johnson is borrowing the "kenosis of patriarchy" concept from Rosemary Radford Ruether, *Sexism and God-Talk: Toward a Feminist Theology* (Boston: Beacon, 1983), 137.

23. This point is one on which Johnson's *Quest for the Living God* was critiqued by the Committee on Doctrine of the U.S. Conference of Catholic Bishops. See Johnson, *Quest for the Living God: Mapping Frontiers in Theology of God* (New York: Continuum, 2007); and USCCB, "Statement on Quest for the Living God: Mapping Frontiers in Theology of God by Sister Elizabeth A. Johnson," March 24, 2011, http://www.usccb.org/about/doctrine/publications/upload/statement-quest-for-the-living-god-2011-03-24.pdf.

highlights an overlooked truth about divine power and vulnerability, for there is great "vulnerability in the ways a woman can be hurt by what damages her child."[24] In other words, the divine power of giving life and freedom to creation brings with it an intense form of vulnerability to that which harms creation. The heart of relationality, then, involves interdependence and mutuality, which means that even the source of all life suffers in solidarity with our lives of conflict and pain.

Johnson concludes her theology of God with a feminist deconstruction of the classical doctrines of divine impassibility and omnipotence. As mentioned in our earlier reflections on divine invulnerability, the barbarous excess of suffering in human history calls these doctrines into question. How can a loving God remain unaffected by or in control of a history in which so much suffering and death has destroyed so many human beings and creation as well? With liberation, feminist, and process theologians, Johnson proposes that we begin to think about God as a suffering God and divine power as characteristically manifested in and through solidarity with human suffering. With women who suffer when they give birth and struggle for justice (and like them), divinity advances the cause of creation in and through suffering. And along with women who suffer affliction and degradation, God sits in dark solidarity, unable to make meaning out of that which has no intelligibility.[25] If God is pure act, then She is the pure act of love. And, though a free act of the will, love, avers Johnson, entails vulnerability to the experience and suffering of the beloved. The relational mystery at the heart of all reality is a God who suffers. In line with my previous reflections on divine invulnerability, however, it is important to remember that Johnson's suffering God is not a powerless God. She is the power of

24. Johnson, *She Who Is*, 178.
25. Cf. ibid., 255.

love at work in women's struggles for justice, healing, freedom, and life. She is the power of comfort and solidarity in the darkest night. She is the power-with of connection and compassion. Though she suffers, it is only in the context of an invulnerable desire for human flourishing. And, ultimately, speaking of She Who Is as a suffering God is not a justification for or solution to the problem of suffering, but rather a never-ceasing call to human responsibility and praxis on behalf of freedom, hope, and love.

Johnson's theology of God is a compelling kenosis of divine invulnerability, but the invulnerability that she deconstructs is not the invulnerability described in the chapter preceding this one. What she rejects is the classically conceived invulnerability of an unfeeling monarch, and the modern isolationism of the autonomous individual. It is important to note, however, that in order not to valorize vulnerability and suffering, Johnson wants to say that God freely *chooses* to enter into relation, vulnerability, and suffering with creation.[26] However, there seems to be a contradiction in Johnson's logic here. In her view, divine love involves a free act of the will, but "as actually lived, and paradigmatically so in the light of women's experience, love includes an openness to the ones loved, a vulnerability to their experience, a solidarity with their well-being, so that one rejoices with their joys and grieves with their sorrows. This is not a dispensable aspect of love, but belongs to love's very essence."[27] While she insists that vulnerability is part of love's essence, Johnson still seems to present the divine choice of relatedness, love, vulnerability, and suffering in a libertarian paradigm, *as if* God could choose otherwise. This insistence on the voluntary nature of divine suffering is puzzling and problematic. If it is in the very essence of love's nature to suffer, then how can divine suffering be a "choice,"

26. Cf. e.g., ibid., 226.
27. Ibid., 266.

the opposite of which God could conceivably desire? Johnson's move here is an unnecessarily anthropomorphic solution to divine suffering vis-à-vis the problem of women's lack of choice when it comes to vulnerability and suffering. This emphasis on free choice is absolutely necessary when it comes to protesting unjustly imposed vulnerability in situations of sexism, poverty, violence, and oppression. However, two problems arise from emphasizing vulnerability as a free choice, whether divine or human. First, there is the aforementioned problem of viewing divine freedom within a libertarian paradigm. It would be more fruitful to move beyond this paradigm, while at the same time offering stronger theology of divine invulnerability: the invulnerability of divine love's free self-expression is most fully manifested in creation when it does precisely what it is in love's essence to do—enter into vulnerable relation with the beloved, even when to do so seems to contradict the invulnerability of the divine essence. Second, on the human side, emphasis on the voluntary nature of vulnerability in God (and in the human will of Jesus, for that matter) fails to deal with the inevitability of certain forms of vulnerability in human life. Human beings need wellsprings of empowerment for freely choosing to be vulnerable in solidarity with those who suffer unjust forms of vulnerability. But we also need models for how to face our past sufferings and *inevitable* vulnerabilities with courage, compassion, and peace. And we need empowerment to inhabit unjust forms of vulnerability not only with a practical commitment to social transformation, but also with a moral center of personal resilience, equanimity, and compassion in the face of suffering. One sadly overlooked place of a divine response to these human needs lies in the Nativity of divine love's incarnation in the flesh and blood of a vulnerable and suffering newborn child.

The Natal Body of Christ:
Finding a Place for Nativity in Theological Anthropology

Contemporary theological reflection on the person and saving work of Christ, along with its implications for theological anthropology, has concerned itself primarily with the adult man Jesus, his life-giving ministry, his consequent death on the cross, and the salvation that his life and death offer to sinful human beings and a broken world marked by grave injustices. Johnson's Jesus-Sophia is a case in point: the seriousness of human sinfulness and the horrors of violence and oppression are problems best met by an autonomous adult agent who empties patriarchy, freely choosing and paying the ultimate price for a dangerous prophetic mission of healing and liberation. Other than noting the oppressed social location of Jesus' birth, scant theological attention is paid to the fullness of divinity and its redemptive power taking on vulnerable human flesh in the newborn Christ-child. But the liberating good news of divine Incarnation does not begin with Jesus' public ministry as an adult, nor with Jesus' shameful torture and death on the cross. Rather, it begins with a socially high-risk pregnancy; with a humble, messy, and painful birth; and with a squalling, dependent, and vulnerable infant. In the words of a 1980s Christmas song that I remember singing in our children's choir: "He was wrinkled and red and he cried just the same as you and I."[28] Like our own human bodies, Christ's fully human body is first and foremost a natal body.

Grace Jantzen is one feminist scholar who attempts to refocus the Western/Christian imaginary on natality in place of what she calls a necrophilic obsession with death and other worlds. I do not think that we can attribute masculinist necrophilia to Johnson or

---

28. "Violet in the Snow," written by Don Mayhew and recorded on the album on *Hi God 2* by Cary Landry.

other feminist and liberation theologians who profess a God of *Life* who struggles against the structural forces of oppression that mete out early and unjust death to the world's poor and marginalized populations. However, Jantzen is on to something that feminists and liberationists have overlooked: namely, the natality of both the human and the divine. In her view, it is natality that actually forms the unacknowledged foundation of the necrophilic imaginary and its masculinist drive for mastery. She therefore hopes that natality can "function as a transformative suggestion, a therapeutic symbol to destabilize the masculinist necrophilic imaginary."[29] It is Jantzen's further hope that her construction of an imaginary of natality will open up new horizons for women's becoming, which has its end in "becoming divine." Jantzen relies heavily on Hannah Arendt here, who argues that natality, more than mortality, is central to human existence and should be considered a primary category of thought. Natality is the condition of human possibility, the foundation of freedom—because we are natals we are free to do new things. However, Jantzen warns that our own beginning as natals is always embodied, and "[t]hus the freedom of natality is not the putative freedom of a disembodied mind, a mind made as free as possible from bodily shackles, as Plato would have it, but rather a freedom that emerges from and takes place within bodily existence. The new things that we can begin are begun out of our bodily and material existence, not *ex nihilo*."[30] This affirms the embodied nature of humanity, along with the inevitability of limits. Human becoming takes place within an inescapably limited existence. Accepting this existence means that we must accept our limits, thus calling into question the valorization of infinity in the Western religious

---

29. Grace Jantzen, *Becoming Divine: A Feminist Philosophy of Religion* (Bloomington: Indiana University Press, 1999), 129.
30. Ibid., 145.

symbolic. "Finitude is not evil. Rather it is the effort to conquer finitude instead of treating it with respect which has been the cause of much evil, much suffering. . . . Rather than squander our energy in a futile struggle against finitude, we can rejoice in the (limited) life we have a natals and act for love of the world."[31] According to Jantzen, as natals, human beings possess the opportunity for a life of becoming, even becoming divine, in a world of finite, yet powerful possibilities.

Jantzen's reorientation of our imaginary toward natality and becoming is a very helpful critique of and alternative to necrophilia and the masculinist drive for mastery in Western and Christian thought and culture. I also take from her focus on natality an implicit, yet helpful suggestion for feminist theology to take in its consideration of the Incarnation. To consider Jesus first and foremost as a *natal*, to reflect on his birth (in addition to his ministry and death) offers a powerful vision of the possibilities embraced by divine love incarnate within the limitations of embodied human finitude. This focus on the natality of the divine in human beings also points to the possibilities open to human beings when they embrace and consciously incarnate their identity and destiny as bearers of divine love in the flesh. However, while Jantzen rightly employs natality as a touchstone for human becoming as embodied and finite creatures, she overlooks the tragic vulnerability implicated in embodied natality. The reality of giving birth and being born is risky business, threatened on all sides by death and other forms of nonbeing. Failure to take the vulnerability of natal life into account unfortunately contributes to the disembodied ethos characteristic of the Western imaginary and the Christian faith. This has had disastrous consequences for theological anthropology.

---

31. Ibid., 155.

Marcia Mount Shoop laments the disembodiment of Christian faith and practice (especially in mainline Protestant denominations). In her view, a "disembodied faith is prone to fear, anxiety, and stasis," all of which are key players in what I have described as the dynamic relationship between vulnerability and violation. As an antidote to disembodiment, Mount Shoop argues that Christians "desperately need to cling to the Incarnation."[32] Theological anthropology, in particular, requires paying close attention to the fleshy, relational, ambiguous, and vulnerable body of Christ as the vulnerable Incarnation of the invulnerable image of divine love. Retrieving an incarnational focus in theological anthropology (along with spirituality and ethics) can help us to inhabit our own fleshy, relational, ambiguous, and vulnerable bodies with less fear, anxiety, and stasis and with more courage, peace, and adventurous compassion. Recovering a place for Nativity in theological anthropology (and Christology) can remind us that divine redemption of human beings in Christ does not begin with redressing social injustice and oppression (though it *must certainly* include that). Rather, redemption—what Jantzen refers to as "becoming divine"—begins with the willingness, both human and divine, to accept our basic natal condition of embodied vulnerability in spite of its perils and because of its infinite promise.

Though I would by no means advocate leaving behind the cross as an image of divine power at work in vulnerability, divine power present in the form of a human baby is a compelling image of redemption within the vulnerable human condition. Nativity (and the theme of natality that it evokes) is a sadly overlooked icon of divine power and human empowerment. The image of the baby Jesus abounds during the Christmas season, but very little reflection

---

32. Marcia Mount Shoop, *Let the Bones Dance: Embodiment and the Body of Christ* (Louisville: Westminster John Knox, 2010), 4.

takes place surrounding the incredibly marvelous import of the idea that God Almighty (!) became a little, tiny, wrinkly, red, squalling, peeing, pooping, drooling, and desperately hungry human creature. The images of the Christ-child are usually robust and rosy-cheeked images of a cherubic older infant or toddler. They are unbearably cute. A newborn baby is beautiful, but at the same time really quite strange, ungainly, and fragile looking. And she makes her needy vulnerability vociferously known. As we saw Gregory of Nyssa and Nicholas of Cusa both indicate, divine power is most gloriously displayed in the coincidence of opposites. When we conceive of divinity as that which is ultimately invulnerable to the sufferings and vicissitudes of human life, what could be more marvelous or powerful than the incarnation of divinity in the figure of a dependent and defenseless newborn child?

Gregory of Nyssa's predecessor, Origen of Alexandria, argues for the greatness of divine power in this same manner, but with a specific significance attached to Christ's vulnerability as a newborn child. In his view, the kenosis of Christ in the vulnerable events of the Incarnation and the cross is what actually reveals the greatness of the godhead. The greatest and most marvelous truths about the divine nature are made evident in the most wondrous and amazing fact of God becoming a particular human being, Jesus. Moreover, that the wisdom of God, creator of heaven and earth, could become a human *baby*, the paramount example of human vulnerability, is confounding indeed. "When, therefore, we consider these great and marvelous truths about the nature of the Son of God, we are lost in the deepest amazement that such a being, towering high above all, should have 'emptied himself' of his majestic condition and become man and dwelt among men."[33] This kenosis of divine invulnerability in the

---

33. Origen of Alexandria, *On First Principles*, trans. G. W. Butterworth (New York: Harper & Row, 1966), 109.

humiliation of humanity begins with the gestation and birth of the baby Jesus:

> But of all the marvelous and splendid things about him there is one that utterly transcends the limits of human wonder and is beyond the capacity of our weak mortal intelligence to think of or understand, namely, how this mighty power of the divine majesty, the very word of the Father, and the very wisdom of God, in which were created "all things visible and invisible," can be believed to have existed within the compass of that man who appeared in Judea; yes, and how the wisdom of God can have *entered into a woman's womb and been born as a little child and uttered noises like those of crying children.*[34]

The power at work here transcends the limits that the Greeks placed on divinity and thus "the human understanding with its narrow limits is baffled, and struck with amazement at so mighty a wonder knows not which way to turn, what to hold to, or whither to betake itself."[35] The greatest display of divinity and the power of divinity to save takes place in the union of invulnerable divinity with its opposite—vulnerable humanity, here characterized as a little child born of a woman's womb who utters noises like those of crying children. This is how the persuasive power of Origen's God works—by gently taking us by our weak and suffering hands and sitting and crying with us in our vulnerable condition. The anthropological truth of the Incarnation seen from the perspective of the Nativity is that we are not alone, that even at our most vulnerable, we are capable of embodying the power of love and becoming divine. As such, this marvelous symbol of divine power-in-vulnerability points to the heart of the human vocation to embody our vulnerability accompanied and empowered by the indomitable power of love.

34. Ibid. Emphasis mine.
35. Ibid.

Jesus of Nazareth—whom Christians hold to be God incarnate—came into this world in the same bloody, messy, and vulnerable manner as the rest of us. He was conceived in one of Mary's fallopian tubes, gestated in her uterus, and was pushed out into the world through her vagina. Gregory argues that there is no shame in this humble and vulnerable manner of redemption that takes place in the incarnation of divinity in the Christ-child's true humanity. The "humiliation" of humanity is not shameful or evil—it is simply vulnerable. In Gregory's time, there were those who objected to the "shameful" manner in which Christians professed God incarnate to enter human existence: through a woman's uterus, cervix, and vagina (oh my!). Gregory dances around naming the anatomical parts involved in reproduction and childbirth, but he does not evade the fact that for human beings there is only one way of entering the world. It is by way of the generative organs that the human race is maintained and it is by the same organs that Almighty God takes on human flesh in the infant Jesus. Where else would Jesus have come from if not from the generative organs of his mother? "'From heaven,' is perhaps the reply of one who despises the method of human birth as something shameful and disgraceful. But in heaven there was no human nature, nor was the disease of evil prevalent in that transcendent life." To avoid the human manner of birth would have compromised redemption of wounded humanity: "He who united himself with man did so with the aim of helping him. How, then, will anyone seek in that sphere where there was no evil and man did not live his life the particular human nature which God assumed—or rather, not the human nature, but some imitation of it?"[36] The Christ child was no imitation of human nature. He was a bona fide human baby who entered the world from a contracting uterus, through

36. Gregory of Nyssa, "An Address on Religious Instruction," 304. Cf. also 306–7.

a stretching cervix, vagina, and perineum, in a vulnerable mess of mucus and blood.

Mary's vagina does not usually grace the stage of Nativity plays.[37] Nor do her breasts. A few years ago, the Vatican issued a statement calling for the rehabilitation of Marian iconography that depicts the Blessed Mother nursing the baby Jesus. According to the statement published in the Vatican newspaper, *L'Osservatore Romano*, such images date back to the early years of Christianity and were very popular during the Middle Ages, but largely disappeared by the end of the seventeenth century. This "vast iconography of traditional Christian art has been 'censored by the modern age' because images depicting Our Lady's naked breast for her child were deemed too 'unseemly,'" too carnal.[38] Paintings in which artists like Leonardo DaVinci (1452–1519), Guido Reni (1575–1642), and Artemisia Gentileschi (1593–1652) depict the Madonna and Child nursing are stunningly beautiful and a welcome antidote to the modern squeamishness about the act of breastfeeding. But even these portraits of the very human act of breastfeeding depict Jesus as an angelic cherub and thus fail to impress upon the viewer's imagination just how tiny, wrinkled, red, and helpless the newborn baby Jesus was. As Sara Ruddick laments, in the Christian story of Jesus' nativity, "the physical realities of birth [and infancy] are at best passed over. The infant, quickly 'wrapped in swaddling clothes,' is quite unlike the crying, shitting, burping, sometimes colicky babies that I have known."[39] If we are to follow Mount Shoop's advice and "cling to

---

37. Perhaps Mary needs her own "Vagina Monologue" in the play by Eve Ensler. See http://www.eveensler.org/plays/the-vagina-monologues/. Portions of what follows appeared in earlier form in my article, "Mary Kept These Things, Pondering Them in Her Heart: Breastfeeding as Contemplative Practice and Source for Theology," in *Spiritus* 13 (2013): 163–86.

38. Carol Glatz, "Marian images need artistic rehabilitation, says Vatican newspaper," *Catholic News Service*, June 19, 2008, http://www.catholicnews.com/data/stories/cns/0803257.htm.

39. Sara Ruddick, *Maternal Thinking: Towards a Politics of Peace* (New York: Ballantine, 1989), 212.

the Incarnation," it is imperative to think more deeply about the significance of divine love taking on flesh in the most vulnerable of human creatures—a baby who is at times passionately miserable about the digestive troubles, the explosive burps and gas and poops, the wet, the cold, the hunger, the teething, the trauma of being born into a life that entails vulnerability and suffering.

Mechthild of Magdeburg does not offer us a piece of iconography on which to gaze, but she does paint an imaginative picture of the Nativity in which the newly born baby Jesus is very much a human newborn baby who cries out in need of his mother's breast. In Mechthild's vision, when Mary laid her son in the manger, he

> immediately began to cry like a newborn child. . . . The virgin was sad, and the Child was hungry and cold. Then the mother had to nurse her Son. This was his Father's will and the Holy Spirit's pleasure. In maternal love, with maidenly bearing, the virgin bent down to her afflicted child and offered him her youthful breast. Now hear of the marvel! The bright blossoming of her fair eyes, the spiritual beauty of her maidenly countenance, the sweetness flowing from her pure heart, and the delightful sparkle of her noble soul: these four things drew together according to the will of the Father, the need of the Son, and the delight of the Holy Spirit in her maidenly breast. And sweet milk flowed forth from her pure heart without any pain. The Child suckled like a human child and his mother rejoiced in a holy manner. The angels sang to God a hymn of praise. The shepherds came and found for all to see our true pledge of redemption in a crib belonging to another.[40]

"Now hear of the marvel!": God cried, God was hungry and cold, God needed human milk for warmth, nourishment, and survival. God suckled at his mother's breast. Nursing mothers know that when a baby is first born, he desperately searches out his mother's breast for that first suckle of colostrum. Little else can placate him, least of all being laid down alone in a cold hard crib. Jesus was no different.

---

40. Mechthild of Magdeburg, *The Flowing Light of the Godhead*, trans. Frank Tobin (Mahwah, NJ: Paulist, 1998), 199.

Out of compassion for suffering humanity, the invulnerability of divine love becomes incarnate in a situation of paramount vulnerability—infancy.

These images of divine vulnerability in the Incarnation and Nativity point to profound anthropological lessons about who we are and how we should aspire to inhabit our vulnerability in a world of great suffering and loss. The exposure to risk that God takes on in the Nativity indicates that it is impossible to seek union with God through a spiritual or material flight to invulnerability alone. Clinging to privilege as a bulwark against vulnerability is paradigmatically anti-incarnational and blocks our union with the One whose love renounces all privilege in becoming human. Union with God is only possible in the renunciation of privilege and in the kenotic coincidence of human vulnerability and the invulnerability of divine love. The vulnerability of the Incarnation, so vividly evident in the Nativity, points to the fact that human beings are all inevitably vulnerable, just as the natal body of Christ was. It also drives home the realization that the human embodiment of divine love does not require the rejection of vulnerability in pursuit of untouchable invulnerability. Indeed such a pursuit is anathema to the theological and anthropological truths of the Nativity and Incarnation. If even God incarnate embraces relationality and embodiment, along with the dependency and vulnerability that they entail, then who are we to attempt to eschew these human realities with assertions of autonomy and unencumbered self-control? As we come to terms with this difficult realization, the Nativity of Christ can comfort and empower us with the confidence that we are not alone in our vulnerability, that divine love enters into compassionate solidarity with our condition. The divine vulnerability manifested in the Nativity of the Christ-child thus urges and empowers human beings to become divine while remaining genuinely human—that is, to inhabit the coincidence of opposites in our own lives by renouncing privilege and making peace with our vulnerable condition.

Peace

Christians hold that invulnerable divine love was united with vulnerable flesh in the body of a human being, born of a woman. The coincidence of opposites that takes place in the incarnation is not simply awe-inspiring proof of a divine power so great that it is able to encompass its opposite. Rather, the Incarnation of the Christ is the manifestation of the coincidence of opposites as the *deepest truth about reality* as a whole and about the place of human beings within reality. The Incarnation reconciles the invulnerability of Being with the vulnerability of human beings. The "Prince of Peace" (Isa. 9:6), who was laid in a cold manger and cried out for succor, is for Christians the one who grants the power to make peace with the vulnerable nature of our lives.

The point of the Incarnation, then, is not to see the awesome power of divinity and bow down to worship it. The point is to recognize and realize ourselves in it and it in ourselves. While Christians see Jesus of Nazareth as a uniquely perfect distillation of divine love incarnate, the Christian tradition equally holds that Christ's divine image is present in all human beings (Matthew 25). The invulnerable divine image resides within vulnerable human beings—embodied, relational, and finite creatures who possess an infinite desire for goodness, beauty, and truth. As Nicholas of Cusa averred, "In all faces the face of faces is seen veiled and in enigma."[41] The first person of the Trinity is the loving God who begets of Godself the second person, whom Nicholas calls the lovable God. All of creation is taken up in this second person, the mediator through

41. Nicholas of Cusa, "On the Vision of God," in *Selected Spiritual Writings*, trans. H. Lawrence Bond (Mahwah, NJ: Paulist, 1997), 244.

whom all things exist and bring pleasure to the loving God: "Nothing pleases a lover, as lover, but the lovable. You, therefore, lovable God are the Son of God, the loving Father. For in you is all the Father's pleasure. Thus, all creatable being is enfolded in you who are lovable God."[42] Human beings are united with the loving God in and through their union with the creatable, cradled presence of God in the vulnerable world. There is a sense in which divine love for creation makes the invulnerable God inherently vulnerable. When we suffer, God suffers. This inherent vulnerability of divinity is expressed most clearly in the Incarnation and Nativity of Jesus. The baby Jesus, whose life began in a pool of blood, who suckled at his mother's breast like any other human child, represents divine power-in-vulnerability incarnate. But the sacramental imagination of the Christian tradition holds that God becomes vulnerable flesh in all children everywhere. Born of my own mother's womb, I too embody the perils and promises of divine love in the flesh. The children that were born of my body and have nursed at my breast are also the image of this vulnerable God. And so too is every child born in this world. The possibility latent in every human birth, in all of human natality, is the possibility of becoming divine. The coincidence of opposites takes place in every nativity.

The problem, however, is that human beings seek to escape the coincidence of opposites through a flight to invulnerability alone. When vulnerability thwarts our desire and causes us suffering and harm, we often seek invulnerability through violence—to ourselves and/or to others. Life inevitably involves suffering, and our attempt to survive the brutality of it all too often destroys us or turns us into destroyers. The Incarnation empowers human beings to embody vulnerability differently: to follow the way of the Incarnation, to

---

42. Ibid., 272.

manifest the coincidence of opposites, to make *peace* with the tragic nature of existence. That invulnerable divine love became vulnerable grants human beings the courage and strength to endure amid suffering and to resist injustice and violence *peacefully*, without recourse to internal or external violence.

Whitehead offers a poignant depiction of Peace as that quality which empowers human beings to survive, and even thrive in the midst of tragedy. For Whitehead, Peace prevents us from following two destructive paths in response to a life marked by finitude and tragedy. Faced with vulnerability, human beings are often tempted to avoid and deny the reality of suffering by responding with either a) apathetic passivity (what Whitehead terms anesthesia) or b) ruthless egotism. The former option avoids conflict and suffering in the hopes that such painful realities will simply go away. The latter seeks to deny and diminish the painful effects of tragic existence on one's own life at the cost of causing greater pain and suffering for others. The mismanagement of human vulnerability in systems of privilege reflects both of these techniques for avoiding and denying the possibility and actuality of suffering and vulnerability. Neither response deals honestly with the fact that human life entails these painful realities. Both refuse to accept our vulnerability and live truthfully with the tragedy of the human condition. But refusing to be vulnerable to pain carries with it the price of closing oneself off to Beauty. Unable to cope with suffering, anesthesia and egotism both cut us off from what is really real, what is really, truly human.

Whitehead offers an alternative. He chooses the path of Peace, that "Harmony of Harmonies," which "crowns the 'life and motion' [the indwelling Eros] of the Soul."[43] Though it is "hard to define and difficult to speak of," he describes Peace as "a broadening of

---

43. Alfred North Whitehead, *Adventures of Ideas* (New York: Macmillan, 1933), 367.

feeling due to the emergence of some deep metaphysical insight, unverbalized and yet momentous in its coordination of values."[44] The metaphysical insight from which Peace emerges puts us in touch with both the Beauty and the Tragedy of real life as vulnerable creatures in a finite and perishing world. Peace entails an understanding and an acceptance of the tragic structure of existence, and thus frees us to appreciate the Beauty that continually and infinitely emerges from the process. Indeed, Whitehead posits that "[i]t is primarily a trust in the efficacy of Beauty."[45] While the creative advance of the Universe inevitably entails "Decay, Transition, Loss, [and] Displacement," Peace gives us a sense of stability, assurance, and purpose:

> As soon as high consciousness is reached, the enjoyment of existence is entwined with pain, frustration, loss, tragedy. Amid the passing of so much beauty, so much heroism, so much daring, Peace is then the intuition of permanence. It keeps vivid the sensitiveness to the tragedy; and it sees the tragedy as a living agent persuading the world to aim at fineness beyond the faded level of surrounding fact.[46]

Whitehead is calling us here to an acceptance of and trust in the service rendered by vulnerability to the ultimate process of Divine Eros persuading reality toward all possible perfections of Beauty and Harmony. The invulnerability of divine love protects our ultimate dignity as *imago dei*, but the progression of all finite, embodied, and relational things to perfect love requires making peace with the vulnerability of our *imago*'s particular, embodied incarnation. It is in this place of peace that we can access the persuasive power of the Divine Eros and participate in its creative and redemptive work for the transformation of the world.

44. Ibid.
45. Ibid.
46. Ibid., 369.

In Whitehead's vision, Peace manifests itself in human life and civilization as a power to survive and even thrive in the midst of tragic existence. It overcomes egotism through self-transcendence, through detachment from the acquisitiveness of undue preoccupation with one's own suffering, and through "self-control at its widest,—at the width where the 'self' has been lost, and interest has been transferred to coordinates wider than personality."[47] It overcomes anesthesia with a calm that widens the sphere of conscious awareness, offers "the subsidence of turbulence which inhibits," and "preserves the springs of energy, [while] at the same time master[ing] them for the avoidance of paralyzing distractions."[48] Peace purifies the emotions and bears fruit in love for humanity. Far from anesthetizing us to or shielding us from suffering, it sensitizes us to tragedy and allows us to feel and act with compassion in the face of the other's pain. Thus freed from preoccupation with our own suffering, we can participate in the persuasive power of Divine Eros to urge all reality toward Beauty and Harmony. The quality of equanimity described by Whitehead here is the very same peace offered in the Nativity of Peace incarnate. Making cosmic peace between invulnerability and vulnerability, divine love incarnate persuades human beings to live at peace with the most basic truth of our "brutiful" lives.[49] It is by the power of the Holy Spirit that we are transformed to live this peace with the luminous power of compassion for the vulnerability and suffering of others.

47. Ibid., 368.
48. Ibid., 367.
49. Glennon Melton, the blogger behind Momastery.com, coined this word to describe the deep truth of life's contradictory nature—vulnerable and terrible and brutal, yet somehow joyous and terrific and beautiful. See http://momastery.com/blog/about-glennon/.

7

Rachel's Lament and Mary's Flight

Love's Longing for Abundant Life

O Mother of mine, Mother of the People
buried with woman's pains, and a thousand times redeemed
in every debased woman who rises in dignity . . .
~Julia Esquivel[1]

A tyrant ruthlessly seeks to blot out the light of divine love that burns as brightly as a star in the vulnerable flesh and blood of Mary's young child. Fearing a messianic rival, Herod orders his soldiers to butcher all the male children in Bethlehem under the age of two. Refugees from the massacre, Mary and Joseph flee to Egypt in order to protect the life of their son. There they remain until Herod dies, at which time the family returns to Nazareth in Galilee, for the despotism of Archelaus, Herod's son and successor to the throne, made them fearful of returning to Judea. Elizabeth Johnson offers riveting images of the terror and bloodshed in Bethlehem: "terrible fear propelling

1. Cited in Jane M. Grovijahn, "Grabbing Life Away from Death: Women and Martyrdom in El Salvador," in *Journal of Feminist Studies in Religion* 7 (1991): 19.

241

escape in the dark from oncoming murder with no guarantee of success; the iron swords, the baby blood, the red pavement stone, the empty look of mothers mute with shock, their piercing wails of inconsolable grief."[2] Hell on earth. While Mary and Joseph have managed to protect Jesus from Herod's murderous intent, their escape from the carnage is not devoid of hardship. Their life in exile could not have been easy, and calls to mind the harsh reality faced by refugees of violent conflict who struggle for survival in foreign lands, "negotiating strange language, customs, and institutions, all the while carrying memories of horror and a feeling of pain for those who did not escape; the recognition that you can't go home again and the brave setting out in a new direction."[3] A survivor of trauma, Mary relies on the creative power of Spirit to move forward and "make a way out of no way."[4]

Divine love, made vulnerable in the image of God borne by the young victims of this massacre, is buried in the violence and traumatic grief of the slaughter. She is buried with the pain of the slain boys' mothers, with the grief of a loss so unfathomably irreplaceable. And yet, the Spirit of love also rises in the defiant dignity of a mother's tears of lamentation:

A voice is heard in Ramah,
weeping and great mourning,
Rachel weeping for her children

---

2. Elizabeth Johnson, *Truly Our Sister: A Theology of Mary in the Communion of Saints* (New York: Continuum, 2004), 243. Johnson directs her readers to graphic reflections on the massacre in Peter Daino, *Mary, Mother of Sorrows, Mother of Defiance* (Maryknoll, NY: Orbis, 1993); and Megan McKenna, *Mary, Shadow of Grace* (Maryknoll, NY: Orbis, 1995), 62–77.

3. Ibid.

4. Cf. Delores Williams, *Sisters in the Wilderness: The Challenge of Womanist God-Talk* (Maryknoll, NY: Orbis, 1995), ix; and Monica Coleman, *Making a Way Out of No Way: A Womanist Theology* (Minneapolis: Fortress Press, 2008). The biblical origin of this phrase seems to be Exod. 14:15–22, in which God makes a way out of no way to free the Israelites from slavery in Egypt. Williams also interprets God's actions on behalf of Hagar in this manner.

and refusing to be comforted,
because they are no more. (Matt. 2:18; Jer. 31:15)

From the depths of this massacre of the Holy Innocents, rise the voices of women whose dignity demands that their complaint be heard. In their voices, and in their weeping, is the Spirit of God, who has compassion for their suffering (Jer. 31:20) and who promises a future in which their mourning will be transformed into dancing and gladness, comfort and joy, abundance and bounty (Jer. 31:13-14).

The Spirit of divine love is also buried in Mary's underground flight to Egypt as a refugee of violence. In Mary's divine child, and in her own self as image of the compassionate one, divine love is hidden away, exiled, expelled from the land in which the Jewish and Christian stories of salvation history are so dramatically concentrated. And yet the Spirit of love rises in the mingling of Mary's tears with Rachel's, in Mary's tenacious refusal to surrender the life of her son to the forces of tyranny and death, and in her pursuit of a future for her family. Matthew's repeated allusions to Mary's presence with her son "keep punctuating the story with a female center of interest which serves to decenter the exercise of male military and political power that governs this narrative. Her character once again opens a fissure in the symbolic universe of patriarchy."[5] The Spirit of love is at work in this fissure, opening a way for the survival of Mary and her family, and offering a vision for the creative transformation of violence and suffering.

Rachel's lament and Mary's tenacity point to the millions of stories of women who suffer the violence of war in contemporary contexts. Jane Grovijahn argues that Salvadoran women during and after El Salvador's brutal civil war (1980–92) have been resolute in their defense of life threatened by the death-dealing forces of tyranny and

---

5. Johnson, *Truly Our Sister*, 246.

greed: "It would seem that each and every suffering, every torture, every defilement propels these women into a deeper affirmation and commitment to life. Such tenacity is salvific."[6] Like Mary, these women offer a survivor's testimony to the God of life:

> While fleeing from the army, a *campesina* gave birth. To continue giving birth in such depravity, poverty and death is a courageous act. "Even though we are persecuted, and the army looks for us to kill us, the birth of this child is a sign that God offers us life." An offering of life is also an offering of salvation. In such dire time, motherhood itself is subversive. Surrounded by lingering death, mothers remain committed to life; embodying presence amidst total absence, they reveal resurrection.[7]

The tears of Rachel, of Mary, of a Salvadoran *campesina*, and of "every debased woman who rises in dignity" to create spaces for life in the midst of death—these are all tears of compassion, tears of the Holy Spirit, which mourn the burial of divine love in the loss of life, which yearn for flourishing, and which "make a way out of no way" for the re-creation of life. These tears point to an anthropology of resilience and resistance that culminates in the work of the Spirit's longing for abundant life, manifested in the human work of lament, perseverance, and compassionate creativity.

Rachel's Lament: The Tears of Holy Longing for Abundant Life

The tears of sorrow in Rachel's maternal lament spring from an innate human desire for the good that cries out in protest at the destruction of the good in situations where vulnerable beings are subjected to suffering, pain, and death.[8] The source of these tears,

---

6. Grovijahn, "Grabbing Life Away from Death," 26.

7. Ibid., 25.

8. Edward Schillebeeckx calls this the "negative contrast experience," in which our "no" to the reality of suffering in the world ultimately presupposes and discloses a divine "yes" to the heart of God's desire for human flourishing. See *God the Future of Man* (New York: Sheed & Ward,

the heart of this desire, is the holy longing of Divine Eros for the flourishing of all creation. Our human tears spring from and produce a thirst for happiness. According to Wendy Farley, this thirst is rooted in the identity of human beings as image of God, flames of divine love, bearers of Christ's spirit of longing for the beauty and well-being of the world. In her words, "It is the unquenchable luminosity of our being that we thirst. In our thirst, we are images of the power that thirsts for the beauty of every existing thing."[9] We long for relief from suffering, but also for knowledge of our true identity. "We long for beauty that is not meretricious and for love that does not betray us. There survives in us human beings a desperate desire for truth. This desire is a burning light in us. It is the image of God in us."[10] The ardent desire of the Holy Spirit is present to human beings and works in and through human beings by way of our desire for freedom from vulnerability and suffering. This desire is often distorted, however, and produces greater vulnerability and suffering when it resorts to the violence that arises from the anxiety of egocentrism. The holy lament of human beings is distorted when it lacks compassion, and it is too often isolated from a recognition of and lament for the interrelated vulnerability of all creatures everywhere.

In the segment of her *Dialogue* titled "Tears," Catherine of Siena calls this distorted type of lament "the tears of death."[11] These tears are productive of spiritual death and separation from God in the one who mourns sensual suffering. They are the tears of sensual sadness, in which the human heart meets the vulnerability of embodied, relational life when it is enslaved to what Farley calls "the illusion

1968), 191; *The Understanding of Faith: Interpretation and Criticism* (New York: Seabury, 1974), 92; and *Church: The Human Story of God* (New York: Crossroad, 1980), 28.

9. Wendy Farley, *The Wounding and Healing of Desire: Weaving Heaven and Earth* (Louisville: Westminster John Knox, 2005), 17.

10. Ibid., 19.

11. Catherine of Siena, *The Dialogue*, trans. Suzanne Noffke, OP (New York: Paulist, 1980), 162.

of egocentrism." Catherine's condemnation of sensuality here is not a criticism of the body itself, or the senses, which can be used for virtue as well as for vice. Rather, the sensuality implicated in the tears of death is directly linked with egocentrism, which places one's own wretchedness and suffering at the center of the universe, to the detriment of charity—love of God and neighbor. This brand of self-centeredness is prone to despair because it concentrates so much on one's own sinfulness that it excludes true knowledge of oneself as loved by God.[12] It also despairs because it cuts off the essential interconnections that are present in the compassionate heart of the Spirit's longing for abundant life for *all*.

Catherine urges the spiritual seeker to rise above such anxious tears to life-giving tears that empty egocentrism from the vessel of the self in order to be filled with divine charity in compassion for her neighbors and affectionate union with God. In the tears of neighborly compassion, the soul draws divine goodness from renunciation of the false self and

> aflame with love, . . . she begins to join and conform her will with mine [God's]. She begins to feel joy and compassion: joy for herself because of this impulse of love, and compassion for her neighbors. . . . Then her eyes, which want to satisfy her heart, weep in charity for me and her neighbors with heartfelt love, grieving only for the offense done to me and the harm to her neighbors.[13]

Having shed the tears of charity, the soul travels the bridge of the Word incarnate, and passes to the stage of union with the Godhead, for which she sheds sweet tears that nourish the soul in its patient, infinite longing for love. In this state, "the vessel of her heart is filled with the sea that is [God's] very self, the most high eternal Godhead! And so her eyes, like a channel trying to satisfy her heart's lead, shed

---

12. Cf. ibid., 79. In Catherine's view, this is the sin of despair: the refusal of divine mercy.
13. Ibid., 163.

tears."[14] Even here, in blissful union with God, the soul is both happy and sorrowful. Filled with divine love for God and neighbor, the soul is grieved at the offense of goodness and "discovers the lover's lament of [God's] divine mercy and sorrow . . ."[15] The soul weeps with divine compassion, then, at the suffering of God's beloved creation.

The tears shed for love of neighbor and love of God intermingle and flavor each other, and Catherine constantly urges the spiritual seeker to remain constant in love of neighbor. It is through such love that she will

> feed the flame of my charity within her, because charity for others is drawn from my [God's] charity, that is, from the knowledge the soul gained by coming to know herself and my goodness to her, which made her see that I love her unspeakably much. So she loves every person with the same love she sees herself loved with, and this is why the soul, as soon as she comes to know me, reaches out to love her neighbors. Because she sees that I love them even more than she does, she also loves them unspeakably much.[16]

The soul that has arrived at this unitive stage is on fire with love of God and compassion for all of God's beloveds. The Holy Spirit nourishes the soul in this love and compassion, "as a mother who nurses her at the breast of divine charity."[17] Set free by the Spirit from slavery to selfish love, the soul is consumed by the sweet fire of holy charity.

Catherine describes these tears as physical tears—actual tears shed by lovers of the divine who cherish the sweetness of union with God and who are thus grieved at suffering and evil. The energy of the Holy Spirit also manifests itself in nonphysical tears, which Catherine

14. Ibid., 163–64.
15. Ibid., 164.
16. Ibid.
17. Ibid., 292.

calls tears of fire, "a weeping of fire, of true holy longing, and it consumes in love." These are the tears of the very Spirit of God:

> I tell you, these souls have tears of fire. In this fire the Holy Spirit weeps in my presence for them and for their neighbors. I mean that my divine charity sets ablaze with its flame the soul who offers me her restless longing without any physical tears. These, I tell you, are tears of fire, and this is how the Holy Spirit weeps. Since the soul cannot do it with tears, she offers her desire to weep for love of me. And if you open your mind's eye you will see that the Holy Spirit weeps in the person of every one of my servants who offers me the fragrance of holy desire and constant humble prayer.[18]

According to Catherine, these are the tears to which Paul refers in Romans 8, where the Spirit "intercedes for us through wordless groans" (Rom. 8:26) because we ourselves know not what to pray for. One might go even further to say that these tears of fire, the tears of the Holy Spirit, are present in the tears of the whole creation, which "has been groaning as in the pains of childbirth right up to the present time" (Rom. 8:21). And they are present in the tears of each of us who eagerly await the transformation of humanity and all of creation in the Spirit of love. Every lament that clamors to the heavens in heartfelt compassion for suffering humanity (and creation) participates in the fiery tears of the Holy Spirit. As Mary Catherine Hilkert observes, Catherine wields the authority of compassion here, calling on human desire to conform itself with divine desire for the flourishing of every existing thing: "Just as in tears of fire the Holy Spirit weeps with love and longing for the well-being of the world, we too are called to participate in the 'lover's lament' of God's own mercy and sorrow through love of neighbor."[19] Catherine focuses here on love of God and neighbor, along with lament for

18. Ibid., 169.
19. Mary Catherine Hilkert, *Speaking with Authority: Catherine of Siena and the Voices of Women Today* (Mahwah, NJ: Paulist, 2008), 100.

the suffering of others, to the seeming exclusion of healthy self-care and lament for one's own suffering and loss. However, her emphasis on the knowledge of oneself as infinitely loved by God opens up space for including healthy, nonegocentric self-regard and grief for oneself as one of God's beloved creatures. Just as the divine response to human vulnerability is compassion, human beings are also called to embody compassion for self *and* others in the face of both inevitable and violated vulnerability. Rachel's lament is the lament of the Spirit, which in turn is the lament of all those who take on the compassionate longing of the Spirit as their own.

Tears of Renewal: Making a Way Out of No Way

The tears of the Holy Spirit that well up in compassionate protest against the suffering of humanity (and creation) are cleansing tears of renewal. These are tears that join Rachel's lament with Mary's tenacious pursuit of a future for herself and her family. The holy longing for life, for justice, for mercy, and for love is a burning fire that effects creative transformation in persons, communities, and societies. The personal transformation described above is wrought by the Spirit of compassion, but it takes place in community and makes way for the transformation of social systems. The Spirit transforms human lives with the power of resilience and resistance, the power to rise together in dignity from the pain of vulnerable existence and make a way out of no way for personal and communal survival, quality of life, and liberation.[20] The Spirit calls vulnerable human beings into relationship and draws us forward to new possibilities for life in the midst of vulnerable existence. Catherine's spirituality of tears is grounded in this ardent fire of active and transformative compassion for the world. In Hilkert's analysis, Catherine was neither

---

20. See Williams, *Sisters in the Wilderness*.

masochistic nor passive in her tears of holy longing: "On the contrary, she operated out of what Schillebeeckx has called 'grace-optimism'—the conviction that despite all evidence to the contrary, God's Spirit of mercy is at work in the world and in our lives, empowering us to be ministers of compassion and healing."[21] Such empowerment in the Spirit is transformative of not only persons, but also communities and whole societies. It is the mediated manner in which God makes a way out of no way for those whose vulnerability exposes them to sufferings that threaten the destruction of lives and spirits.

Johnson offers a helpful analysis of the pneumatological origins of both desire for wholeness and empowerment for transformation. In her view, divine mystery is always experienced through the mediation of history. Christians name as Spirit "this movement of the living God that can be traced in and through experience of the world."[22] The yearning of the Spirit for the existence, beauty, and abundant life of creation is present in human beings as an energy for renewal and empowerment. The renewing and empowering Spirit is at work opening up new paths in the midst of brokenness and injustice. Spirit's life-giving power "comes into expression most intensely in fragmentary moments of renewing, healing, and freeing when human imbecility and destructive will are held at bay or overcome and a fresh start becomes possible."[23] Drawing on the wisdom of Hildegard of Bingen, Johnson further describes the Spirit's invigorating power as

> life, movement, color, radiance, restorative stillness in the din. She pours the juice of connection into hardened hearts. Her power makes dry twigs and withered souls green again with the juice of life. She purifies,

21. Hilkert, *Speaking with Authority*, 114.
22. Elizabeth Johnson, *She Who Is: The Mystery of God in Feminist Theological Discourse* (New York: Crossroad, 1992), 124–25.
23. Ibid., 135.

absolves, strengthens, heals, gathers the perplexed, seeks the lost. She plays the music in the soul, being herself the melody of praise and joy. She awakens mighty hope, blowing everywhere the winds of renewal in creation.[24]

The power of Spirit for creative transformation is especially mediated through human praxis of freedom on behalf of justice and peace. However, it is important to remember here that Spirit is also at work in the experience of personal transformation as "the power of person making among those diminished by pain who do not know their own dignity."[25] The Spirit empowers vulnerable beings with the desire to rise in dignity from the abasement of privilege and/or marginalization to meet human vulnerability with compassionate and transformative action for healing, connection, and flourishing.

The power of Spirit described here has been recognized as "Eros" by many contemporary feminist and womanist scholars. Audre Lorde set the foundation for discourse on Eros over three decades ago in her essay "Uses of the Erotic: The Erotic as Power." Lorde explains "the erotic" as a deeply female and spiritual resource within all of us, a powerful force that "arises from our deepest and nonrational knowledge."[26] As the personification of love and the creative power born of Chaos, eros is a life-giving force that empowers creative energy for life, work, love, dancing, history, and language. The erotic functions in several ways: as a power that emerges from sharing a meaningful pursuit with another person; as a capacity for joy that "heightens and sensitizes and strengthens"[27] all experience; as a refusal to accept powerlessness and other "supplied states of being which

---

24. Elizabeth Johnson, "Remembering Creative Spirit," in *Women's Spirituality: Resources for Christian Development*, ed. Joann Wolski Conn (New York: Paulist, 1996), 372.

25. Johnson, *She Who Is*, 138.

26. Audre Lorde, "Uses of the Erotic: The Erotic as Power," in *Sister Outsider* (Berkeley, CA: Crossing, 1984), 53. The essay was originally a paper delivered at the Fourth Berkshire Conference on the History of Women, Mount Holyoke College, August 25, 1978.

27. Ibid., 56.

are not native to me such as resignation, despair, self-effacement, depression, self-denial";[28] and as a deep participation in the feeling of others. This is a power that, when acknowledged and accepted, can empower women (and all human beings) for the transformation of the world: "Recognizing the power of the erotic within our lives can give us the energy to pursue genuine change within our world, rather than merely settling for a shift of characters in the same weary drama. For not only do we touch our most profoundly creative source, but we do that which is female and self-affirming in the face of a racist, patriarchal, and anti-erotic society."[29] The personal transformation that takes place in recognizing the power of the erotic within empowers and energizes participation in the transformation of systems of privilege that trample the vulnerability of the marginalized.

Lorde's vision here is nontheological. In fact, she insists that the satisfaction experienced in eros need not be called *god*.[30] However, Christian feminists and womanists have adopted this language of eros in their efforts to correlate women's lives and the sacred power of divine love.[31] Much further back in the Christian tradition, Pseudo-Dionysius describes Eros as the divine yearning for the creation of the world and the yearning for the Beautiful and the Good instilled in creation by God. For Pseudo-Dionysius, this divine yearning is the power of true desire for unity with God and creation, "a simple self-moving power directing all things to mingle as one."[32] I

---

28. Ibid., 58.
29. Ibid., 59.
30. Cf. ibid., 57.
31. For example, see Rita Nakashima Brock, *Journeys by Heart: A Christology of Erotic Power* (New York: Crossroad, 1988); Carter Heyward, *Touching Our Strength: The Erotic as Power and the Love of God* (San Francisco: Harper & Row, 1989); Anne Bathurst Gilson, *Eros Breaking Free: Interpreting Sexual Theo-ethics* (Cleveland: Pilgrim, 1995); Farley, *The Wounding and Healing of Desire*; and Mary C. Grey, *Sacred Longings: The Ecological Spirit and Global Culture* (Minneapolis: Fortress Press, 2004).

borrow Eros here as a way of naming the indwelling power of holy longing that draws human beings both out of unhealthy acceptance of vulnerability and into transformative communities seeking compassionate ways of inhabiting universal vulnerability together as individuals and societies. In Christian language, what Lorde calls "our most profoundly creative source" can be interpreted as the Spirit of divine love, our deepest longing for beauty, goodness, and truth in union with God and all of creation. This longing is what brings vulnerable human beings together in love, and out of the Spirit-filled communities that emerge, divine love makes possible new paths for coping with our shared vulnerabilities and responding to suffering with ever-widening, radical compassion.

As Pseudo-Dionysius indicates, Eros is first and foremost a divinely instilled longing for union, for connection, for relationship. Human beings are essentially relational, but so too is all of creation. Everything that exists is what it is only in relationships of interdependence with the rest of creation. Maternal experience has shown us that interdependence generates profound vulnerability (see chapter 1), but it is also the condition for the possibility of life itself, of love, meaning, and virtue. The Spirit of God instills in human beings the desire to embody this deep reality of interconnectedness in intentional and compassionate bonds of love. In Mary Grey's ecofeminist theology, the Holy Spirit is the drive to connect that awakens us "to awareness of the many-leveled interconnectedness of all living systems" and draws us into relationships of mutuality and justice.[33] Grey's Spirit is a "boundary-crosser," urging "the formation of community across the boundaries of faith and nation. . . . Through

32. Pseudo-Dionysius, "The Divine Names," in *The Complete Works*, trans. Colm Luibheid (New York: Paulist, 1987), 79–84.
33. Grey, *Sacred Longings*, 111–12. Grey's relational pneumatology is a helpful corrective to Pseudo-Dionysius' hierarchical understanding of Eros as integrating that which is superior with that which is subordinate.

a process of healing the splits and dualisms of patriarchal history that set men over against women, mind as superior to body, human beings as superior to animals and the natural world, the Spirit prompts an integration which promotes the flourishing of all."[34] At once a peaceful dove and the disruptive presence of a Wild Bird, the Spirit of God revels in the chaotic unity of diverse peoples and all life-forms.[35] There is no easy or invulnerable unity here though. Rather, as a disruptive and challenging presence, the Wild Bird of holy longing goes before us calling us to do the difficult work of creative transformation in the midst of vulnerability. The relationships of mutuality and justice into which we are called, however, are Spirit's transformative answer to the anxiety we experience surrounding our vulnerability.

Monica Coleman's postmodern womanist theology also places heavy emphasis on communities as the work of the Spirit for creative transformation. Drawing on the wisdom of both process thought and womanist theology, Coleman explores black women's experience of God as the one who "makes a way out of no way."[36] This expression has its roots deep in the African American community and, according to Coleman, it also has deep resonances with the concept of creative transformation in process theology. According to Coleman, the womanist expression of God making a way out of no way "acknowledges God's presence in providing options that do not appear to exist in the experiences of the past. It is a weaving of the past, future, and possibilities offered by God; a weaving that leads to survival, quality of life, and liberating activity on the part of black women."[37] Coleman's engagement with process thought,

---

34. Ibid., 114.

35. Cf. ibid., 116–17.

36. Coleman, *Making a Way Out of No Way*. Coleman is particularly indebted to Delores Williams in her adoption of this experience as a central locus of theological reflection. See Williams, *Sisters in the Wilderness*, ix.

however, leads her to affirm that the divine process of making a way out of no way is not exclusive to black women's experiences. Rather, it is a characteristic of the way in which "the aim of God is always toward survival, quality of life, and justice in every context," including nonhuman environments.[38] The context of salvation in Coleman's framework is always communal. In a process world, creative transformation can only happen in and through community, and community is also the goal of creative transformation.[39] In and through relationships of mutual respect and compassion for vulnerability and suffering, the Spirit of Divine Eros forges a path forward, creating new possibilities for life and flourishing in community. Tears of death are shed in anxiety-filled isolation. The Holy Spirit's tears of renewal are shed in creative and life-giving relationships with others, thus joining our maternal witnesses in pointing to an anthropology in which embodied relationality is both the ground of our personhood and the place of our liberation and transformation in the Spirit of Love's holy and compassionate longing for abundant life.

Compassion

Compassion is the redemptive power of divinity to liberate human beings from the tyranny of vulnerability and suffering.[40] The power of compassion at work in the Spirit's persuasive, indwelling presence

---

37. Coleman, *Making a Way Out of No Way*, 33.
38. Ibid., 94.
39. Ibid., 98.
40. For an extensive phenomenology of compassion (divine and human), see Wendy Farley, *Tragic Vision and Divine Compassion: A Contemporary Theodicy* (Louisville: Westminster John Knox, 1990). Maureen O'Connell's *Compassion: Loving Our Neighbor in an Age of Globalization* (Maryknoll, NY: Orbis, 2009) offers an excellent overview of compassion in philosophical and theological ethics, along with a proposal for Christian compassion in the face of global injustice and oppression. Of particular relevance to my own treatment of privilege in theological anthropology, O'Connell's ethical work confronts the injustice of white privilege with the challenge of political compassion.

is the selfsame power of holy longing at work in the Incarnation of divine love—what Nicholas of Cusa calls the coincidence of opposites—described in chapter 6. Christians hold that, by the power of the Holy Spirit and out of compassion for the world, invulnerable divine love became vulnerable flesh in the body of a human being who was born, grew to maturity, and suffered a violent death as the result of his ministry of radical compassion and his prophetic annunciation of the kingdom of God. By the same power of the Holy Spirit, the incarnation of divine love is repeated in the compassion of every Rachel who laments the absence of abundant life and of every Mary who tenaciously forges a way out of no way. The power of compassion at work in lament and creative transformation is the Spirit-filled way in which human beings are called to incarnate divine love in a wounded and wounding world. In and through compassion, human beings live the deepest truth of reality—the coincidence of opposites. The indwelling presence of divine compassion makes it possible to inhabit the vulnerability of the human condition with spirit and grace. In and through compassion, divine love becomes incarnate in human beings and human beings become divine.

As the Holy Spirit of longing for the universal realization of abundant life, compassion meets vulnerability with assets for both resilience to harm and resistance to the unjust management of vulnerability in systems of privilege. The Spirit of God empowers resilience through a creative conversion of the human heart from the illusion of egocentrism—whether this is manifest in the conventional understanding of egocentrism as arrogant and aggressive pride, or in the self-enclosures of passivity and despair—to the reality of interdependence and mutuality. When compassion for the suffering of others wells up in tears of holy longing for universal flourishing, anxiety dissipates and it is hard to remain locked in either the paralysis of self-pity or the hostility of self-importance. Such is the beginning of healing and resilience described by Mary Karr when she relates how she momentarily experienced a surge of compassion for fellow addicts at a meeting of Alcoholics Anonymous:

> Standing at the [coffee] urn, I hear a tweedy classics professor say to a big black marine with patches from Khe Sanh on his bulging arms: It's hard to be an articulate ghost. Illogically, as I hear this, some frozen inner aspect thaws enough that a small surge of pity swells through me. I head my watery coffee with powdered cream and stop thinking about myself long enough to come alive a little. I notice in the professor's baggy face his red-rimmed eyes, and the care in the marine's gaze starts to plug me in to something invisible that rivers among these strangers. It's like running from my cardiac area, I've been dragging a long extension cord unplugged from all compassion, and it's suddenly found a socket. The room comes breathing to life.[41]

Munching on cookies provided by the kindness of strangers, Karr experiences pleasure in this upsurge of compassion: "Pleasure, I feel—mouth to spine to head. A small uprush of pleasure. This, I think, is why other people aren't screaming. I've briefly forgotten to feel sorry for myself, to worry, to generate any kind of report on my own performance."[42] Emptying the self of the anxiety induced by vulnerability and suffering, the Spirit of love fills the self with the unitive power of divine charity.[43] The abandonment of egocentrism, however momentary at first, clears away self-loathing and self-aggrandizement as modes of dealing with the anxiety of vulnerable existence. Thus freed from the tyranny of vulnerability and suffering, the self can begin to plug in to that invisible current of divine love

---

41. Mary Karr, *Lit: A Memoir* (New York: HarperCollins, 2009), 189.
42. Ibid.
43. Feminist concerns regarding the dangers of kenosis are relevant here. Sarah Coakley and Beverly Lanzetta both offer feminist retrievals of kenosis and vulnerability before God as opening up spaces in the human psyche for divine empowerment. See Sarah Coakley, *Powers and Submissions: Spirituality, Philosophy and Gender* (Malden, MA: Blackwell, 2002); and Beverly Lanzetta, *Radical Wisdom: A Feminist Mystical Theology* (Minneapolis: Fortress Press, 2005). I will address the practice of contemplative kenosis at length here in chapter 8.

that breathes life into all existing things. Compassion's kenosis of egocentrism makes way for fulfillment of the self in the power-invulnerability of divine love. In Catherine's words, "[b]ecause she has left all she finds all."[44]

Freed from anxiety by the Holy Spirit, the self is empowered to go outside of herself in ardent compassion for all of God's creatures, meeting their vulnerability with active care and resisting the violation of vulnerability with nonviolent tenacity of spirit. Kenosis empowers ekstasis. Emptied of anxiety, holy longing fills the heart with divine charity such that it burns and weeps for the anxiety and violation of all humanity and creation. In this kenotic and ecstatic state of union with divine love, the human heart cannot bear the suffering of its beloved. It cries out with Rachel in a maternal lament for human suffering, and with Mary it rises in dignity from the ashes of vulnerability and suffering to resist unjust forms of vulnerability and seek a future of abundant life. The Spirit of compassion weeps with passionate womb-love and struggles for the survival, quality of life, and liberation of all of humanity. The vulnerability, suffering, and compassion of Rachel and Mary is expanded by compassion to include all those who suffer: "'Mother' does not mean being the woman who gives birth to and cares for a child; to be a mother is to feel in your own flesh the suffering of all the children, all the men, and all the young people who die as though they had come from your own womb."[45] Entering into communities of compassion, human beings are empowered both to cope with vulnerability and suffering in healthy ways, and to resist the destructive forces of mismanaged vulnerability in systems of privilege. This divine desire for human flourishing does not offer an escape from vulnerability, for

44. Catherine of Siena, *The Dialogue*, 292.

45. Luz Beatriz Arellano, quoting Nicaraguan mother Idania Fernandez, in "Women's Experience of God in Emerging Spirituality," in *With Passion and Compassion: Third World Women Doing Theology*, ed. Virginia Fabella and Mercy Amba Oduyoye (Maryknoll, NY: Orbis, 1988), 142.

holy longing can in fact expose the heart (and the body) to greater suffering. But such vulnerability is the condition for the possibility of creative transformation, new life, and even joy in the midst of a vulnerable and suffering world.

Conclusion: Might We Be Overcome?

In these three chapters, I have constructed a theological anthropology rooted in an outline of three dimensions of divine love's redemptive response to the vulnerability of the human condition. To sum up, there are three ways in which God empowers human beings with assets for resilience and resistance in the midst of an existence marked by vulnerability, suffering, anxiety, and violence. The primordial dimension of divinity is invulnerable love that preserves the fundamental dignity of the human person as *imago dei*, even in the midst of the most heinous violations of vulnerability. This love can grant human beings the courage to endure suffering, to assert themselves as persons made in the divine image, and to resist the forces of worldly power and privilege that violate the vulnerability of God's precious creation. The invulnerability of divine love, however, tempers courage with peace when its self-manifesting dimension becomes incarnate as a lowly, vulnerable infant born of a Palestinian peasant woman. Without incarnation as vulnerable flesh, divine invulnerability would remain impotent to save vulnerable humanity, for the invulnerable image of divine love is paradoxically vulnerable in human flesh. And without the advent of peace, human courage too easily slides to self-assertion at the cost of vulnerable others. Finally, the courageous peace of divine love flowers forth in compassion, as the Spirit of creative transformation softens hearts that have been hardened by suffering, anxiety, and violation. Freed from the prison of fearing vulnerability, human beings lament the suffering of all creatures everywhere and are capacitated for incarnating divine love in creative communities of mutual compassion.

As powerful as the Trinitarian dynamics of divine love are, this theological vision is not a panacea. Human beings remain vulnerable, and life still involves horrific suffering and, in the end, death. According to Julian of Norwich, the root of the human problem is not vulnerability or suffering or death per se, but that we are blind to the love with which God meets and empowers us in our vulnerability and suffering. Our blindness to this love and its redemptive power leads us both to become impatient with our vulnerable condition and to succumb to despair or doubtful fear.[46] In all of her visions, Julian found that this message of divine love that casts out impatience and fear was most clear. Love was the meaning of all that was shown to her, by love and for love: "So I was taught that love is our Lord's meaning. And I saw very certainly in this and in everything that before God made us he loved us, which love was never abated and never will be."[47] In these revelations of divine love, Julian received a promise that she would not be overcome, nor would any of us ultimately be overcome by the harm to which we are exposed in our vulnerability and suffering. Yet Julian cautions that she was not told that she would not be troubled, or that we would not know distress. The words "You will not be overcome" were revealed to her not as a magical force field to make her invulnerable and protect her from all harm, but as an assurance uttered "very insistently and strongly, for certainty and strength against every tribulation which may come."[48] Julian urges her readers to tend to these words and "to be strong in faithful trust, in well-being and in woe, for he loves and delights in

---

46. Julian of Norwich, *Showings*, trans. Edmund Colledge and James Walsh (Mahwah, NJ: Paulist, 1978), 322.
47. Ibid., 342.
48. Ibid., 315.

us, and so he wishes us to love him and delight in him and trust greatly in him, and all will be well."[49]

And yet today, as in Julian's time, all is *not well*: untold millions *have been* overcome, despairing of meaning or dying an unjust and dehumanizing death. Christian wisdom hopes against hope that vulnerability, suffering, and death will not, cannot ultimately destroy even those among us who have been overcome. To trust in divine love is the primary Christian means of empowerment for resilience to harm and resistance to violence in the midst of contexts plagued by vulnerability, anxiety, and violence. In divine love, Christians find the courage, peace, and compassion to reach out to a suffering world in love. And, as Julian reminds us, even when these resources are inaccessible or invisible to our vulnerable and suffering hearts, divine love continues to preserve and protect our inherent worth and dignity as beloved sons and daughters of God. There is no blame or punishment if or when we are overcome due to the vulnerability of our condition, but there is always compassion and an offering of hope, even if that offer remains hidden.

Mothers inhabit an especially vulnerable position in our world due to biological and socially produced factors that expose them to particularly intense forms of suffering, anxiety, victimization, and participation in the violation of vulnerable others. The vulnerability of mothers (and their dependent children) is an icon of universal human vulnerability and the dynamic relationship between vulnerability, anxiety, and violence. Intensely connected to the origins of human life, maternity and natality point to the vulnerability of all human beings, along with the anxious attempts of human beings to stave off vulnerability with control. On the other hand, the maternal witnesses that grace these pages also provide

49. Ibid.

windows into how divine grace is manifested in maternal and natal vulnerability, especially the maternal vulnerability of Mary and the natal vulnerability of her son Jesus. Vulnerability is not only or always or necessarily a precursor to violation. It is also the site of human empowerment and redemption, experienced as a Trinitarian set of resources for resilience and resistance. We now turn our attention to maternal narratives of suffering and empowerment that unveil practical means—both contemplative and active—for human beings to access these graced resources for confronting vulnerability with the courage, peace, and compassion of their true identities as unique and sacred reflections of divine love.

PART III

To Suckle God with Exercises of Love

8

Practices of Resilience and Resistance

Memory, Contemplation, and Solidarity

Divine love, by definition, does not impose itself on human beings as the "answer" to vulnerability, suffering, anxiety, and violence. The lofty aspirations of theological anthropology are not guaranteed fulfillment by divine fiat. Nor can human beings be transformed for love by an act of the will, an intellectual assent to religious dogma, or verbal acceptance of divine love into their hearts. Human beings are practical animals and, as such, becoming one with God in human life requires practice—spiritual disciplines that slowly, achingly give birth to the courage, peace, and compassion of divine love in the midst of a vulnerable and suffering world. Divine invulnerability means that nothing can ever separate us from the love of God, but this is on the divine side of things. On the human side, the realization of our union with divine love is fragile and even dependent on efforts we put forth to make space for divine love and to nurture the growth of love in our lives. From desert ascetics, to medieval contemplatives, to contemporary liberation theologians, Christians through the ages have held that, though grace is a free and unearned gift, human beings do not do nothing in the process of working out our salvation (Phil. 2:12). In light of this divine need for human cooperation, Hadewijch of Brabant exhorted her readers to carry God maternally, and to "suckle God with exercises of love."[1] Although it is divine love that ultimately does the work within us, human collaboration is required for love's gestation, birth, and nurturance in our lives. An incarnational faith—a faith that takes seriously the vulnerability of Christ's natal body—recognizes the fragility of divine love's embodiment in human flesh. It is by way of practices that human beings suckle divine love in their own vulnerable selves and care for the vulnerability and dignity of others. Practices of contemplation and action that nurture the divine image within and honor the divine image in others are powerful resources for resilience and resistance in the face of both ordinary vulnerability and radical suffering. These practices are not always explicitly Christian, religious, or even "spiritual," since as Wendy Farley notes, living the incarnation permeates everything we do.[2]

In this chapter, I draw on two maternal narratives of vulnerability, resilience, and resistance to propose three families of practices that nurture the growth of divine love in vulnerable human lives and relationships. These families of practices are: memory of suffering, contemplative kenosis, and solidarity with vulnerable others. The mothers whose stories I highlight here—American memoirist Mary Karr and Liberian peacemaker Leymah Gbowee—both rely on various manifestations of these practices in order to cultivate the

---

1. Cf. Hadewijch, *The Complete Works*, trans. Mother Columba Hart (Mahwah, NJ: Paulist, 1980), 119.
2. Wendy Farley, *Gathering Those Driven Away: A Theology of Incarnation* (Louisville: Westminster John Knox, 2011), 188.

courage, peace, and compassion necessary for human beings to embody divine love in the midst of vulnerability and suffering.

There is a triadic and dynamic structure to the relationship between these practices of memory, contemplation, and solidarity. Memory is primarily active, kenosis is primarily contemplative, and solidarity is primarily active (though there are certainly contemplative elements to memory and solidarity, as well as active elements to kenosis). The structure of my analysis in this chapter (as in the book as a whole) thus echoes the relationship between contemplation and action present in liberationist pastoral and theological methodology, which moves from practice to theory to practice.[3] The threefold, cyclical pattern of "see-judge-act" that explicitly characterizes liberationist theologies and communities of faith is also implicit in the movement from a) memorial observation of vulnerability and suffering to b) contemplation of divine love as the personal, relational, and even cosmic milieu in which vulnerability and suffering reside, and c) solidarity as the practical and active incarnation of divine love in the midst of a broken and breakable world. Contemplation and action thus intertwine to form an inextricable matrix in which the presence of divine love heals and empowers fragile human beings to inhabit our vulnerable condition with courage, peace, and compassion.

Two Maternal Narratives of Vulnerability, Resilience, and Resistance

Before examining the matrix of practices in which divine love can be nourished by human beings, it will be helpful to pause and introduce

---

3. See Clodovis Boff, "Epistemology and Method of the Theology of Liberation," in *Mysterium Liberationis: Fundamental Concepts of Liberation Theology*, ed.Ignacio Ellacuría and Jon Sobrino (Maryknoll, NY: Orbis, 1993), 57–84. An excellent summary of the method is offered by Elaine Graham, Heather Walton, and Frances Ward in *Theological Reflection: Methods* (London: SCM, 2005), 182ff.

the testimonies of the mothers whose narratives inform my practical theological analysis. Here I briefly relay the stories of Mary Karr and Leymah Gbowee, with reference to the three sets of practices that empower these particular women to inhabit, accept, and resist the vulnerability, pain, and injustice of their respective situations.

The first woman whose story informs my analysis is the American memoirist, Mary Karr. As we saw in previous chapters, Karr experienced a tortured childhood in the hardscrabble world of Leechfield, East Texas, mostly due to the depressive alcoholism of her psychologically abusive mother. Through the practice of remembering both her childhood and her mother's own traumatic past, Karr comes to understand that she was not to blame for her mother's lack of care and compassion. This memorial process also brought Karr to an awareness of her mother's own "blamelessness"[4] in the cycle of violated vulnerability. Charlie Karr herself had been deeply wounded by the disappearance of her first two children, who were kidnapped by their father at a young age. Writing her first memoir, *The Liars' Club*, was the discursive memorial practice through which Karr's memory of the painful truth about the past had a liberating effect on both mother and daughter in their quest for healing and wholeness.

Karr's past did not cease to have a debilitating hold on her psyche, however, until she engaged in contemplative practices of prayer, gratitude, and surrender to the divine. Her second memoir, *Cherry*,[5] narrates the lurid sexual and pharmacological escapades of her adolescence and young adulthood. As Karr left her childhood behind, she coped with her pain, anger, depression, and persistent

---

4. In an open letter to her son Dev, Karr writes, "Just as you're blameless for the scorched parts of your childhood, I'm equally exonerated for my own mother's nightmare. Maybe I can show you how I came to peace, how she and Daddy wound up as blameless in my story as you are." Mary Karr, *Lit: A Memoir* (New York: HarperCollins, 2009), 5–6.

5. Mary Karr, *Cherry: A Memoir* (New York: Viking, 2000).

vulnerability through a steady stream of sex, drugs, and alcohol. It is when she becomes a mother herself that she begins the long, hard road of recovery, detailed in her most recent memoir *Lit*. This road is riddled with relapse after relapse, until Karr finally takes the advice offered by fellow addicts in Alcoholics Anonymous to engage in daily spiritual practices that would place her in the hands of a "higher power." These practices re-member Karr as one loved by God, shot through with "the force that infuses every petal," and continually lured to realize her fullest potential of life and love, even in the face of radical vulnerability.[6]

Karr's recovery from her traumatic childhood and subsequent alcoholism takes place in solidarity with her mother, her son, her fellow addicts, and her readers. While her memoirs are brutally honest about the damaging effects of her mother's behavior, Karr writes of her own pain in solidarity with her mother's pain. Furthermore, Karr strives for sobriety and sanity in part for the sake of her son Dev's well-being. She also seeks recovery in solidarity with fellow addicts, whose vulnerability draws her out of her own paralyzing pain into a compassionate awareness of the needs of others. Finally, Karr's writing is an act of solidarity with her readers. While this may not have been Karr's intention from the start, her readers have experienced the offering of solidarity in her memoirs. When Karr set out on the road to promote *The Liars' Club*, ordinary folks from every walk of life confided in her "about childhoods that certainly differed from [hers] in terms of surface pyrotechnics—fires set and fortunes squandered. But the feelings were identical." She sensed "a community assembling around [her]" of people who, like her, were struggling to lead healthy adult lives while coping with the feelings of anger, guilt, and depression induced by their turbulent and

6. Karr, *Lit*, 385–86.

traumatic childhoods.[7] Karr's memoirs confirm many of her readers' own experiences in a flawed family and thus feed them "the way the bread of communion does, with a nourishment that seems to form new flesh."[8] While writing itself is her primary practice of solidarity, she is also physically present to those with whom she is in solidarity (to varying degrees).

The second maternal narrative that informs my analysis is that of Liberian peace activist and Nobel laureate, Leymah Gbowee. Gbowee experienced a relatively comfortable childhood in a middle-class family in Liberia's capital city of Monrovia. Though her mother was emotionally distant and her father had children with three other women on the side, Gbowee grew up with confidence in her own worth and abilities. In 1989, she graduated from high school with plans to study medicine at university and with a sense of personal strength and limitless possibility. The violent onset of Liberia's fourteen-year civil war shattered not only Gbowee's plans for the future, but also her sense of purpose, dignity, and self-worth. Just barely escaping a massacre committed by President Samuel Doe's troops, Gbowee's family fled the violence in Monrovia to a refugee camp in Ghana. It was there that she first met Daniel, the man who would later become father to four of her five children. Although the children they had together are "the center of [her] world," being with this man "nearly destroyed [her]."[9] About a year into their relationship, Daniel became violent, controlling, and demeaning toward Gbowee. Soon after she began thinking of leaving him, she discovered that she was pregnant with their first child. After years of abuse, Gbowee took her children and left Daniel, returning to her family in Liberia, pregnant with her fourth child.

---

7. Mary Karr, *The Liars' Club: A Memoir* (New York: Penguin, 1995), xiii.
8. Ibid., xiv.
9. Leymah Gbowee, *Mighty Be Our Powers: How Sisterhood, Prayer, and Sex Changed a Nation at War* (New York: Beast Books, 2011), 42.

Having been trained previously in social services, Gbowee began working for the Trauma Healing and Reconciliation Program of the Lutheran Church in Liberia and the Lutheran World Federation. One of her primary tasks in this job was to lead workshops that provided women with a safe space in which to share the trauma wrought in their lives by the brutality of Liberia's civil war. The work of sharing their memories of suffering through both discursive and embodied practices contributed to the process of healing, helping the victims of war to become "strong again,"[10] capable of resilience and resistance to violence. Gbowee found healing for herself in this practice of remembering suffering—referred to by Liberian women as "The Shedding of the Weight." Gbowee writes that, after sharing her own story at the first meeting of the Women in Peacebuilding Network (WIPNET), "I felt purged of shame. Like the women in the groups I'd led myself, I felt as if a great wound in me had healed."[11] Remembering the past helped to move Gbowee forward, into a future of great promise.

Gbowee also regained strength and confidence in her own potential through contemplative practices of prayer and meditation on Scripture. The violence Gbowee witnessed during the early days of Liberia's civil war rocked her faith and existential identity to the core. In her words, "When you move so quickly from innocence to a world of fear, pain and loss, it's as if the flesh of your heart and mind gets cut away, piece by piece, like slices taken off a ham. Finally, there is nothing left but bone."[12] In this state of shock and numbness, Gbowee's relationship with Daniel begins and evolves into an abusive and paralyzing trap. Her faith in God was destroyed by the war and her faith in herself was replaced by self-loathing and

10. Ibid., 82.
11. Ibid., 113.
12. Ibid., 39.

shame during her experience with Daniel. One night, when Daniel became sexually violent, Gbowee escaped, grabbed her Bible and locked herself in the bathroom, where she asked God to guide her with a verse. She let the book fall open and was met with the promise of Isaiah 54: "*For the Lord has called thou as a woman forsaken and grieved in spirit . . . O thou afflicted, tossed with tempest, and not comforted, behold, I will lay thy stones with fair colors, and lay thy foundations with sapphires. . . .*"[13] When Daniel saw the passage and laughed in her face, Gbowee paid him no mind: "*Stones with fair colors. Foundations with sapphires.* I came back to Isaiah again and again over the next decade. I knew it was my promise."[14] Contemplation of this promise—with its power to cast out fear of shame (Isa. 54:4) and its rootedness in the kindness of God (Isa. 54:8b)—contributed to the renewal of Gbowee's strength and confidence to become a leader of the Liberian women's peace movement and an eventual recipient of the Nobel Peace Prize.

Memory of suffering and contemplation of divine love required the addition of solidarity for Gbowee to rise from the status of victim to the stature of a strong and courageous woman capable of leading a community of women in the struggle for an end to Liberia's brutal civil war. Solidarity with her own children impelled her to pull herself out of depression and into a life of purpose and action. The love she had for her own children also extended her circle of concern to include solidarity with all of Liberia's children, thus motivating her to do something positive to achieve peace for her country. Finally, and perhaps most significantly, Gbowee's solidarity with other Liberian women is what has played the most definitive role in banishing the fear, loneliness, and depression that had kept her paralyzed for so long. Gbowee's own words, written about how she felt while reading

13. Ibid., 47.
14. Ibid.

a vision for peace to the women of WIPNET, convey the power of this transformation best:

> I remember the crowd listening intently and hundreds of heads nodding. I had no idea where we were going next in our alliance, our quest. But I did know this: I had lived in fear for a long time. . . . I'd seen friends, whole families, wiped out, and never lost the awareness that I could be next. I'd been depressed for a long time, too, isolated in my own world. When I had to send my children away, I felt the worst kind of loneliness. But now, as the women of WIPNET gathered together, my fear, depression and loneliness were finally, totally, wiped away. Others who felt the way I did stood beside me; I wasn't alone anymore. And I knew in my heart that everything I had been through, every pain, had led me to this point: leading women to fight for peace was what I was meant to do with my life.[15]

The solidarity Gbowee experienced in Liberian women's peace movement was transformative of not only her own spirit and the spirits of thousands of other women; it was also transformative of the Liberian armed conflict. The women's mass action for peace, with its relentless demands for an end to the senseless violence committed by both government and rebel forces, played a constitutive role in the process of moving through Liberia's ceasefire, disarmament, and democratic elections.[16] For Gbowee, practicing solidarity offered not only personal healing, but also an enduring commitment to determined action for healing and reconciliation in Liberian society as a whole.

With this biographical and practical background in mind, the remainder of this chapter brings this theological anthropology to its culmination with a practical theological analysis of how practices of memory, contemplation, and solidarity are powerful resources for

---

15. Ibid., 130.
16. A powerful depiction of Liberia's women peacemakers can be viewed in the documentary film, *Pray the Devil Back to Hell*, DVD, directed by Gini Reticker (New York: Fork Films, 2009).

empowering human beings to live with their individual and shared vulnerabilities in more courageous, peaceful, and compassionate ways. The narratives of Mary Karr and Leymah Gbowee will inform my analysis as examples of individuals who refused to allow their identity as women and mothers to be determined by their pain. Rather, they were able to make peace with their vulnerability and rise courageously to live lives of compassion for both their own vulnerable children and for the vulnerability of the human condition as a whole. The following analysis will offer a practical theological account of how such resilience and resistance can be possible, how human beings can find a way to make manifest their luminous identity as bearers of divine love's incarnate image, even in the midst of tremendous suffering.

Memory of Suffering: Naming Vulnerability and Violation

One of the defining characteristics of the Christian faith is the remembrance of suffering.[17] In our Scriptures and church practices, Christians remember the slavery of the Hebrews in Egypt, the exile of Israel in Babylon, the massacre of the Holy Innocents, the crucifixion of Jesus, and the suffering of the early Christian martyrs. However, the Christian tradition always and only remembers these sufferings in relation to the Exodus, the return from exile, the Incarnation, and the Resurrection. Thus Christian memory of suffering is always linked to the promise of a future in which suffering will not have the last word. This promise can offer courage for endurance, and it encourages living with the peace and compassion of the "kin-dom of God" that is already present, but not yet fulfilled. However, the

---

17. An earlier version of the material presented in this section was published in my article, "Remembering the Massacre at El Mozote: A Case for the Dangerous Memory of Suffering as Christian Formation in Hope," in *The International Journal of Practical Theology* 17, no. 1 (2013): 1–26.

narratives of Karr and Gbowee demonstrate that courage, peace, and compassion experienced in the memory of suffering do not arise simply or only from the comforting assurance of a divine pledge to make things right (though this promise can have beneficial effects, to be sure). Rather, there is something about the memory of suffering, *in and of itself*, that can empower individuals (or at least begin to empower them) for resilience and resistance to vulnerability and suffering. Narration of the painful memory itself, or other embodied means of grappling with it, can give birth to courage, peace, and compassion even in the face of tragedy. Karr and Gbowee are formed and transformed by their memory of suffering, then, because remembering the suffering of human beings (and, arguably, creation) has cognitive and practical value in and of itself. The knowledge and praxis that flow from this memory is capable of empowering human beings to inhabit the vulnerability of our basic condition with greater love and justice for ourselves and others.[18]

There are at least four ways in which memorial practices empower resilience and resistance within the vulnerable condition marked by suffering and anxiety: they *interrupt* prevailing conceptions of personal and collective history and reality; they empower formation in a liberating *identity*; they nurture a new moral *imagination* and vision of an alternative future; and they *inspire* those who remember to compassionate action in the present on behalf of that future. Through these four functions, the dangerous memory of suffering demonstrates itself to be a powerful, even integral component in the

---

18. The memory of suffering provides much fodder for theological and ethical reflection on difficult questions such as how Christians should remember, and it is imperative to warn against the potentially destructive abuses of memory that engender hatred and violence. By no means is the memory of suffering an unqualified good, nor is it morally ambiguous. However, for the sake of focus and brevity, I will focus on how the practice of memory of suffering can be a positive, empowering force for good.

process of healing and learning to inhabit vulnerability with courage, peace, and compassion, rather than fear, violence, and isolation.

Interruption

At first glance, it might seem that memory has an inherently conservative impulse that would reinforce a painful status quo and encourage resignation to it. Would not revisiting memories of childhood trauma and neglect simply further paralyze someone like Karr, on whom the past had such a debilitating hold? Similarly, would not Gbowee's shameful memories of surviving a massacre and enduring domestic violence simply reaffirm her status as a passive victim and her consequent feelings of shame and self-loathing? Facing a painful past reiterates a person's vulnerability in the present. How could subjecting oneself to greater vulnerability possibly empower resilience and resistance?

Perhaps we might begin to understand the liberating effect of memorial practices by referencing the pervasive manipulation of collective memory by the privileged and powerful in order to maintain their influence and minimize resistance. Totalitarian regimes, for example, rely heavily on the destruction and control of their victims' memory by wiping out the evidence of their crimes, intimidating or eliminating those who would bear witness, employing euphemisms in place of the plain truth, and asserting outright falsehoods.[19] Victims' memories of the past are replaced by an official memory that serves the interests of the powerful. This manipulation of memory culminates in the erasure of memory, especially the memory of suffering, in order to effect the total domination of individuals, communities, and whole peoples. In the words of Johann Baptist Metz, "It is no accident that the destruction

---

19. Cf. Tzvetan Todorov, *Hope and Memory: Lessons from the Twentieth Century* (Princeton: Princeton University Press, 2003), 113ff.

of memory is a typical measure taken by totalitarian governments. People's subjugation begins when their memories are taken away. Every colonization takes its principle here."[20] Similarly, for Karr and Gbowee to have repressed their memories of suffering and remained silent about their past would have had the effect of accepting the prevailing narratives of male privilege, women's passivity, and personal failure surrounding their respective vulnerabilities. Memory of the past *interrupts* these oppressive macro- and micro-narratives.

Metz argues that memory of past suffering is of practical and cognitive value and is the key to resisting political violence, injustice, and oppression. He advocates the practice of narrating "dangerous memories, memories that challenge. These are memories in which earlier experiences flare up and unleash new dangerous insights for the present. For brief moments they illuminate, harshly and piercingly, the problematic character of things we made our peace with a long time ago and the banality of what we take to be 'realism.'"[21] While Metz and other contemporary theologians who follow his lead[22] refer primarily to the need for collective memory of structural violence and injustice, there is a direct connection with the healing effects of remembering personal suffering. The memorial interruption of narratives in which violated vulnerability and patriarchal privilege are somehow "natural" to the order of things must be undertaken in relation to the very intimate and delicate process of remembering personal vulnerability and suffering.

Susan Brison, who reflects philosophically on the experience of trauma (including her own), brings together the personal and political meaning of memory in her groundbreaking work *Aftermath:*

20. Johann Baptist Metz, *Faith in History and Society: Toward a Practical Fundamental Theology* (New York: Crossroad, 2007), 105.
21. Ibid.
22. Jon Sobrino, Elizabeth Johnson, and M. Shawn Copeland are three examples of contemporary theologians influenced by Metz's concept of "dangerous memory."

Violence and the Remaking of the Self. In her view, memory of personal trauma is central to the struggle against violent and oppressive power in part because it "unravels whatever meaning we've found and woven ourselves into." Listening to the stories of those who have suffered trauma is "an experience in *un*learning; both parties are forced into the Dantean gesture of abandoning all safe props as they enter and, without benefit of Virgil, make their uneasy way through its vague domain."[23] For example, in remembering the painful truth about her family's past, Karr unlearns everything she thought she knew about her mother's poisonous personality. While Karr had always suspected that she herself was to blame for her mother's unhappiness, the memory of what really happened interrupted her narrative of self-blame and set her on a new course toward healing. When Karr's readers encounter her memoirs, they too experience healing through interruption of the narrative of loneliness and isolation that tells them that they are alone in their vulnerability and painful experiences.

Gbowee's memorial interruption of her self-loathing narrative had similarly healing personal effects, as did the memorial practices of her Trauma Healing and Reconciliation groups. But Gbowee's public memory of women's roles in Liberia's armed conflict also publicly interrupts the conventional narrative of modern war stories, which reflect male privilege in that men are at the center of the story as perpetrators and saviors, while women are portrayed only in the background as victims.[24] Gbowee begins her autobiography with a damning description of the conventional narrative:

23. Susan Brison, *Aftermath: Violence and the Remaking of the Self* (Princeton: Princeton University Press, 2002), 58.
24. This public memory is most widely known in the film *Pray the Devil Back to Hell*, which features Gbowee as its main protagonist. Her autobiography and speaking engagements are also venues for sharing this public memory.

Commanders are quoted offering confident predictions of victory. Male diplomats make serious pronouncements. And the fighters—always men, whether they are government soldiers or rebels, whether they are portrayed as heroes or thugs—brag, threaten, brandish grisly trophies and shoot off their mouths and their weapons. . . . [L]ook more carefully, at the background, for that is where you will find the women. You'll see us fleeing, weeping, kneeling before our children's graves. In the traditional telling of war stories, women are always in the background. Our suffering is just a sidebar to the main tale; when we're included, it's for "human interest." If we are African, we are even more likely to be marginalized and painted solely as pathetic, hopeless expressions, torn clothes, sagging breasts. Victims. That is the image of us that the world is used to, and the image that sells.[25]

Interrupting this narrative, Gbowee's memorial practice shows the world the truth about Liberian women's agency in the midst of violated vulnerability:

How we hid our husbands and sons from soldiers looking to recruit or kill them. How, in the midst of chaos, we walked miles to find food and water for our families—how we kept life going so that there would be something left to build on when peace returned. And how we created strength in sisterhood, and spoke out for peace on behalf of all Liberians. This is not a traditional war story. It is about an army of women in white standing up when no one else would—unafraid, because the worst things imaginable had already happened to us. It is about how we found the moral clarity, persistence and bravery to raise our voices against war and restore sanity to our land. You have not heard it before, because it is an African woman's story, and our stories are rarely told. I want you to hear mine.[26]

The interruption effected by remembered suffering (and subjectivity) forces individuals and communities to unlearn their received

---

25. Gbowee, *Mighty Be Our Powers*, ix. Metz advocates the memory of suffering in a way that actually seems to echo the conventional (oppressive) dichotomy between victims and perpetrators, leaving little room for recognizing the subjectivity enacted by those who suffer. This is despite his concern for creating a world in which the subjectivity of all is honored and encouraged.

26. Ibid., x.

understandings of reality, especially those understandings that further violate human vulnerability and legitimate domination by those who hold positions of privilege and power.[27] While the unveiling of personal demons, sexual injustice, and socio-political power structures can certainly have depressing effects, it can and does also bring about resilience and resistance in that it awakens individuals and communities from what Jon Sobrino often calls "the sleep of cruel inhumanity," the soporific state that prevents both understanding the realities of violated vulnerability and privilege, and working to overcome them.

Identity

In the history of philosophy, John Locke famously made the connection between our memory of the past and our present self-identity.[28] Edward Casey sums up this association between memory and identity quite clearly: "It is an inescapable fact about human existence that we are made of our memories: *we are what we remember ourselves to be.*"[29] While our memory is never completely within our own control, Casey affirms that there is a certain freedom entailed in this relationship of self to memory—that is, the freedom to participate in the construction of our present self-identity: "I am free in establishing my ongoing and future personal identity by means of my

27. I have argued elsewhere that the conventional understanding of women (especially mothers) as passive victims of violence serves to legitimate violent conflict and undermine peacebuilding. See my article, "Motherhood, Violence, and Peacemaking: A Practical-Theological Lesson from Liberia," in *Violence, Transformation and the Sacred: They Shall Be Called Children of God* [College Theology Society 2012 Annual Volume], ed. Margaret R. Pfeil and Tobias L. Winright (Maryknoll, NY: Orbis, 2012), 160–74.

28. Cf. John Locke, *An Essay Concerning Human Understanding*, ed. J. Yolton (New York: Dutton, 1965), ch. 27, sec. 10. For an in-depth discussion of the connection between memory and identity, cf. also Jeffrey Blustein, *The Moral Demands of Memory* (Cambridge: Cambridge University Press, 2008), 41ff.

29. Edward Casey, *Remembering: A Phenomenological Study* (Bloomington: Indiana University Press, 1987), 290.

own remembering."[30] In situations of severe vulnerability, trauma, and violence, however, victims experience a shattering of self-identity. The freedom of memorial self-definition of which Casey speaks is hindered by a subsequent enslavement to a definition of identity imposed by the victimizer. This is accomplished not only by the violence itself, but by a variety of discourses surrounding that violence and the moral status of its victims. Discourses of privilege, domination, and violence rob victims of the freedom to define their own subjectivity and thus can serve to construct subjects who are passive, acquiescent, self-destructive, and sometimes even destructive toward others.

For those who survive violence, for those who are vulnerable to it, and for those who stand in solidarity with the victims of violence (both living and dead), the practice of remembering suffering can empower resilience and resistance insofar as it effects a rejection of received self-understandings that fragment, devalue, and destroy personal and communal identity. In doing so, it forms and affirms those who remember in a personal and communal identity that asserts their fundamental dignity, worth, and value as relational, embodied, and agential beings. Brison explains that trauma causes an "undoing of the self"; it not only destroys one's sense of a cohesive self, it also severs the relation of the self to one's own body, to others, to the larger community and to humanity as a whole. Indeed, given that the self is essentially embodied and relational, the severing of such ties is part of what undoes the personal identity of the individual.[31] To remember suffering in certain harmful ways could perpetuate this fragmentation and devaluation of identity, to be sure. But the dangerous memory of suffering performed by both Karr and Gbowee is a courageous means of "saving threatened identity" and restoring

30. Ibid., 291.
31. Cf. Brison, *Aftermath*, 39ff.

subjectivity to themselves and others who have been similarly affected by violence. In Metz's words,

> The destruction of memory turns out systematically to hinder identity, to prevent people from becoming subjects or continuing to be subjects in their social-historical contexts. Uprooting slaves and deporting them always tends to destroy their memories, and precisely in this way serves as a powerful reinforcement of their state of being as slaves, their systemic disempowerment in the interest of effecting their complete subjugation. On the other hand, the formation of identity always begins with the awakening of memory.[32]

For Karr and Gbowee, narrating their memories of vulnerability and suffering served to affirm and assert the worth and dignity of their respective personal identities, over and against their intended negation by violence.

On one of her book tours for *The Liars' Club*, Karr met a woman from Chicago who had been raised by a schizophrenic who "received orders from God himself" about what she was to wear on a given day. This woman, Karr relates, survived through stories: "From narratives about childhood, this woman manufactured a self, neither cut off from her past nor mired in it."[33] This insight echoes Karr's own experience. As long as she remained cut off from the past, she was unable to become a healthy and resilient self, capable of facing the vulnerability of her present. It is through telling the stories of her family's past that Karr not only interrupted the myths she and her mother had "cobbled together out of fear," but also constructed a self-identity that would eventually become as luminous as the sunset that she and her mother darkly drove into on the night the truth was revealed.[34] Releasing the pain of the past through memorial practice makes possible the construction of a self-identity capable of

---

32. Metz, *Faith in History and Society*, 75.
33. Karr, *The Liars' Club*, xiv.
34. Ibid., 320.

dealing with the vulnerability of the present. As Gbowee remarks, "[W]omen can't become peacemakers without releasing the pain that keeps them from feeling their own strength."[35] Interrupting—indeed, rejecting—the guilt and self-loathing that characterizes conventional narratives of vulnerability and suffering is thus accompanied by an affirmation of their dignity, self-worth, and identity as women of strength and mothers of promise.

Imagination

Thus far, we have seen that the memory of suffering can empower resilience and resistance insofar as it both interrupts toxic explanations of suffering that we have received from the past and informs and transforms the dignity of our identity in the present. We now turn our attention to the future. Memory of suffering is also productive of resilience and resistance insofar as it engenders an alternative imagination that envisions the possibility of an alternative future. This function of memory involves both the dream that "*otro mundo es posible*" ("another world is possible") and a process of critical discernment as to what that world should look like. In Brison's words, "It is only by remembering and narrating the past—telling our stories and listening to others'—that we can participate in an ongoing, active construction of a narrative of liberation, not one that confines us to a limiting past, but one that forms a background from which a freely imagined—and desired—future can emerge."[36] Empowerment for resilience and resistance is in large part determined by a specific vision of the future informed by the memory of suffering: that is, by a vision of a future in which the suffering of the past and present is

---

35. Gbowee, *Mighty Be Our Powers*, 114.
36. Brison, *Aftermath*, 98.

transformed into an alternative already-but-not-yet world in which the courage, peace, and compassion of divine love reign.

In and of itself, the very act of remembering suffering empowers resilience and resistance because it minimally contains the hope, based on an alternative moral imagination, that the protest will be heard and answered, that one's vulnerability will be recognized and respected, that suffering will not have the last word, that evil is not invincible, and that a better life is on the horizon. Avishai Margalit makes this point well. In his view, the hope of the moral witness to suffering is so heroic because

> people who are subjected to evil regimes intent on destroying the fabric of their moral community easily come to see the regime as invincible and indestructible and stop believing in the very possibility of a moral community. Being a helpless inmate in a Nazi concentration camp or a Bolshevik gulag can make you believe that the thousand years Reich or the unstoppable juggernaut of communist triumph is just the way of the world. The disparity of power between victim and perpetrator confirms every minute what seems to be the invincibility of the regime.[37]

Such is the heroism of the women in Gbowee's Trauma Healing and Reconciliation workshops, who refused to resign themselves to silence in the face of an invincible regime of violence. During one session, when things got particularly painful and intense, Gbowee suggested that they stop. But "[a] very old woman rose up on her walking stick. 'Don't let us stop!' she said. 'The UN brings us food and shelter and clothes, but what you have brought is much more valuable. You've come to hear the stories from our bellies. Stories that no one else asks about. Please, don't stop. Don't ever stop.'"[38] In women like Karr, Gbowee, and the old lady on her walking stick, the memory of suffering (and subjectivity) fosters an alternative

---

37. Avishai Margalit, *The Ethics of Memory* (Cambridge, MA: Harvard University Press, 2002), 155.
38. Gbowee, *Mighty Be Our Powers*, 121.

imagination in which the tyrannical regime of vulnerability, anxiety, privilege, and violence is not invincible and in which a moral community of shared vulnerability and subjectivity is possible.

Indeed, the memory of suffering is essential to imagining that community, since without journeying into the past, there can be no vision for the future. Such is the argument of Andreas Huyssen, who asserts that "memory discourses are absolutely essential to imagine the future and to regain a strong temporal and spatial grounding of life and imagination in a media and consumer society that increasingly voids temporality and collapses space."[39] Karr's narration of her mother's pain, for example, counters the imagination of male privilege that takes as natural a man's right both to dictate his wife's identity and actions and to punish her for her transgression of his privilege. Similarly, Gbowee's memory of both political and domestic violence counters the necrophilic imagination of male domination and masculinist militarism. The imagination fostered by these memories, on the other hand, takes very seriously the need for a vision of the future grounded in equality, nonviolence, and respect for the vulnerability and dignity of each person.

For the Christian imagination, the temptation to abstraction from time and space is an ever-present danger. The hope for an end to suffering in the next world can tend to foster a vision of the future that tempts Christians to ignore the urgency of suffering in the here and now. Remembering concrete suffering—past and present—is an essential corrective to this tendency. It is even more so when situated within what Metz calls the dangerous memory of Jesus Christ and his Passion, Death, and Resurrection. The imagination that emerges from this dangerous memory does not neglect suffering here and now, but rather

---

39. Andreas Huyssen, *Twilight Memories: Marking Time in a Culture of Amnesia* (New York: Routledge, 1995), 6.

holds a particular anticipation of the future as a future for the hopeless, the shattered and oppressed. In this way it is *a dangerous and liberating memory*, which badgers the present and calls it into question, since it does not remember just any open future, but precisely this future, and because it compels believers to be in a continual state of transformation in order to take this future into account.[40]

This moral-religious imagination has the power to prevent abstract flight from the here and now because its vision of the future "grows from the soil of the memory of suffering."[41] When Christians remember suffering, such as the suffering of domestic and political violence, they anticipate "a specific future for humankind as a future for the suffering, for those without hope, for the oppressed, the disabled, and the useless of this earth."[42] But Christians do not simply and passively hope for that future without a transformed moral imagination in which the future of freedom promised by God both demands and empowers true freedom for and reconciliation with perpetrators of violence in social and political life. To remember the perpetrator's vulnerability and pain (such as the vulnerability and pain of Mary Karr's mother Charlie, or the child soldiers of Liberia) can be a powerful means of resisting violation, while remaining hopeful for reconciliation.

Inspiration for Action

According to the foregoing analysis, the memory of suffering in general, and of personal trauma in particular, can empower resilience and resistance insofar as it serves a) to interrupt and critique a harmful status quo, b) to nurture and form those who remember in liberating rather than oppressive personal identities, and c) to foster an

---

40. Metz, *Faith in History and Society*, 88–89. I would distance myself from the apocalypticism of Metz here though.
41. Ibid., 108.
42. Ibid., 112.

alternative moral imagination, or vision of a more just future. Each of these hope-filled functions of this kind of memory would be incomplete, however, without their basis and culmination in the social and political praxis of struggle *against* the injustice of the present reality and *for* the construction of a more just and peaceful world. The memorial practices of both Karr and Gbowee nurture and provide inspiration for that struggle.

This practical function of remembering suffering corresponds to Huyssen's and Young's arguments that the ways in which human communities memorialize the past should have political consequences for both their visions of the future and their actions in the present. For Huyssen, human beings need to remember the past in order to construct their present identities and imagine the future. But, in his view, memorial discourses should be also and especially oriented toward action on behalf of the future, "which will not judge us for forgetting, but for remembering all too well and still not acting in accordance with those memories."[43] Similarly, for James E. Young, who is specifically interested in the art of monuments, memorial practices should serve to function as the basis for social and political action.[44] He suggests that those who remember should always concern themselves with the concrete consequences of memorialization. In other words, they should always ask themselves "to what ends we have remembered. That is, how do we respond to the current moment in light of our remembered past? This is to recognize that the shape of memory cannot be divorced from the actions taken in its behalf, and that memory without consequences contains the seeds of its own destruction."[45] Insofar as Karr's and

43. Huyssen, *Twilight Memories*, 260.
44. Cf. James E. Young, *The Texture of Memory: Holocaust Memorials and Meaning* (New Haven: Yale University Press, 1993), 13.
45. Ibid., 15.

Gbowee's practices of remembering suffering are oriented toward recognizing and respecting vulnerability, as well as overcoming the damaging structures and effects of privilege and violence, they form a basis for compassionate action and thus have concrete historical consequences. We soon will see that the solidarity their memorial practices produce and grow out of is the primary vehicle for these consequences.

Contemplative Kenosis: Re-Membering the Self

According to the foregoing analysis, memory of suffering has the potential to interrupt harmful narratives of vulnerability and privilege, and to re-member a person's dignity and worth as a vulnerable, yet potentially luminous human being. Contemplative practices of silent prayer, meditation on Scripture, and even supplication have the potential to fill out the content of human luminosity and solidify the courage, peace, and compassion of divine love as defining aspects of personal identity. Human vulnerability, the anxiety it begets, and the resultant structures of violence and privilege that produce further vulnerability—these forces all conspire to construct subjects defined by pain and unhealthy personal and structural responses to it. However, Susan Dunlap argues that construction of subjectivity by various oppressive discourses is not cause for despair or resignation. Drawing on Michele Foucault and citing Chris Weedon, she asserts that agential choice in favor of alternative discourses is possible, based on the memory of alternative sources of knowledge:

> In the battle for subjectivity and the supremacy of particular versions of which it is a part, the individual is not merely the passive site of discursive struggle. The individual who has a memory and an already discursively constituted sense of identity may resist particular interpellation or produce new versions of meaning from the conflicts

and contradictions between existing discourses. Knowledge of more than one discourse and the recognition that meaning is plural allows for a measure of choice on the part of the individual and even where choice is not available, resistance is still possible.[46]

Contemplation of divine love can have this effect of re-membering the subject by tapping into an alternative source of previously "forgotten" knowledge. The transformative knowledge attained in contemplation both rejects dominant discourses that devalue personal identity, and opts for subversive discourses that construct subjects whose identity is based on freedom, dignity, and respect.

In the Christian perspective, contemplation as an alternative discourse is situated within the larger alternative discourse and formative practices of the church as a community of memory. The church remembers suffering not as an isolated practice, but within in the context of remembering God's creative and redemptive love for all humanity. Miroslav Volf provides a lengthy but poignant analysis of how the Christian framework thus interpreted can effect healing and hope for wounded self-identity. He argues that, while wrongdoing can distort and paralyze human identity in harmful ways, Christians believe

> that neither what we do nor what we suffer defines us at the deepest level. Though the way we think of and treat ourselves and the way others think of and treat us does shape our identity, no human being can make or unmake us. Instead of being defined by how human beings relate to us, we are defined by how *God* relates to us. We know that fundamentally we are who we are, as unique individuals standing in relation to our neighbors and broader culture because God loves us—to such a great extent that on the cross Jesus Christ, God incarnate, shouldered our sin and tasted our suffering.[47]

---

46. Susan Dunlap, "Discourse Theory and Pastoral Theology," in *Feminist and Womanist Pastoral Theology*, ed. Bonnie J. Miller-McLemore and Brita L. Gill-Austern (Nashville: Abingdon, 1999), 137. Dunlap is citing Chris Weedon, *Feminist Practice and Poststructuralist Theory* (New York: Blackwell, 1987), 106.

Situating the contemplation of divine love within the "dangerous memory" of divine solidarity with human suffering in creation, Incarnation, and the cross affirms the value of human persons, made in the divine image, as loved by God over and against any attempts to violate that love.

What is more, contemplation can be understood as *resistance* to the violation of vulnerability and human dignity insofar as it affirms, forms, and transforms practitioners into their God-given identity as not only loved by God, but as sacred *loci* of divine presence and activity in the world. In Christian language, the contemplative chooses to be defined and transformed by her status as God-bearer, temple of the Holy Spirit, and the body of Christ, as opposed to being defined by the actions of those who have harmed or seek to harm her. In Volf's words again,

> We remember wrongs suffered as people with identities defined by God, not by wrongdoers' evil deeds and their echo in our memory. . . . [B]ehind the unbearable noise of wrongdoing suffered, we can hear in faith the divinely composed music of our true identity. When this happens, memories of mistreatment lose much of their defining power. They have been dislodged from the place they have usurped at the center of the self and pushed to its periphery. They may live in us, but they no longer occupy us; they may cause us pain, but they no longer exhaustively define us.[48]

Remembering suffering within this contemplative framework "re-members" and reclaims bodies, identities, and subjectivities as infused with the power of divine love. This empowers and forms practitioners in an identity that opts for courage, peace, and compassion in the face of vulnerability, pain, and suffering.

---

47. Miroslav Volf, *The End of Memory: Remembering Rightly in a Violent World* (Grand Rapids: Eerdmans, 2006), 79.
48. Ibid., 80.

How does this work? The contemplative practices performed by Karr and Gbowee demonstrate that what facilitates the remembrance of the *imago dei* in the midst of vulnerability and violence is a process of transformative kenosis before the divine. Contemplation empties the subject of harmful discourses and fills her with the power to inhabit her vulnerability with resilience to harm and resistance to violence. Despite her doubts and anger with God, Gbowee's reliance on Isaiah 54 allowed the power of divine love to slowly, gently remove her shame and self-loathing as a victim of war and domestic violence. When Daniel's insults were at their worst—"Stupid. Stupid. Stupid. He used the word so often that even the kids picked up on it"—Gbowee "would cross the road to sit under a palm tree with a young girl who sold fruit. Or huddle in the bedroom and open the Bible to Isaiah. '*I will lay thy stones with fair colors, and lay thy foundations with sapphires.*' Asking God—begging—'Where are you? Where is the promise you made to me?'"[49] When she left Daniel for good and returned to Liberia to live with her family, her father's "description of her as a 'damned baby machine' . . . lodged in [her] like a barb that still gave off poison" even years later.[50] "My sadness and self-hate grew. It seemed that every page I turned was darkness. I was nothing. . . . I was a damned baby machine."[51] Contemplation of Isaiah 54 gave Gbowee a chance to empty out the shame and humiliation of her situation in order to be filled by the promise of divine kindness and the assurance of her identity as a royal and dignified daughter of God. "*Do not be afraid. You will not suffer shame. Do not fear disgrace, you will not be humiliated.*"[52] The kenosis of a false self—and its attendant fear and

---

49. Gbowee, *Mighty Be Our Powers*, 66.
50. Ibid., 80.
51. Ibid., 72.
52. Ibid., 188.

shame—made way for Gbowee to re-member her true self as a strong and courageous woman, at peace with her vulnerability and capable of great compassion for the suffering of others.

Karr, too, was able to re-member her true self only through kenotic practices of what she calls "surrender" to the divine. An avowed atheist, Karr scoffed at the mention of God, prayer, and spirituality in general, until she was finally desperate enough to get down on her knees and snidely ask her higher power, "Where the fuck have you been?"[53] Despite her skepticism, Karr practices and practices this simple act of kneeling before the universe to express gratitude for her blessings and pray for the strength to stay sober. She becomes more convinced of the necessity of practicing surrender in a moment of terrifying temptation when she flees to the bathroom, kneels on the dirty floor, counts her breaths, says a few prayers, and begs for God to keep her away from a drink. Karr remarks on the powerful effect of this practice:

> Those of you who've never prayed before will cackle like crows and scoff at the change I claim has overtaken me. But the focus of my attention has been yanked from the pinballing in my head to south of my neck, where some solidity holds me together. I feel like a calmer human than the one who'd knelt a few minutes before. The primal chattering in my skull has dissipated as if some wizard conjured it away. I walk back to the table with a pearl balanced in my middle. And Lord am I hungry.[54]

Here Karr's practice of spiritual surrender empties her of desperation and fills her with the divine "pearl" of inner peace and confidence, however momentary. Even more powerful is Karr's experience of surrender after admitting herself to the hospital for suicidal intentions:

---

53. Karr, *Lit*, 219.
54. Ibid., 250.

Behind a door, my body bends, and the linoleum rises. I lay my face on my knees in a posture almost fetal. It is, skeptics may say, the move of a slave or brainless herd animal. But around me I feel gathering—let's concede I imagine it—spirit. Such vast quiet holds me, and *the me I've been so lifelong worried about shoring up just dissolves like ash in water.* Just isn't. In its place is this clean air. There's a space at the bottom of an exhale, a little hitch between taking in and letting out that's a perfect zero you can go into. There's a rest point between the heart muscle's close and open—an instant of keenest living when you're momentarily dead. You can rest there.[55]

Karr claims that it was there in the hospital (in her words, "the loony bin") that she truly surrendered—"not full bore, the way saints do, once and for all, blowing away my ego in perfect service to God—not even close. . . . Before, I'd feared surrender would no doubt swerve me into concrete. Before, I'd feared surrender would sand me down to nothing. Now I've started believing it can bloom me more solidly into myself."[56]

As solidly and beautifully as Karr begins to bloom from the soil of her surrendered self, her aging mother's cruel words still could send her reeling back to the hyper-vulnerability and woundedness of her childhood. After an episode in which she responded to her mother's bile with angry and vindictive words, Karr is unable to sleep or even to pray and so she rises to find her mother's old Bible and look up the two verses assigned to her by a friend and fellow recovering addict. What happens astounds her. The exact verses of both passages are underlined in child's blue chalk. The first is particularly poignant and relevant to the present discussion of contemplative kenosis. It is the "Hanging Psalm": "Cleanse me with hyssop, that I may be pure; wash me, make me whiter than snow. Let me hear sounds of joy and gladness; let the bones you have crushed rejoice. Turn

---

55. Ibid., 296. Emphasis mine.
56. Ibid., 299.

away your face from my sins; blot out all my guilt. A clean heart create for me, God; renew in me a steadfast spirit [Ps. 51:7-12]."[57] In this instant, the anger is siphoned out of Karr like poison from a snakebite, as she realizes, "I could be made new, that I am—have always been—loved." In her words, "Maybe all any of us wants is to feel singled out for some long, sweet, quenching draft of love, some open-throated guzzling of it—like what a baby gets at the breast. The mystery of the Bible passages, marked just for me, does that." Allowing divine love to fill her with love, Karr becomes existentially aware of and transformed by her own worth. "I start to arrive in the instant as never before, standing up in it as if pushed from behind like a wave, for it feels as if I was made—from all the possible shapes a human might take—not to prove myself worthy but to refine the worth I'm formed from, acknowledge it, own it, spend it on others."[58] Kenotic surrender to the power of divine love does not eliminate Karr's vulnerability, but rather empowers her to inhabit it and the pain it has caused her with greater courage, peace, and compassion for the vulnerability of others, including her mother.

Surrender, kenosis, acceptance of vulnerability. These are all dangerous words for feminists concerned with undoing hierarchies of domination and putting an end to the abuses of power that violate the humanity and dignity of women and other oppressed persons. The last thing women in general and mothers in particular need is to be asked to empty themselves or surrender to a power other than themselves. Sarah Coakley's work can help us to understand how practices of contemplative kenosis like those performed by Gbowee and Karr need not perpetuate patterns of women's self-abnegation, but rather have the potential to empower practitioners in the resilience and resistance that comes from union with divine love.

57. Ibid., 381.
58. Ibid., 384.

In Coakley's view, powerlessness and dependency are problems in society that feminist theologians have rightly attempted to redress. However, Coakley avers that our Enlightenment-inspired fear of heteronomy and vulnerability is symptomatic of a dangerous spiritual crisis and can actually lead to the continuation of oppression.[59] Patriarchy and its hierarchies of oppression need to be overturned, it is true. And vulnerability to raw power can be (has been) horrifically damaging to women. But Coakley sets out to investigate how women might empty the powers of patriarchy without turning around and filling themselves up with the very same kind of abusive power they oppose. She thus seeks theoretical and practical ways of holding together appropriate forms of kenosis and empowerment. She seeks a means by which women might be empowered to resist domination while at the same time emptying *themselves* of the desire to meet vulnerability with a will to dominate vulnerable others. What Coakley argues is needed to resolve this seeming opposition between power and vulnerability is a kenotic stance of openness and vulnerability to God, who alone can fill the human person up with the nonabusive divine power necessary for confronting, deflecting, and discerning the violation of vulnerability wrought by worldly powers and principalities (such as privilege).

What Coakley describes here is the need for a spiritual extension of Christic kenosis. This places us in the paradoxical, and for most feminists, problematic realm of losing one's life in order to save it. This is precisely the kenotic paradox Karr began to inhabit as she more and more thoroughly sought to embody the Prayer of St. Francis: "It is in dying to self that we are born to eternal life."[60] In response to Daphne Hampson's critique of kenosis as perhaps

59. Sarah Coakley, *Powers and Submissions: Spirituality, Philosophy, and Gender* (Malden, MA: Blackwell, 2002).
60. Cf. Karr, *Lit*, 297.

appropriate for men, but damaging to women, Coakley offers a detailed history of various interpretations of Christ's kenosis in the Incarnation and on the cross. A thorough examination of these interpretations and how they measure up to Hampson's critique far exceeds the scope of the task at hand. Coakley herself ascribes to the interpretation of Christic kenosis as a choice from the start to renounce worldly (that is, abusive) forms of power, which are in fact false powers and are sometimes wrongly identified as divine. This interpretation of kenosis as a refusal to grasp at abusive power (as in clinging to privilege) represents a way of uniting human vulnerability with divine empowerment. The human choice of Jesus never to have certain forms of power kenotically opens up the space for nonabusive divine strength to be made perfect in what appears to be human weakness.

Though this interpretation is not the real butt of Hampson's critique, the feminist concern with women's self-effacement and vulnerability to worldly powers could easily apply here, and with just cause. But Coakley argues that we must not fall into the same trap of gender stereotypes that we seek to upend. We should not assume that patterns of domination and the need for kenosis only apply to men and never to women. Nor should we assume that the power that men (generally) hold should be sought by way of compensation by women. We are all capable of abusing worldly power and are all thus in need of some form of *askesis* to avoid doing so. Therefore, Coakley argues that the feminist presumption of women's need for power must be accompanied by both an account of what kind of power we need and a practical means of avoiding the "masculinist" power we rightly denounce.

The kind of power we need, according to Coakley, is not abusive and domineering power, not the power of privilege, but the nonbullying power of a God who works most perfectly through human vulnerability and weakness. The spiritual practice that Coakley advocates as a means of women's empowerment through kenosis is the practice of silent prayer. This form of contemplative practice is the spiritual extension of the Christic kenosis described above. Coakley never describes this practice in detail, but she does explain that, in wordless prayer, the believer empties herself of the human tendency to grasp at worldly power. Here the practitioner makes the ascetical commitment to lay herself bare and cede to the divine, thus patiently opening herself up to self-transformation through divine empowerment. There is certainly risk and pain involved in this type of contemplative practice, but it is the empowering risk and pain that engages the believer in the pattern of cross and resurrection. It is not an invitation to be battered by God or by other human beings. Nor does it lead to submission to unjust suffering or self-abnegation. Rather it is the place of human transformation in the divine and a means of empowerment to give prophetic voice in the face of abuse. The kenosis that takes place in this practice of contemplative kenosis is not the essentialist's stance of "feminine" passivity and receptivity. It is not the "complement" to the masculinist power or privilege, but rather its undoing. In the end, the fruits of this practice are what is most important. For Coakley, they include prophetic and courageous resistance to oppression and nonviolent destruction of the false idol of patriarchy. Through kenotic prayer, the practictioner is filled with the power to struggle against hierarchies of domination without giving in to their ever-present allure. In other words, contemplative kenosis has the potential to empower both privileged and marginalized persons to renounce their own desires to grasp at privilege, while at the same time resisting the manifestations of privilege in the structural injustice and violence of prevailing social and political systems.

On the one hand, Coakley's argument for contemplative kenosis offers a helpful analytic tool for understanding the process of self-emptying and empowerment experienced by Karr and Gbowee. Both women were unduly vulnerable as a result of the violence and abuse they had experienced. Both, however, could have easily taken their anger and pain out on vulnerable others in their care—for both women, their children, and for Karr, her aging mother. In fact, for both women, the realization of the harm that they were causing their own children led them to desire transformation. Certainly their spiritual kenosis was in part intended to empty them of the temptation to wield "worldly power" in the form of child (or elder) abuse. On the other hand, Coakley overlooks the more predominant object of the contemplative kenosis experienced by both Gbowee and Karr. For both women, it was the pain and anxiety caused by internal discourses of self-loathing and self-blame that needed to be annihilated in order for their true selves as recipients and bearers of divine love to bloom. Indeed, it is only the removal of such destructive barriers to self-transcendence that would prevent both women from turning into the monsters that they were running from.

Beverly Lanzetta offers a helpful analysis of this particular need for the self-emptying of harmful discourses that produce soul-suffering in women (and other marginalized persons). According to Lanzetta, the problem of violated vulnerability is not solely a structural problem, but also a spiritual one, since "violence against a woman is directed first and foremost to the core of her nature—to her unique embodiment of the divine in this world."[61] Spiritual and material violation are intertwined such that "[w]hat harms a woman's soul reverberates in her physical, emotional, and mental spheres, generating suffering in every area of her life. At the same time,

---

61. Beverly Lanzetta, *Radical Wisdom: A Feminist Mystical Theology* (Minneapolis: Fortress Press, 2005), 2.

violations of a woman in the material realm have a direct impact on women's integrity, health, and moral agency."[62] For this reason, Lanzetta argues for the need to understand spiritual practices that "confront and alleviate the misogyny that inhabits [women's] consciousness."[63] In conversation with contemporary feminist theological scholarship, she analyzes the contemplative practices of Julian of Norwich and Teresa of Avila as techniques employed by marginalized souls to achieve their spiritual potential. The resultant feminist mystical theology, which Lanzetta calls the *via feminina*, follows a mystical path of apophasis, or un-saying, of that which negatively defines women:

> *Via feminina* traces a feminist path of the apophasis—or un-saying—of "woman." In using the term "un-saying" to refer to women's liberation, I intend a mystical path that enters into and moves through a woman's "nothingness"—that is, what diminishes, injures, humiliates, or shames her—to a positive affirmation of her dignity and worth. By negating all that falsely defines her, a woman steps outside the symbolic order of culture, religion, *and* God, giving up and subverting her capacity to be identified by patriarchal cultures.[64]

Responding to potential critics who might dismiss her mystical claims as limited by the privilege of her social location, Lanzetta suspects that what she describes may be actually present in spiritual practices across diverse contextual landscapes. Her experience and knowledge lead her to wonder if this apophatic process that "transforms soul oppression is not implicitly present, even as it has remained unnamed, in the lives and spiritual experiences of a great many mystics and ordinary people today."[65] The above analysis of kenotic practices employed by Karr and Gbowee would seem to confirm this suspicion

62. Ibid.
63. Ibid.
64. Ibid., 22.
65. Ibid., 24.

that diverse methods of overcoming soul-suffering may well share in common some form of un-saying or kenosis of the harmful power that systems of privilege and violence previously granted to vulnerability and pain in the life of the practitioner.

Solidarity: Re-Membering Communities of Shared Vulnerability

The practices of memory and contemplation described and analyzed above are fulfilled (and, in turn, reinvigorated) in the ordinary and extraordinary practice of solidarity. Overcoming anxiety and coping with vulnerability in healthy, nonviolent ways requires both interpersonal and structural solidarity, defined here as the lived commitment to sharing the burdens of vulnerability in community (Gal. 6:2).[66] This is the opposite of privilege, described in chapter 2 as the structural mismanagement of vulnerability in which various resources for coping with vulnerability are concentrated in the hands of certain populations and denied to others. Communities of solidarity ultimately lighten the burden of vulnerability for all their members, even while entering into such vulnerability-sharing situations seems to require a certain degree of self-sacrifice for some. Both Karr and Gbowee risk the adventure of entering into solidarity with vulnerable others, and the result is a lightened spiritual load for both of these women and the vulnerable others with whom they form community.

---

66. This section is primarily concerned with the liberating *interior* effects of solidarity. An extensive body of literature on solidarity exists in Christian ethics, liberation theology, and Catholic social thought. See, e.g., Jon Sobrino and Juan Hernandez Pico, *Theology of Christian Solidarity* (Maryknoll, NY: Orbis, 1985); Gregory Baum and Robert Ellsberg, eds., *The Logic of Solidarity: Commentaries on Pope John Paul II's Encyclical "On Social Concern"* (Maryknoll, NY: Orbis, 1989); Anselm Kyongsuk Min, *The Solidarity of Others in a Divided World* (New York: T. & T. Clark, 2004); Gerald Beyer, *Recovering Solidarity: Lessons from Poland's Unfinished Revolution* (Notre Dame: University of Notre Dame Press, 2010).

Gbowee writes very honestly about the effect that solidarity had on her ability to meet her own pain and vulnerability with courage, peace, and compassion.

> When you're depressed, you get trapped inside yourself and lose the energy to take the actions that might make you feel better. You hate yourself for that. You see the suffering of others but feel incapable of helping them, and that makes you hate yourself, too. The hate makes you sadder, the sadness makes you more helpless, the helplessness fills you with more self-hate. Working at the THRP [Trauma Healing and Reconciliation Project] broke that cycle for me. I wasn't sitting home thinking endlessly about what a failure I was; I was doing something, something that actually helped people. The more I did, the more I could do, the more I wanted to do, the more I saw needed to be done.[67]

In concert with memory and contemplation, solidarity broke the cycle of vulnerability, anxiety, and depression for Gbowee. It is what gave her (and her fellow peacemakers) the personal strength to build a communal movement of women taking action for peace in her country. The healing experienced in remembering personal trauma was an initial form of solidarity that found its fulfillment in the solidarity of collective action for peace. Gbowee remarks of the more than two thousand women who gathered each day to pray for and demand peace that "[t]he women of Liberia had been taken to our physical, psychological and spiritual limits. But over the last few months, we had discovered a new source of power and strength: each other."[68] These women made the decision to share the burden of their vulnerability in a community of action that resisted the heinous violations of vulnerability taking place in Liberia's armed conflict. Solidarity gave them the power and strength to step out and "do the impossible."[69] In Gbowee's words, "We hadn't [yet] brought peace to

---

67. Gbowee, *Mighty Be Our Powers*, 85.
68. Ibid., 137.
69. *Pray the Devil Back to Hell*, DVD.

Liberia, but our work was emboldening the nation. God's hands were under our effort and I saw daily how right it had been to begin the work by mobilizing at the bottom. You can tell people of the need to struggle, but when the powerless start to see that they really can make a difference, nothing can quench the fire."[70] Solidarity set these ordinary women on fire with the luminosity of divine love in action.

Solidarity follows from and flows into both memory of suffering and kenotic contemplation. The self-identity described above as empowered by the memory of suffering and the contemplative remembrance of the self is not that of an isolated monad, but of radically social human beings constituted by and called into solidarity with one another. Brison affirms that victims of violence cannot find healing and liberation in seclusion, but only in relation to a community that listens to their stories and thus enables the victim to become a subject again.[71] Furthermore, relating memories of suffering is also an act of solidarity in itself—an act in which the storyteller is the agent of transformation for the listening/reading community. As Karr observes, stories of suffering "feed us the way the bread of communion does, with a nourishment that seems to form new flesh."[72] In the community of readers she has assembled around her memoirs of vulnerability and recovery, Karr has achieved her "dream response" as a writer: "to plug a reader into some wall outlet deep in the personal psychic machine that might jumpstart him or her into a more feeling way of life."[73] There is a reciprocity that takes place in such a memorial exchange. Collective memory of suffering affirms the identity and worth of those who suffer by and with the result of reintegrating them into the web of social relations that constitute relational subjectivity. In turn, however, the

70. Gbowee, *Mighty Be Our Powers*, 151.
71. Cf. e.g., Brison, *Aftermath*, xi, 56, and 64.
72. Karr, *The Liars' Club*, xiv.
73. Ibid., xv.

identity of the community is also constituted and fostered in and through the practice of listening and remembering.[74] The burden of vulnerability—in its generic and specific forms—is shared by all in this memorial form of solidarity.

There is also a connection between contemplation and solidarity. From a Christian perspective, the self-identity realized in kenotic contemplation begins with an individual's personal subjectivity before God but also, in the words of Metz, "has to be concerned precisely with how [all] persons can become and live as subjects in situations of misery and oppression."[75] Indeed, it is largely in and through solidarity—a compassionate and empowering response to the vulnerable other—that the identity of human beings as *imago dei* is constituted and union with the divine is realized. Although contemplative practices are often solitary and focus on the individual, the empowered identity that they construct can only be formed and continually realized and re-formed in solidarity and community with others. The specific formation of Christian identity—both individual and communal—is therefore necessarily rooted in solidarity. The power of this identity is derived from divine love's solidarity with humanity, which empowers human beings to realize their oneness with the divine, with humanity, and with all of creation. This unitive love extends to the living and the dead; memory of those who have suffered and of those who continue to suffer today is central to manifesting that love. More radically still, it also extends solidarity to the violators of vulnerability and the perpetrators of harm.

---

74. According to James E. Young, "[M]emorials provide the sites where groups of people gather to create a common past for themselves, places where they tell the constitutive narratives, their 'shared' stories of the past. They become communities precisely by having shared (if only vicariously) the experiences of their neighbors. At some point, it may even be the activity of remembering together becomes an event in itself that is to be shared and remembered" (*The Texture of Memory*, 6–7).

75. Metz, *Faith in History and Society*, 64.

Both Karr and Gbowee struggled to extend solidarity to include perpetrators of harm. Practices of both memory and contemplation helped them in this process. Karr's commitment to memorial understanding of her mother's "blamelessness" in her traumatic childhood is itself an extension of solidarity to a vulnerable and suffering woman. Furthermore, Karr's contemplative kenosis of the anger she felt toward her mother is what finally gave her peace and allowed her to extend compassion to and enter into solidarity with even the tangible source of her own pain. The practice of getting on her knees in surrender to the divine is what finally facilitated this expansion of compassion and solidarity. Kneeling before the divine had the de-centering effect described by a recovering addict Karr met at a halfway house during her period of resistance to acknowledging a "higher power." Karr asked this woman,

> What kind of God wants me to get on my knees and supplicate myself like a coolie? Janice busts out with a cackling laugh, You don't do it for God. You do it for yourself. All this is for you . . . the prayer, the meditation, even the service work. I do it for myself too. I'm not that benevolent.

> How does getting on your knees do anything for you? I say. Janice says, It makes you the right size. You do it to teach yourself something. When my disease has ahold of me, it tells me my suffering is special or unique, but it's the same as everybody's. I kneel to put my body in that place, because otherwise, my mind can't grasp it.[76]

In solidarity, individuals live out this divine truth: that their own vulnerability and pain is not located at the center of the universe. Recognizing this truth in community with others means respecting, protecting, understanding, and even sharing in the vulnerability of others. Both memory and contemplative kenosis cultivate the courage, peace, and compassion necessary for this to happen.

76. Karr, *Lit*, 241.

Gbowee also extends solidarity to perpetrators of harm—specifically the former child soldiers she meets through her work with the Trauma Healing and Reconciliation project. Although she doubts that she ever truly will be able to forgive these boys, she recognizes that peacemaking requires solidarity with them, that they might "rediscover their humanity so they can once again become productive members of their communities."[77] When Gbowee demonstrated unflinching courage in the face of their threatening postures, the former child soldiers started calling her "General" and began talking to her about their past experiences and current problems. Gbowee was then able to get "to know them as something more than their frightening poses." Her contemplative approach to their otherness—her desire to listen to, understand, and enter into relationship with them—led her to appreciate their plight as wounded and vulnerable beings:

> The boy who'd bragged about the fun of raping middle-aged women had joined a rebel group at twelve because he thought it would make him a man. Now he was an amputee, and his mother had turned her back on him, saying she never gave birth to a one-leg child.
>
> Sam Brown had been eight or nine when his family fled their village during the war; his mother had so many children she didn't notice that she'd left him behind. The fighters who moved in used him to fetch water, and when he was ten, he joined a Small Boys Unit. One day, he fell into an ambush and was shot in the arm. Infection set in, and the arm had to come off. Now he was fifteen and an alcoholic.
>
> Some of the girls who picked up guns did so because it was a way to protect themselves from rape. A number of the ex-combatants' girlfriends and wives had been abducted as young girls. Raped repeatedly. Violence was the only language they new. And yet . . . at times they talked to their children with love the way I talked to mine.

---

77. Gbowee, *Mighty Be Our Powers*, 82.

> Like me, they hoped their kids would lead better lives. I could see my younger self in them—the broken dreams, the rage.[78]

Listening to these stories was itself a form of solidarity: simply recognizing the pain of another is a powerful way to lighten the load of his psychic vulnerability by sharing even just a small piece of it. Gbowee also did what she could to help these "enemies" face their vulnerability through material assistance and social services.

The radically universal nature of divine love extends solidarity to all vulnerable beings, including those who have violated the vulnerability and dignity of others. Human participation in the universality of divine solidarity is no easy task. It is incredibly difficult to recognize the vulnerability of and extend compassion and care to individuals (and groups) who have raped, pillaged, and terrorized even the most vulnerable members of society. But it is even difficult to remain in solidarity with nonperpetrators who share similar goals of peace, justice, and equality. For instance, Gbowee relates that the women's movement in Liberia appeared effortlessly united from the outside, but was plagued with divisions on the inside. Almost everything the movement did "required endless work" and the politics of the movement were "exhausting." According to Gbowee, age, class, and education-related differences contribute to the fact that "[i]n Liberia, as in the US and other countries, it's a sad truth that we often spend more time fighting each other than anyone else."[79] The divisions that she faces in the movement, and the enormity of the work to be done, take their toll. Gbowee struggled with excessive alcohol consumption for years until a recent health incident forced her to quit drinking, but she still battles with bouts of depression and loneliness: "I still don't sleep easily and I still wake up too early." Solidarity, then, requires more than contemplative kenosis. It requires

78. Ibid., 91–92.
79. Ibid., 144.

relational kenosis, in which the individuals entering into a community of shared vulnerability are willing to pay a certain price for solidarity, which according to Metz is "a commitment, without counting the cost, to shattered lives."[80] The cost involved for Gbowee has been primarily psychological and emotional. For others, it may be material, political, financial, or social. As Nussbaum points out, and as the Incarnation reveals, the virtuous life exposes its practitioners to increased vulnerability.[81] This is especially true of the virtue of solidarity.

Mary Grey argues from an ecofeminist perspective that the sacrifice involved in solidarity is "not only redeemable [as a concept] but also essential [as a practice] within a life-style that chooses life for all, joy and justice for all, sustainable living for all." Such sacrifice is "inevitable because it will visibly and dramatically clash with the status quo."[82] Grey, too, uses the language of kenosis to indicate the very real difficulties that accompany recognizing vulnerability and sharing in the vulnerability and suffering of others. For her, though, kenosis is what makes theologically possible the incarnation of Christ and the enablement of "a new vital force of divine presence."[83] I interpret the concluding words of Gbowee's autobiography to be a powerful, though implicit, description of how this vital, kenotic force

---

80. Metz, *Faith in History and Society*, 209. Metz takes a self-sacrificial approach to solidarity, insisting that solidarity should not be thought of in terms of equal exchange between partners forming an alliance of interest. From the perspective of Christian discipleship, he argues, there should be no thought of serving one's own interests when entering into relationships of solidarity with others, especially suffering others. While I agree with his critique of pragmatic humanism here, the main goal of this section on solidarity has been to demonstrate how solidarity actually contributes to the healing and flourishing of the individual entering into community. Solidarity, at least ideally, *is* of benefit to *all* participants in its bonds, despite (or perhaps because of?) the kenosis it entails.

81. See Martha Nussbaum, *The Fragility of Goodness: Luck and Ethics in Greek Tragedy and Philosophy* (Cambridge: Cambridge University Press, 1986), 336.

82. Mary Grey, *Sacred Longings: The Ecological Spirit and Global Culture* (Minneapolis: Fortress Press, 2004), 188.

83. Ibid., 201.

of divine love has been unleashed by the solidarity embodied in the Liberian women's peace movement. Gbowee states that, because of the solidarity of the women of this movement,

> I believe that in the end, tyranny will never succeed, and goodness will always vanquish evil. Although I may not see it in my lifetime, peace will overcome. I believe, I *know*, that if you have unshakable faith in yourself, in your sisters, and in the possibility of change, you can do almost anything. The work is hard. The immensity of what needs to be done is discouraging. But you look at communities that are struggling on a daily basis. *They* keep on—and in the eyes of the people there, you are a symbol of hope. And so you, too, must keep on. You are not at liberty to give up. *Don't stop*, echoes the older Liberian lady's voice. *Don't ever stop*. My answer to her: I never will.[84]

In these words Gbowee brings together both the cost and the promise that solidarity holds for overcoming the personal and societal effects of violently managed vulnerability. Solidarity is hard work. It requires sacrifice. But it instills hope, alleviates anxiety, and empowers its practitioners to inhabit their own vulnerability with courage, peace, and compassion for the vulnerability of others. This is because, sacramentally speaking, solidarity signifies and manifests our greatest hope for communion with God and all of humanity.

Conclusion: Embracing the Human Condition

In this chapter I have drawn on the narratives of Mary Karr and Leymah Gbowee to propose and analyze three families of practice that have the potential to fill human beings in general, and Christians in particular, with the power of divine love in the midst of a vulnerable existence. Memory of suffering, contemplative kenosis, and solidarity all work together to function in the narratives of Karr and Gbowee as resources for resilience and resistance. These practices

---

84. Gbowee, *Mighty Be Our Powers*, 229–30.

offer access to the courage, peace, and compassion necessary for inhabiting vulnerability with less anxiety and greater awareness of the vulnerability of others. It is important to note that these practices are not magical cures for the problem of anxiety; much less do they "solve" the problem of vulnerability. Furthermore, like all human performances, these practices have multiple outcomes within and across contexts. What is helpful in the experience of one practitioner can be experienced as unhelpful or even downright oppressive for another.[85] Discernment is necessary. The criterion for discernment is how well a given practice allows for the practitioner to cope with her own particular vulnerability in healthy, rather than self-destructive or violent ways. For Karr and Gbowee, memory, contemplation, and solidarity have proven to be liberating forces for good in their own lives as mothers and more, as well as in the lives of their

85. According to literature in performance theory, a given human practice is capable of creating multiple outcomes and multiple subjectivities in and across contexts. This dynamic view of human practice rests on the fundamental claim of performance theory, which insists that the performance of ritual action does not simply symbolize something, it *creates* something for practitioners and their audiences. Every ritual performance creates something different; the same ritual performance can create different outcomes for different people at the same time; and the same ritual performance can even create something different for the same person over the course of time. According to Catherine Bell's article on performance, there can be no one definitive interpretation of a set of ritual actions. Each action, rather, is intended and experienced in a plurality of ways. See Catherine Bell, "Performance," in *Critical Terms for Religious Studies*, ed. Mark Taylor (Chicago: University of Chicago Press, 1998), 218. Joyce Burkhalter Flueckiger's work on performance in her book *Gender and Genre in the Folklore of Middle India* provides a key insight into how and why this creation of multiple outcomes occurs, even within the same basic genre of performance. She employs the communication model set forth by Roman Jakobson and adapted by ethnographers of speaking to identify several key variables that influence the outcome of any given speech act, performance, or ritual action. These variables include addresser, addressee, context, message, contact and code. According to Flueckiger, "The model sets up the variables of context and text as interdependent components of a system, so that any one of components may shift depending on the identity or content of any one of the others." Since a change in any one of the variables involved in performance can produce a shift in outcome, performance is inherently dynamic. A comparative study of the same ritual genre performed in two different contexts, for example, will thus show that the genre is capable of producing multiple results. And a comparative study of different genres from within the same repertoire might highlight this multiplicity even further. Joyce Burkhalter Flueckiger, *Gender and Genre in the Folklore of Middle India* (Ithaca, NY: Cornell University Press, 1996), 22.

respective families and communities. The practical insights gleaned from Karr's and Gbowee's narratives are applicable to the mission of Christian churches as communities of shared vulnerability. These communities and their members are charged with the task of bearing one another's burdens (Gal. 6:2) and sharing with anyone in need (Acts 2:4). While a blueprint for ecclesial sharing of vulnerability in practices of memory, contemplation, and solidarity exceeds the scope of this volume, I would like to end this chapter with the following suggestion: Perhaps faith communities ruled in the name of the Father would benefit from lessons learned from mothers like Mary Karr and Leymah Gbowee, whose practices of resilience and resistance have empowered them to replace the pursuit of total control with the courage, peace, and compassion necessary for embracing the human condition in all of its tragic and beautiful vulnerability.

9

Conclusion

Contemplating Vulnerability

In his contemplative writings, Nicholas of Cusa encounters God in the "coincidence of contradictories," a reality that lies beyond the wall of paradise, where infinity and finitude, truth and image, God and creation, meet.[1] Nicholas perceives that Jesus resides within that wall, for in him the divine creating nature and the human created nature are visibly and lovably one.[2] In the language of this theological anthropology, Nicholas would say that the Incarnation represents the divine embrace of human vulnerability, without ceasing to possess the power of divine goodness and love. On the one hand, this theological project has drawn on maternal experiences to demonstrate that this coincidence of opposites in human life is unlikely, if not impossible. Human existence in this world is marked by embodiment, relationality, perishing, and moral ambiguity. All

---

1. Nicholas of Cusa, "On the Vision of God," in *Selected Spiritual Writings*, trans. H. Lawrence Bond (Mahwah, NJ: Paulist, 1997), 251.
2. Ibid., 276.

of these elements of our condition render human beings vulnerable to bodily pain, psychic anguish, spiritual suffering, moral demise, and ultimately death. Vulnerability lays us bare to forces beyond our control, forces that can have the power to destroy our ability to choose goodness and love, forces that can destroy our lives and the lives of those we love. Human happiness, especially when it is understood as *eudaemonia*, is a fragile and contingent endeavor. In the words of Reta Winters, whose maternal grief haunts the pages of Carol Shields's novel *Unless*, "Unless you're lucky, unless you're healthy, fertile, unless you're loved and fed, unless you're clear about your sexual direction, unless you're offered what others are offered, you go down in the darkness, down in despair."[3] Even the luckiest among us are threatened with darkness and despair due to the anxiety that accompanies the universal vulnerability of the human condition. Anxiety breeds violence, which begets further vulnerability for self and for others. It seems that Nicholas's coincidence of opposites is impossible in this life, even for those whose only misfortune lies in the eventual necessity of death.

On the other hand, resources in the Christian tradition testify that the coincidence of opposites found in God and embodied in Jesus is precisely the deepest truth of the human condition. With all the beauty that his sacramental imagination can offer, Nicholas professes that God has led him to a place in which he sees God's "absolute face to be the natural face of all nature, the face which is the absolute entity of all being, the art and the knowledge of all that can be known."[4] The nature of divine love is characterized by the impossible coincidence of power and vulnerability. Jesus is the human manifestation of that coincidence. His embodiment of divine love in the midst of a vulnerable, wounded, and wounding

3. Carol Shields, *Unless* (New York: Fourth Estate, 2002), 224.
4. Nicholas of Cusa, "On the Vision of God," 246.

world points to the profound truth of divine love's image, presence, and potentiality in each and every vulnerable human being. The power of divinity upholds the divinity of humanity, even in the most vulnerable of situations. The face of divine love is irrevocably—even if inconceivably—"the face of all faces."[5] This is a vulnerable face, a face that experiences and mourns the violation and destruction of creation. But it is also a face whose loving gaze never abandons suffering humanity, even in the darkest night when we can only see dimly, as if through a mirror (1 Cor. 13:12), or not at all.

Human life and human love takes place within this coincidence of vulnerability and power, darkness and luminosity, fragility and beauty. Mothers live and breathe this reality in their very flesh, and in their conflicted and ambiguous and often loving hearts. By no means do women's experiences of maternity and natality offer "proof" of the concurrence between power and vulnerability in human life and love. However, the mothers whose narratives and analyses grace these pages do point to this profound truth about the paradoxical nature of human existence. This very truth is offered eloquently and in more pedestrian terms by recovering addict and bulimic, writer, and mother of three, Glennon Melton: "Life is brutal. But it's also beautiful. Brutiful, I call it. Life's brutal and beautiful are woven together so tightly that they can't be separated. Reject the brutal, reject the beauty. So now I embrace both, and I live well and hard and real."[6] The women highlighted in these pages—from Mary of Nazareth to Leymah Gbowee to Mary Karr—witness to the possibility of embodying divine love, of living well and hard and real, in the midst of vulnerable, painful, and frightening circumstances. These women reveal the spark of divinity that catches fire and shines through persons and communities who learn, slowly and painfully,

5. Ibid.
6. Glennon Melton, "Meet Glennon," http://momastery.com/blog/about-glennon/.

to inhabit human vulnerability with courage, peace, and compassion. Their resilience in the wake of harm and their resistance to the violation of themselves and vulnerable others is a powerful testament to the possibility of passing beyond the wall of paradise and embodying the power and vulnerability of love. When Leymah Gbowee describes what she and her sister peacemakers did to demand peace in their country, she remarks that they "stepped out to do the impossible."[7] Their witness—a maternal witness, but also a more broadly human witness—demonstrates the coincidence of the impossibility and possibility, the tragedy and beauty, the vulnerability and immense power of love.

The witness of courageous women who inhabit vulnerability with the power of love offers a glimpse of what redemption looks like within the finite and fragile conditions of human existence in this life. Their witness also offers a glimmer of hope for a world in which human beings might manage their individual and collective vulnerability with greater respect and compassion for themselves and for the vulnerability of others. However, it would be overly optimistic to end on this hopeful note. In his considerations of suffering and the human condition, Edward Schillebeeckx points out that human resistance to suffering and evil is always relativized by the transitory nature of human life and the inevitability of death. In his words, "[A]t the deepest level, at the level of our outline of an earthly, human future, we are . . . confronted with the final fiasco of our efforts at resisting evil. Death above all shows that we are deluded if we think that we can realize on earth a true, perfect and universal salvation for all and every individual."[8] The maternal experience of fistula as a living death, the loss of a child to the violent mechanisms of

---

7. *Pray the Devil Back to Hell*, DVD, directed by Gini Reticker (New York: Fork Films, 2009).

8. Edward Schillebeeckx, *Christ: The Experience of Jesus as Lord* (New York: Crossroad, 1980), 726–27.

slavery and patriarchy, the massacre of innocents, the ravages of war, and the horror of sexual violence. These are but a few examples of vulnerability as the impingement of death—of nonbeing—on human life. These experiences cannot be erased or justified by any theology or spiritual practice of divine love. At least in this lifetime, "perfect and universal salvation" is an impossibility.

Furthermore, Schillebeeckx continues his remarks on the futility of resistance to evil with the assertion that "human salvation is only salvation, *being whole*, when it is universal and complete. There cannot really be talk of salvation as long as there is still suffering, oppression and unhappiness alongside the personal happiness that we experience, in our immediate vicinity or further afield."[9] The experience of redemption at work in the narratives of Mary of Nazareth, Mary Karr, and Leymah Gbowee is powerful, and offers profound lessons for embodying the power and vulnerability of divine love in this finite and fragile world. However, Schillebeeckx reminds us that this localized experience of redemption is relativized not only by one's own personal confrontation with death, but also by the suffering, oppression, and unhappiness of vulnerable others in our wounded and wounding world. The challenge of this reminder is to meet the vulnerability of others with ever-expanding, radical compassion. It is to recognize that personal resilience is incomplete without concern for the resilience of others, and that even communal resistance to the violation of vulnerability is incomplete without vigilance for the vulnerability of all others, including our enemies. This is a tall order for human beings, who tend to experience greater concern for "a broken mirror at home than a burning house abroad."[10] The vulnerability of our own *philia* is of ultimate concern, and our *eros* for those we love can easily eclipse the vulnerability of

---

9. Ibid., 727. Emphasis mine.
10. David Hume, *A Treatise of Human Nature* (London: Oxford University Press, 1960), 428–29.

others. Mothers exemplify this tension in the difficulty they often experience transcending their passionate love for their own children to embrace the well-being of all humanity as cause for care and concern. The particularity of human *philia*, then, is a challenge to expanding compassion and solidarity beyond our immediate vicinity. For this reason, the Christian tradition has often seen a tension between *agape*, on the one hand, and *philia* and *eros* on the other.[11] But the particularity of passionate love for our family and friends can also be a powerful resource for cultivating universal compassion and enacting a more extensive network of solidarity. A maternal perspective once again proves to be illustrative of how this might work.

Before she was killed, a Nicaraguan revolutionary woman wrote to her daughter, "A mother isn't just someone who gives birth and cares for her child. A mother feels the pain of all children, of all peoples, as if they had been born from her womb."[12] While I appreciate the sentiment of these words, and can easily get caught up in the poetry of their revolutionary fervor, I am not sure they convey the truth about the powerful resources that the *particularity* of maternal passion and practice can offer in the moral struggle to extend compassion and care beyond one's inner circle to the vulnerability of distant and different others (including enemies). That struggle—and it is a struggle, not something that comes naturally—is rooted in the particularity of intimate relationships of care for one's own children and remains rooted there as it expands in solidarity to embrace the particular importance of every mother and every mother's child. Women who have banded together in solidarity based on their

---

11. See Anders Nygren, *Agape and Eros: A Study of the Christian Idea of Love* (Philadelphia: Westminster, 1953).

12. Idania Fernandez, quoted by Luz Beatriz Arellano in "Women's Experience of God in Emerging Spirituality," in *With Passion and Compassion: Third World Women Doing Theology*, ed. Virginia Fabella and Mercy Amba Oduyoye (Maryknoll, NY: Orbis, 1988), 142.

identities as mothers to protest poverty, oppression, war, and violence have done so as an extension of their particular love for their own particular children.[13] As Sara Ruddick points out, such women do not "'transcend' their particular loss and love; particularity [is] the emotional root and source of their protest. It is through acting on that particularity that they [extend] mothering to include sustaining and protecting any people whose lives are blighted by violence."[14] Rooting solidarity in the intimate particularity of one's own special relations can not only nurture an expansive sense of concern for vulnerable and suffering others. It can also contribute to ensuring that we view those others not as abstractions or objects, but as real, particular people in relationships of interdependency and care with other real, particular people.[15] For Christians, keeping the particular passion of maternal practice in focus need not detract from our vocation to agapeic love. Rather, it can serve as a reminder to make that love real in concrete care and compassion for others. In Bonnie Miller-McLemore's words, "It is precisely this impulse of self-extension for our most proximate loved ones, those most closely related to us, that Christianity has commanded us to extend to our neighbors at large. We are to build on such passion, not reject it."[16]

I conclude with a practical suggestion for building on our passion for our most proximate loved ones to extend compassion to vulnerable others further afield. While I would not venture to offer myself as an example of how to successfully cultivate universal compassion (I am a humble and perpetually frustrated novice on

13. Leymah Gbowee and the women peacemakers of Liberia are just one example of mothers banding together in protest of violence and injustice. Two other examples include Argentina's "Mothers of the Plaza de Mayo" and El Salvador's "Co-Madres."

14. Sara Ruddick, *Maternal Thinking: Towards a Politics of Peace* (New York: Ballantine, 1989), 231.

15. Cf. Rita C. Manning, *Speaking from the Heart: A Feminist Perspective on Ethics* (Lanham, MD: Rowman & Littlefield), 157.

16. Bonnie Miller-McLemore, *In the Midst of Chaos: Care of Children as Spiritual Practice* (San Francisco: Jossey-Bass, 2006), 113.

this journey), the practice that I suggest here grows out of my own maternal experience of breastfeeding my first child—an experience that approximated contemplative meditation on a sacred icon of divine love.[17] Across from the chair in which I reclined to breastfeed my daughter hung two pieces of religious art: an icon of Our Lady of Guadalupe standing over the crib of her son, the baby Jesus; and a postcard print of a painting depicting a young peasant Mary kissing her baby's cheek, titled "Kissing the Face of God." As a new mother enjoying the privilege of uninterrupted time to sit in silence with my suckling child, I spent countless hours contemplating these images. But the most powerful icon that transfixed my gaze was my own daughter, safe in my arms and content at my breast. I never grew tired of studying the beautiful contours of her face, the raw vulnerability of her desperate hunger, the perfect formation of her miniature limbs, the ever-increasing chubbiness of her cheeks, hands, and knees. I meditated on every detail of her body, down to her long eyelashes, delicate wrists, and tiny toes. She was (and still is, along with her younger brothers) the image of God for me. When I would bend down to kiss her face, I truly felt myself to be kissing the face of God. At the same time, I came to know at a deeply immediate, undeniable, and visceral level what I had previously assented to at an intellectual and functional level: that every child is this precious, and this vulnerable. Every child is the image of God, a vulnerable and powerful manifestation of divine love in the world. Meditation on my own infant icon heightened my awareness of the presence of the divine in all children and, indeed, in all of creation.

Not every mother has the time, energy, or desire to sit with a calmly nursing infant in silent contemplation of her divine beauty.

---

17. For an earlier, expanded version of this reflection, see my article "Mary Kept These Things, Pondering Them in Her Heart: Breastfeeding as Contemplative Practice and Source for Theology," *Spiritus: A Journal of Christian Spirituality* 13 (2013): 163–86.

There are very few moments for such quiet in our household these days. Furthermore, not every woman (or man) has the opportunity or the desire to interact directly with children. What my experience points to, though, is the potential for contemplation on the particularity of vulnerable beauty to expand our awareness of universal vulnerability and cultivate our compassion for vulnerable others outside our circles of intimate concern. Within the Christian narrative, contemplation on icons, images, and stories of Christ's Nativity can facilitate this process. The Nativity is not simply a story of divine incarnation in one human being (however unique and salvific Jesus' incarnation of divine love may be). Rather, the Nativity calls our attention to the presence of the divine in every vulnerable child and human being. In his short work titled *Christmas Eve: Dialogue on the Incarnation*, Friedrich Schleiermacher makes this point in a compelling and original fashion. Gathered at a Christmas Eve party, the women and men present commence to discuss the meaning of Christmas. The women's Christmas stories all center around the idea that "every mother is another Mary. Every mother has a child divine and eternal."[18] My experience as a mother confirms Schleiermacher's insight here. While I would not seek to deny the uniqueness of God's Incarnation in Jesus, the visceral and embodied experience of cradling my babies in my arms impels me to insist that God did not only dwell among us in human flesh two thousand years ago. Each and every child born of woman is God incarnate, divine desire made flesh.

While divine love invulnerably preserves the divine image in human flesh, divine love's incarnation in humanity (and, indeed, all of creation) also makes God inherently vulnerable. When we suffer, God suffers. This inherent vulnerability of divinity is expressed most

---

18. Friedrich Schleiermacher, *Christmas Eve: Dialogue on the Incarnation*, trans. Terrence N. Tice (Lewiston, NY: Edwin Mellen, 1990), 48.

clearly in the Incarnation and Nativity of Jesus. The baby Jesus, who desperately suckled at his mother's breast like any other human child, represents divine power-in-vulnerability incarnate. But God becomes vulnerable flesh in all children, all mothers, and all persons everywhere. The children that nursed at my breast are the image of God. So too is every child. Because divinity is vulnerable, we are called to nurture God, to carry God maternally and suckle God "with exercises of love,"[19] especially in our care for God in ourselves and vulnerable others everywhere. It is in such care—fragile and limited as it may be—that we might embody the deepest truth of the human condition, the coincidence of opposites, the power of divine love, in our own vulnerable human flesh.

19. Cf. Hadewijch, *The Complete Works*, trans. Mother Columba Hart (Mahwah, NJ: Paulist, 1980), 119.

Bibliography

Adams, Marilyn McCord. *Christ and Horrors: The Coherence of Christology.* Cambridge: Cambridge University Press, 2006.

_____. *Horrendous Evils and the Goodness of God.* Ithaca, NY: Cornell University Press, 1999.

Amaya, Rufina, Mark Danner, and Carlos Henríquez Consalvi. *Luciérnagas en El Mozote.* San Salvador, El Salvador: Ediciones Museo de la Palabra, 1996.

Arendt, Hannah. *The Human Condition.* Chicago: University of Chicago Press, 1958.

Aristotle. *Nicomachean Ethics.* Second Edition. Translated by Terence Irwin. Indianapolis: Hackett, 1999.

Arellano, Luz Beatriz. "Women's Experience of God in Emerging Spirituality." In *With Passion and Compassion: Third World Women Doing Theology*, edited by Virginia Fabella and Mercy Amba Oduyoye, 135–50. Maryknoll, NY: Orbis, 1988.

Augustine of Hippo, *City of God.* Translated by Henry Bettenson. London and New York: Penguin, 1972.

_____. *Confessions.* Translated by Henry Chadwick. Oxford and New York: Oxford University Press, 1991.

_____. *Enchiridion.* http://www.newadvent.org/fathers/1302.htm.

Bareth, Narayan. "Indian Mother Arrested for 'Selling 11-Year Old Daughter for $12,000." BBC News Service, January 25, 2013. http://www.bbc.co.uk/news/world-asia-india-21191819.

Baum, Gregory, and Robert Ellsberg, eds. *The Logic of Solidarity: Commentaries on Pope John Paul II's Encyclical "On Social Concern."* Maryknoll, NY: Orbis, 1989.

BBC News, "America's Child Death Shame." BBC News Service, October 17, 2011. http://www.bbc.co.uk/news/magazine-15193530.

Bell, Catherine. "Performance." *Critical Terms for Religious Studies*, edited by Mark Taylor, 205–24. Chicago: University of Chicago Press, 1998.

Beyer, Gerald. *Recovering Solidarity: Lessons from Poland's Unfinished Revolution.* Notre Dame: University of Notre Dame Press, 2010.

Blustein, Jeffrey. *The Moral Demands of Memory.* Cambridge: Cambridge University Press, 2008.

Boff, Clodovis. "Epistemology and Method of the Theology of Liberation." In *Mysterium Liberationis: Fundamental Concepts of Liberation Theology*, edited by Ignacio Ellacuría and Jon Sobrino, 57–84. Maryknoll, NY: Orbis, 1993.

Boff, Leonardo. *Trinity and Society.* Maryknoll, NY: Orbis, 1988.

_____. *Holy Trinity, Perfect Community.* Maryknoll, NY: Orbis, 2000.

Bonhoeffer, Dietrich. *Letters and Papers from Prison.* London: SCM, 1967.

Brison, Susan J. *Aftermath: Violence and the Remaking of the Self.* Princeton: Princeton University Press, 2002.

Brock, Rita Nakashima. *Journeys by Heart: A Christology of Erotic Power.* New York: Crossroad, 1988.

Burke, Kevin. "The Crucified People as 'Light for the Nations': A Reflection on Ignacio Ellacuría." In *Rethinking Martyrdom*, edited by Teresa Okure et al., 120–30. London: SCM, 2003.

_____. *The Ground Beneath the Cross: The Theology of Ignacio Ellacuría.* Washington, DC: Georgetown University Press, 2000.

Cannon, Katie G. *Black Womanist Ethics*. Atlanta: Scholars, 1988.

Casey, Edward. *Remembering: A Phenomenological Study*. Bloomington: Indiana University Press, 1987.

Council of Trent. *Catechism for Parish Priests*. http://www.fordham.edu/halsall/mod/romancat.html.

Catherine of Siena. *The Dialogue*. Translated by Suzanne Noffke, OP. New York: Paulist, 1980.

Chase, Susan, and Mary Frances Rogers, eds. *Mothers and Children: Feminist Analyses and Personal Narratives*. New Brunswick, NJ: Rutgers University Press, 2001.

Child Welfare Information Gateway. "Understanding the Effects of Maltreatment on Brain Development" (2009). http://www.childwelfare.gov/pubs/issue_briefs/brain_development/effects.cfm.

Coakley, Sarah. *Powers and Submissions: Spirituality, Philosophy and Gender*. Malden, MA: Blackwell, 2002.

Coleman, Monica. *Making a Way Out of No Way: A Womanist Theology*. Minneapolis: Fortress Press, 2008.

Cullinan, Colleen Carpenter. "In Pain and Sorrow: Childbirth, Incarnation, and the Suffering of Women," *Cross Currents* (Spring 2008): 95–107.

Collins, Patricia Hill. *Black Feminist Thought: Knowledge, Consciousness, and the Politics of Empowerment*. New York: Routledge, 1991.

Daino, Peter. *Mary, Mother of Sorrows, Mother of Defiance*. Maryknoll, NY: Orbis, 1993.

De Marneffe, Daphne. *Maternal Desire: On Children, Love, and the Inner Life*. New York: Little, Brown & Co., 2004.

DeParle, Jason. *American Dream: Three Women, Ten Kids, and a Nation's Drive to End Welfare*. New York: Penguin, 2004.

Dunlap, Susan. "Discourse Theory and Pastoral Theology." In *Feminist and Womanist Pastoral Theology*, edited by Bonnie J. Miller-McLemore and Brita L. Gill-Austern, 133–48. Nashville: Abingdon, 1999.

Dykstra, Craig. "Reconceiving Practice." In *Shifting Boundaries*, edited by Barbara Wheeler and Edward Farley, 35–66. Louisville: Westminster John Knox, 1991.

Ellacuría, Ignacio. "The Crucified People." In *Mysterium Liberationis: Fundamental Concepts of Liberation Theology*, edited by Ignacio Ellacuría and Jon Sobrino, 580–603. Maryknoll, NY: Orbis, 1993.

_____. "Discernir el 'signo' de los tiempos," *Diakonía* 17 (1981).

_____. "Hacia una fundamentación filosófica del método teológico latinoamericano," *Estudios Centroamericanos*, 322–23 (1975).

Eliot, Lise. *What's Going On in There? How the Brain and Mind Develop in the First Five Years of Life*. New York: Bantam, 1999.

Erdrich, Louise. *The Blue Jay's Dance: A Birth Year*. New York: HarperCollins, 1995.

Farley, Wendy. *Gathering Those Driven Away: A Theology of Incarnation*. Louisville: Westminster John Knox, 2011.

_____. *Tragic Vision and Divine Compassion: A Contemporary Theodicy*. Louisville: Westminster John Knox, 1990.

_____. *The Wounding and Healing of Desire: Weaving Heaven and Earth*. Louisville: Westminster John Knox, 2005.

Feuerbach, Ludwig. *The Essence of Christianity* [1841]. Cambridge: Cambridge University Press, 2012.

Fineman, Martha. *The Autonomy Myth: Towards a Theory of Dependency*. New York: New Press, 2004.

_____. *The Neutered Mother, the Sexual Family and Other 20th Century Tragedies*. New York, Routledge, 1995.

_____. "The Vulnerable Subject: Anchoring Equality in the Human Condition," *Yale Journal of Law and Feminism* 20, no. 1 (2008).

_____. "The Vulnerable Subject and the Responsive State," *Emory Law Journal* 60 (2011).

Fletcher, Jeannine Hill. *Motherhood as Metaphor: Engendering Interreligious Dialogue.* New York: Fordham University Press, 2013.

Flueckiger, Joyce Burkhalter. *Gender and Genre in the Folklore of Middle India.* Ithaca, NY: Cornell University Press, 1996.

Friedan, Betty. *The Feminine Mystique.* New York: W. W. Norton, 1963.

Fulkerson, Mary McClintock. *Places of Redemption: Theology for a Worldly Church.* Oxford: Oxford University Press, 2007.

Gbowee, Leymah. *Mighty Be Our Powers: How Sisterhood, Prayer, and Sex Changed a Nation at War.* New York: Beast Books, 2011.

Gillies, Val. *Marginalized Mothers: Exploring Working Class Experiences of Parenting.* New York: Routledge, 2007.

Gilson, Anne Bathurst. *Eros Breaking Free: Interpreting Sexual Theo-ethics.* Cleveland: Pilgrim, 1995.

Glatz, Carol. "Marian images need artistic rehabilitation, says Vatican newspaper." *Catholic News Service,* June 19, 2008. http://www.catholicnews.com/data/stories/cns/0803257.htm.

Graham, Elaine, Heather Walton, and Frances Ward. *Theological Reflection: Methods.* London: SCM, 2005.

Greenberg, Irving. "Cloud of Smoke Pillar of Fire: Judaism, Christianity, Modernity After the Holocaust." In *Auschwitz: Beginning of a New Era? Reflections on the Holocaust,* edited by Eva Fleischner. New York: Ktav, 1977.

Gregory of Nyssa. "Address on Religious Instruction." In *Christology of the Later Fathers,* edited by Edward Roche Hardy. Philadelphia: Westminster, 1954.

Grenholm, Cristina. *Motherhood and Love: Beyond the Gendered Stereotypes of Theology.* Grand Rapids: Eerdmans, 2011.

Grenz, Stanley. *The Social God and the Relational Self: A Trinitarian Theology of the Imago Dei.*Louisville: Westminster John Knox, 2001.

Grey, Mary C. *Sacred Longings: The Ecological Spirit and Global Culture.* Minneapolis: Fortress Press, 2004.

Grovijahn, Jane M. "Grabbing Life Away from Death: Women and Martyrdom in El Salvador," *Journal of Feminist Studies in Religion* 7 (1991): 19–28.

Gutiérrez, Gustavo. *A Theology of Liberation.* Maryknoll, NY: Orbis, 1988.

_____. *The God of Life.* Maryknoll, NY: Orbis, 1991.

_____. "Reflections from a Latin American Perspective: Finding Our Way to Talk about God." In *Irruption of the Third World: Challenge to Theology* [Papers from the Fifth International Conference of the Ecumenical Association of Third World Theologians, August 17–29, 1981, New Delhi, India], edited by Sergio Torres and Virginia Fabella. Maryknoll, NY: Orbis, 1983.

_____. *We Drink from Our Own Wells: The Spiritual Journey of a People.* Maryknoll, NY: Orbis, 1992.

Hadewijch. *The Complete Works.* Translated by Mother Columba Hart. Mahwah, NJ: Paulist, 1980.

Harding, Sandra, ed. *The Feminist Standpoint Theory Reader: Intellectual and Political Controversies.* New York: Routledge, 2004.

Hartstock, Nancy. "The Feminist Standpoint: Developing the Ground for a Specifically Feminist Historical Materialism." In *Discovering Reality*, edited by Sandra Harding and Merrill B. Hintikka, 283–310.Dordrecht: Kluwer Academic, 1983.

Hebblethwaite, Margaret. *Motherhood and God.*London: Cassell, 1984.

Heidegger, Martin. *Being and Time.* Translated by Joan Stambaugh. Albany: State University of New York Press, 2010.

Held, Virginia. *The Ethics of Care: Personal, Political, and Global.* New York: Oxford University Press, 2006.

Heyward, Carter. *The Redemption of God: A Theology of Mutual Relation.* Lanham, MD: University Press of America, 1982.

_____. *Touching Our Strength: The Erotic as Power and the Love of God.* San Francisco: Harper & Row, 1989.

Hilkert, Mary Catherine. *Speaking with Authority: Catherine of Siena and the Voices of Women Today.*Mahwah, NJ: Paulist, 2008.

Hochschild, Arlie. "Global Care Chains and Emotional Surplus Value." In *On the Edge: Living with Global Capitalism,* edited by W. Hutton and A. Giddens. London: Jonathan Cape, 2000.

_____. "The Nanny Chain," *The American Prospect,* December 19, 2001.

Human Rights Watch. "I Am Not Dead, But I Am Not Living: Barriers to Fistula Prevention and Treatment in Kenya" (2010). http://www.hrw.org/node/91514.

Hume, David. *A Treatise of Human Nature.* London: Oxford University Press, 1960.

Huyssen, Andreas. *Twilight Memories: Marking Time in a Culture of Amnesia.* New York: Routledge, 1995.

Jantzen, Grace. *Becoming Divine: A Feminist Philosophy of Religion.* Bloomington: Indiana University Press, 1999.

_____. *God's World, God's Body.* Philadelphia: Westminster, 1984.

John Paul II. Apostolic Exhortation, *Reconciliation and Penance* (1984). http://www.vatican.va/holy_father/john_paul_ii/apost_exhortations/ documents/hf_jp-ii_exh_02121984_reconciliatio-et-paenitentia_en.html.

Johnson, Elizabeth A. *Quest for the Living God: Mapping Frontiers in Theology of God.* New York: Continuum, 2007.

_____. "Remembering Creative Spirit." In *Women's Spirituality: Resources for Christian Development,* edited by Joann Wolski Conn. New York: Paulist, 1996.

_____. *She Who Is: The Mystery of God in Feminist Theological Discourse.* New York: Crossroad, 1992.

_____. *Truly Our Sister: A Theology of Mary in the Communion of Saints.* New York: Continuum, 2004.

Julian, John. *The Complete Julian of Norwich.* Brewster, MA: Paraclete, 2001.

Julian of Norwich. *Showings.* Translated by Edmund Colledge and James Walsh. Mahwah, NJ: Paulist, 1978.

Karr, Mary. *Cherry: A Memoir.* New York: Viking, 2000.

_____. *The Liars' Club: A Memoir.* New York: Penguin, 1995.

_____. *Lit: A Memoir.* New York: HarperCollins, 2009.

Keller, Catherine. *Face of the Deep: A Theology of Becoming.* New York: Routledge, 2003.

Kierkegaard, Søren. *The Concept of Anxiety: A Simple Psychologically Orienting Deliberation on the Dogmatic Issue of Hereditary Sin* [1841]. Macon, GA: Mercer University Press, 2008.

Kimmel, Michael S., and Abby L. Ferber, eds. *Privilege: A Reader.* Boulder, CO: Westview, 2003.

Kinser, Amber. *Motherhood and Feminism.* Berkeley: Seal, 2010.

Kirby, Peadar. "Theorising Globalisation's Social Impact: Proposing the Concept of Vulnerability," *Review of International Political Economy* 13, no. 4 (October 2006): 632–55.

_____. *Vulnerability and Violence: The Impact of Globalisation.* Ann Arbor, MI: Pluto, 2006.

Kittay, Eva Feder. *Love's Labor: Essays on Women, Equality, and Dependency.* New York: Routledge, 1999.

Kristeva, Julia. *Powers of Horror: An Essay on Abjection.* New York: Columbia University Press, 1982.

LaCugna, Catherine. *God for Us: The Trinity and Christian Life.* New York: HarperCollins, 1991.

Lanzetta, Beverly. *Radical Wisdom: A Feminist Mystical Theology.* Minneapolis: Fortress Press, 2005.

Locke, John. *An Essay Concerning Human Understanding.* Edited by J. Yolton. New York: Dutton, 1965.

López, Ian F. Haney. "The Social Construction of Race: Some Observations on Illusion, Fabrication, and Choice," *Harvard Civil Rights-Civil Liberties Review* 29, no. 1 (1994): 1–62.

Lorde, Audre. *Sister Outsider.* Berkeley, CA: Crossing, 1984.

Manning, Rita C. *Speaking from the Heart: A Feminist Perspective on Ethics.* Lanham, MD: Rowman & Littlefield, 1992.

March, Kathryn. "Childbirth with Fear." In *Mothers and Children: Feminist Analyses and Personal Narratives*, edited by Susan E. Chase and Mary Frances Rogers, 168–73. New Brunswick, NJ: Rutgers University Press, 2001.

Margalit, Avishai. *The Ethics of Memory.* Cambridge, MA: Harvard University Press, 2002.

Maynard, Jane F. *Transfiguring Loss: Julian of Norwich as a Guide for Survivors of Traumatic Grief.* Cleveland: Pilgrim, 2006.

McFague, Sallie. *Models of God: Theology for an Ecological, Nuclear Age.*Philadelphia: Fortress Press, 1987.

_____. *A New Climate for Theology: God, the World, and Climate Change.* Minneapolis: Fortress Press, 2008.

McIntosh, Peggy, "Working Paper No. 189: White Privilege and Male Privilege: A Personal Account of Coming to See the Correspondence Through Work in Women's Studies." Wellesley, MA: Center for Research on Women, 1988.

McKenna, Megan. *Mary, Shadow of Grace.* Maryknoll, NY: Orbis, 1995.

Mechthild of Magdeburg. *The Flowing Light of the Godhead.* Translated by Frank Tobin. Mahwah, NJ: Paulist, 1998.

Melton, Glennon. "Meet Glennon." http://momastery.com/blog/about-glennon/.

Metz, Johann Baptist. *Faith in History and Society: Toward a Practical Fundamental Theology*. Translated by J. Matthew Ashley. New York: Crossroad, 2007.

Miller-McLemore, Bonnie. *Also a Mother: Work and Family as a Theological Dilemma*. Nashville: Abingdon, 1994.

_____. *In the Midst of Chaos: Care of Children as Spiritual Practice*. San Francisco: Jossey-Bass, 2006.

_____. *Let the Children Come: Reimagining Childhood from a Christian Perspective*. San Francisco: Jossey-Bass, 2003.

Min, Anselm Kyongsuk. *The Solidarity of Others in a Divided World*. New York: T. & T. Clark, 2004.

Morrison, Toni. *Beloved*. New York: Plume, 1987.

_____. *A Mercy*. New York: Vintage, 2008.

Mount Shoop, Marcia. *Let the Bones Dance: Embodiment and the Body of Christ*. Louisville: Westminster John Knox, 2010.

Nelson, Derek R. *What's Wrong with Sin: Sin in Individual and Social Perspective from Schleiermacher to Theologies of Liberation*. New York: T. & T. Clark, 2009.

Nicholas of Cusa. *Selected Spiritual Writings*. Translated by H. Lawrence Bond. Mahwah, NJ: Paulist, 1997.

Niebuhr, Reinhold. *The Nature and Destiny of Man* [1941]. Louisville: Westminster John Knox, 1996.

Noddings, Nel. *Caring: A Feminine Approach to Ethics and Moral Education*. Berkeley: University of California Press, 1984.

Norris, Thomas. *The Trinity: Life of God, Hope for Humanity*. New York: New City Press, 2009.

Nussbaum, Martha. *The Fragility of Goodness: Luck and Ethics in Greek Tragedy and Philosophy*. Cambridge: Cambridge University Press, 1986.

Nygren, Anders. *Agape and Eros: A Study of the Christian Idea of Love*. Philadelphia: Westminster, 1953.

O'Reilly, Andrea, Marie Porter, and Patricia Short, eds. *Motherhood: Power and Oppression*. Toronto: Women's Press, 2005.

Origen of Alexandria. *On First Principles*. Translated by G. W. Butterworth. New York: Harper & Row, 1966.

Parreñas, Rhacel Salazar. *Servant of Globalization: Women, Migration, and Domestic Work*. Stanford: Stanford University Press, 2001.

Pseudo-Dionysius. *The Complete Works*. Translated by Colm Luibheid. New York: Paulist, 1987.

Placher, William. *Narratives of a Vulnerable God: Christ, Theology, and Scripture*. Louisville: Westminster John Knox, 1994.

Plaskow, Judith. *Sex, Sin and Grace: Women's Experience and the Theologies of Reinhold Niebuhr and Paul Tillich*. Lanham, MD: University Press of America, 1979.

Rahner, Karl. *Foundations of Christian Faith: An Introduction to the Idea of Christianity*. New York: Seabury, 1978.

_____. *Theological Investigations, Vol. XXIII*. Baltimore: Helicon, 1992.

Rapp, Emily. "Notes from a Dragon Mom," *New York Times*, October 15, 2011.

_____. *The Still Point of the Turning World*. New York: Penguin, 2013.

Rich, Adrienne. *Of Woman Born: Motherhood as Institution and Experience*. New York: W. W. Norton, 1976.

Ross, Susan. "God's Embodiment and Women: Sacraments." In *Freeing Theology: The Essentials of Theology in Feminist Perspective*, edited by Catherine Mowry LaCugna, 185–210. New York: HarperCollins, 1993.

Ruddick, Sara. *Maternal Thinking: Towards a Politics of Peace*. New York: Ballantine, 1989.

Ruether, Rosemary Radford. *Sexism and God-Talk: Toward a Feminist Theology*. Boston: Beacon, 1983.

Saiving, Valerie. "The Human Situation: A Feminine View," *The Journal of Religion* 40, no. 2 (April 1960): 100–112.

Saracino, Michele. *Being About Borders: A Christian Anthropology of Difference.* Collegeville, MN: Liturgical, 2011.

Sawicki, Marianne. *Crossing Galilee: Architectures of Contact in the Occupied Land of Jesus.* New York: Continuum, 2000.

Schaberg, Jane. *The Illegitimacy of Jesus: A Feminist Theological Interpretation of the Infancy Narratives, Expanded 20th Anniversary Edition.* Sheffield, UK: Sheffield Phoenix Press, 2006.

Schillebeeckx, Edward. *Christ: The Experience of Jesus as Lord.* New York: Crossroad, 1980.

_____. *Church: The Human Story of God.* New York: Crossroad, 1996.

_____. *God the Future of Man.* New York: Sheed & Ward, 1968.

_____. *Interim Report on the Books Jesus and Christ.* New York: Crossroad, 1981.

_____. *The Understanding of Faith: Interpretation and Criticism.* New York: Seabury, 1974.

Schleiermacher, Friedrich. *Christmas Eve: Dialogue on the Incarnation.* Translated by Terrence N. Tice. Lewiston, NY: Edwin Mellen, 1990.

Shields, Carol. *Unless.* New York: Fourth Estate, 2002.

Shulman, Alix Kates. "A Mother's Story." In *Mothers and Children: Feminist Analyses and Personal Narratives,* edited by Susan E. Chase and Mary Frances Rogers, 21–24. New Brunswick, NJ: Rutgers University Press, 2001.

Sobrino, Jon. *Jesucristo Liberador.* San Salvador: UCA Editores, 1991.

_____. *Jesus the Liberator: A Historical Theological View.* Maryknoll, NY: Orbis, 1993.

_____. *No Salvation Outside the Poor: Prophetic-Utopian Essays.* Maryknoll, NY: Orbis, 2008.

_____. *Where Is God: Earthquake, Terrorism, Barbarity, and Hope.* Maryknoll, NY: Orbis, 2004.

_____. *Witnesses to the Kingdom: The Martyrs of El Salvador and the Crucified Peoples*. Maryknoll, NY: Orbis, 2003.

Sobrino, Jon, and Juan Hernandez Pico. *Theology of Christian Solidarity*. Maryknoll, NY: Orbis, 1985.

Spitz, René. *Dialogues from Infancy: Selected Papers*. Edited by R. N. Emde. New York: International Universities Press, 1983.

Stack, Carol. "Different Voices, Different Visions: Gender, Culture, and Moral Reasoning." In *Uncertain Terms: Negotiating Gender in American Culture*, edited by Faye Ginsburg and Anna Lowenhaupt Tsing, 19–27. Boston: Beacon, 1990.

Stamm, Jill. *Bright from the Start: The Simple, Science-Backed Way to Nurture Your Child's Developing Mind from Birth to Age 3*. New York: Gotham, 2007.

Steingraber, Sandra. *Having Faith: An Ecologist's Journey to Motherhood*. Cambridge, MA: Perseus, 2001.

Tanner, Kathryn. *Jesus, Humanity and the Trinity: A Brief Systematic Theology*. Minneapolis: Fortress Press, 2001.

Thonneau, Patrick et al. "Ectopic pregnancy in Conakry, Guinea," *Bulletin of the World Health Organization* 80, no. 5 (2002). http://www.scielosp.org/scielo.php?script=sci_arttext&pid=S0042-96862002000500006.

Tillich, Paul. *The Courage to Be*. New Haven: Yale University Press, 1952.

_____. *Systematic Theology, Vol. 1*. Chicago: University of Chicago Press, 1973.

_____. *Systematic Theology, Vol. 3*. Chicago: University of Chicago Press, 1976.

Townes, Emilie M. *Breaking the Fine Rain of Death: African American Health Issues and a Womanist Ethic of Care*. Eugene, OR: Wipf & Stock, 2006.

Tronto, Joan C. *Moral Boundaries: A Political Argument for an Ethic of Care*. New York: Routledge, 1993.

Todorov, Tzvetan. *Hope and Memory: Lessons from the Twentieth Century.* Princeton: Princeton University Press, 2003.

Traina, Cristina. *Erotic Attunement: Parenthood and the Ethics of Sensuality between Unequals.* Chicago: University of Chicago Press, 2011.

UNICEF. *State of the World's Children 2012.* New York: United Nations, 2012.

USCCB. "Statement on Quest for the Living God: Mapping Frontiers in Theology of God by Sister Elizabeth A. Johnson." March 24, 2011. http://www.usccb.org/about/doctrine/publications/upload/statement-quest-for-the-living-god-2011-03-24.pdf.

U.S. Department of Health and Human Services. "Child Maltreatment 2009." December 31, 2009. http://www.acf.hhs.gov/programs/cb/pubs/cm09/cm09.pdf.

U.S. Department of Labor, Department of Labor Statistics. "Employment Characteristics of Families Summary." April 26, 2012. http://www.bls.gov/news.release/famee.nr0.htm.

U.S. Environmental Protection Agency. "Mercury: Health Effects." http://www.epa.gov/hg/effects.htm.

Volf, Miroslav. *The End of Memory: Remembering Rightly in a Violent World.* Grand Rapids: Eerdmans, 2006.

Ward, Benedicta. "Julian the Solitary." In *Julian Reconsidered*, edited by Kenneth Leech and Benedicta Ward. Oxford: Sisters of the Love of God Press, 1988.

Warner, Judith. *Perfect Madness: Motherhood in the Age of Anxiety.* New York: Riverhead, 2005.

Weedon, Chris. *Feminist Practice and Poststructuralist Theory.* New York: Blackwell, 1987.

Whitehead, Alfred North. *Adventures of Ideas.* New York: Macmillan, 1933.

Willett, Cynthia. *Maternal Ethics and Other Slave Moralities.* New York: Routledge, 1995.

Williams, Delores. *Sisters in the Wilderness: The Challenge of Womanist God-Talk.* Maryknoll, NY: Orbis, 1995.

World Health Organization. "10 facts on obstetric fistula." March 2010. http://www.who.int/features/factfiles/obstetric_fistula/en/#.

_____. "Maternal Mortality." http://www.who.int/making_pregnancy_safer/topics/maternal_mortality/en/.

Young, James E. *The Texture of Memory: Holocaust Memorials and Meaning.* New Haven: Yale University Press, 1993.

Zizioulas, John D. *Being as Communion: Studies in Personhood and the Church.* Crestwood, NY: St. Vladimir's Seminary Press, 1997.

Zucchino, David. *Myth of the Welfare Queen: A Pulitzer Prize-Winning Journalist's Portrait of Women on the Line.* New York: Touchstone, 1997.

Audio-Visual Resources

Lim, Louisa. "Painful Memories for China's Footbinding Survivors." Interview aired on National Public Radio's "Morning Edition," March 19, 2007. http://www.npr.org/templates/story/story.php?storyId=8966942.

National Committee on Pay Equity. "The Wage Gap over Time: In Real Dollars, Women See a Continuing Gap." http://www.pay-equity.org/info-time.html.

Palin, Sarah. "Mama Grizzlies." http://www.youtube.com/watch?v=fsUVL6ciK-c.

_____. "Remarks by Sarah Palin." http://www.youtube.com/watch?v=vKgNrb3baNM.

_____. "Transcript: Gov. Sarah Palin at the RNC." National Public Radio. http://www.npr.org/templates/story/story.php?storyId=94258995.

Pray the Devil Back to Hell. DVD. Directed by Gini Reticker. New York: Fork Films, 2009.

Spitz, René. "Psychogenic Diseases in Infancy." 1952. http://www.archive.org/details/PsychogenicD.

Warren, Elizabeth. "Elizabeth Warren on the Myth of Class Warfare."
http://www.youtube.com/watch?v=XcFDF87-SdQ.

Index